WHAT CANADIANS THINK...

ABOUT ALMOST....

EVERYTHING

DARRELL BRICKER & JOHN WRIGHT
OF IPSOS-REID

 DOUBLEDAY CANADA

Doubleday Canada and colophon are trademarks.

LIBRARY AND ARCHIVES CANADA CATALOGUING IN PUBLICATION

Bricker, Darrell Jay, 1961–
    What Canadians think about almost everything / Darrell Bricker, John Wright.

ISBN 0-385-65985-7

1. Canada—Social conditions—21st century. 2. Canada—Civilization—21st century. I. Wright, John II. Title.

HN110.Z9P8 2005   971.07   C2004-907426-1

Cover image: David Trood Pictures/Getty Images
Printed and bound in Canada

Published in Canada by
Doubleday Canada, a division of
Random House of Canada Limited

Visit Random House of Canada Limited's website: www.randomhouse.ca

TRANS 10 9 8 7 6 5 4 3 2 1

Dedicated to those incredible people in North America who spend a total of 1.3 million hours a year answering our questions when they could be doing other things. You create the future's understanding of us, today.

Contents

Introduction

IT HAPPENS, INEVITABLY, at every public, business or social event we go to.

Someone discovers that we work for Ipsos-Reid, and during the course of small talk they ask THE QUESTION: "So, what are you polling about today?"

Back when we began working at the Angus Reid Group, the predecessor to Ipsos-Reid, the company was small enough that you'd actually be able to sort through the topics in your head and pretty much (apart from proprietary work for clients) tell people the list. That was back when we were doing maybe $5 million in research a year and most thought we weren't doing much more than conducting polls for the media on the topic of the day. Some still do.

And nothing could be farther than the truth.

In Canada this year Ipsos-Reid will conduct about $100 million worth of research on almost every dimension of Canadians' opinions on just about every subject possible. Ninety-five percent of our business—truly the bread and butter of our industry—consists in exploring things like which kind of diaper a new mother would prefer, how many credit cards you have in your wallet, what new lottery game you prefer to play, which car you'd like to see made, what you'd like for lunch, or where you'd like to vacation. And because clients hire us to do the work, you rarely hear about it. Which is as it should be. That's our job.

But it slowly dawned on us that each of our public media releases was like a dab of paint in an enormous life-sized portrait of Canada. So we thought we'd step back from the canvas to see what

Canada looks like from that vantage, something we hadn't previously done.

Until now. Here is the portrait. It's a work in progress, of course. Opinions are always changing, and there is no way anyone could even dream of filling in every last detail of everything Canadians actually think. And we haven't included all of the information we could have here. That would run to volumes and volumes. Instead we've chosen the best bits—the salient points, the telling facts, and the strange things we thought you'd want to know.

We ask about government policy and current issues; we ask about favourite t.v. shows, and drinking beer and going to the cottage; we ask about topless sunbathing and healthcare policy; we ask about raising kids and investing for retirement; we ask about fears and hopes and bad hair days.

So today, when someone asks THE QUESTION, there is really only one accurate answer: "What Canadians Think . . . About Almost Everything."

We think (and we hope you agree) that all Canadians want to know what Canadians think. And while no Canadian is exactly like any other, when we begin to put one opinion beside another, then add another belief, and put that beside a preference or an aversion, and so on, and we let the numbers add up, after all the years we've been at this, we get a pretty good idea of what is on Canadians' minds.

Now you can too.

If we've learned one thing from our years of prying into the minds of Canadians, it is that they're a fascinating lot—mostly reasonable, usually congenial, sometimes exasperating, from time to time simply bizarre. (And we ought to know—we're Canadian too.) Not a day goes by that we are not surprised by something we stumble across in our research, and I hope we never stop being surprised.

We are surprised by the strength of some replies. For example, when editorials, pundits and others were screeching that Canadians should saddle up with our friends across the border and join them in Iraq *or else,* and almost 7 in 10 told us they'd rather stay here, we think a finding like that shows that, right or wrong, Canadians are capable of thinking for themselves, even when the so-called experts are telling them something quite different. The same goes for other issues like labelling GMOs: we found that 90% of Canadians want to know when they're buying and eating genetically modified food (and that goes for trans fat as well). Or what they want in their healthcare system—the Romanow Report was given public vindication with 82% support, despite being dumped on in many quarters of the country by political, media or special interests when it was released.

We are often surprised by regional variations. For example, a Manitoban is twice as likely as an Ontarian to oppose a ban on pellet guns. And which province is most likely to support the decriminalization of marijuana? You might feel justified in guessing British Columbia. But you would be wrong. The answer is Quebec. How about the province that feels most burdened by the tax man? You might guess Alberta this time. Nope. Quebec again.

We also see striking variations across all the demographic categories. Someone with a high school education is 50% more likely than someone with a university education to believe that decriminalized marijuana will lead to an increase in crime. A young Canadian is twice as likely as an older Canadian to invest monthly. A woman is twice as likely to floss than is a man. A woman is 50% more likely than a man to believe that high oil prices are a form of vengeance for the American invasion of Iraq. And so on.

Some of the stuff we come across is simply bizarre. In the course of a day's work we may have to determine what percentage of Canadian men mow the lawn in open-toed shoes, or how many of us believe the devil has a hand in humanity's day-to-day affairs, or the percentage of Canadians who would like to change their hair colour. In which province are women most likely to sunbathe topless? Read on and find out.

Sure, some of these numbers make perfect sense, and are not surprising at all—let's say that 99.9% of Canadians put their pants on one leg at a time. But even the fact that 0.1% of Canadians have found some other procedure for getting dressed is pretty interesting—that's 24,000 very ambitious adult Canadians.

Sometimes we see stereotypes shattered (women are more likely than men to leave a fiancé standing at the altar) and sometimes we see them hilariously confirmed (men are more likely than women to allocate discretionary spending to the consumption of beer).

All of which is to say that every one of these facts and graphs tells a story; each is a window into the everyday lives of our friends and neighbours and families and clients and perhaps even our enemies. And it's another dab of paint on the canvas as to who we, as Canadians, are.

Now, you can read this book cover to cover. But we also think you can enjoy just sticking your finger in anywhere, and start reading. We think the first thing you come across should be enough to get you thinking, and certainly to get you talking, perhaps even laughing out loud.

We want to thank the people at Doubleday Canada for taking this project on—especially the publisher, Maya Mavjee, and Nick Massey-Garrison, who was the editor of this publication and who ultimately figured out how to make it work. Without Nick, there wouldn't have been a book. Top kudos also go to journalist and writer Dan Turner, who we've had the pleasure of working with before on numerous studies, and who improved our early drafts by making our numbers more human and interesting, and to C. Scott Richardson, who designed the cover and the pages you are reading. Also a very special thanks to Elaine Roberts, who worked with us every step of the way in the production of the manuscript, and to our agent, Robert Mackwood.

Thanks as well to all of our colleagues who have worked on these polls during the past several years and to the clients who have sponsored them—especially CTV and the *Globe and Mail,* true partners in discovering and reporting what Canadians think. As well, we thank the management of Ipsos-Reid for giving us the latitude to do something that we truly enjoy every day—learning more about this great country and the people who live in it.

But we also want to pay a special tribute to the people that answer our surveys every single day (and evening). For the 1.3 million North Americans who this year will answer our call and spend a few minutes of their very hectic days, thank you. Without you giving up the time we wouldn't know how wonderful, rich and diverse, funny and just plain interesting we all are in this great country, Canada. Your portrait is what appears in the pages that follow.

A special tribute must be paid to Dr. Angus Reid, who established the Angus Reid Group over a 7-11 store in Winnipeg in 1979 and turned it into a national icon and household name. An incredible experience for all of us who worked with him—thanks, Angus. Thanks as well to the crew that pounds out our public releases year after year: Jennifer, Paul, Sarah, Justin, Rose, Sue, Glen and Mags: quite the legacy, eh?

Finally, at the end of the day, both of us have the privilege of going home to the most important people in our lives. For Darrell, a very special thanks goes to Nina, his wife of twenty-three years, and daughter Emily. As for John, a heartfelt thanks goes to his wife, Jennifer, the "brood"—Olivia, Josh, Katie and James—and Grandma Eileen Wright. For each of you, your opinions count the most.

Darrell and John

Crime and Punishment

Crimes, like virtues, are their own rewards.

—George Farquhar

No one *likes* crime. That is, even criminals do not enjoy being robbed or defrauded or assaulted. No one likes being a victim of crime, or being accused of committing one (being convicted of one even less). The effects of crime—grief, anxiety, increased policing, incarceration and insurance—are as bad as its effects—poverty, lack of education, stupidity, greed, egotism, mental illness, discrimination. There is really very little to recommend crime, except that it sometimes seems like a promising way to get ahead.

Every now and then a little bit of humour creeps into the world of crime. Take, for example, the story about the thief who stole an electronic device worth $2,500 off the front porch of a woman who had placed it there for a few minutes while she was cleaning up inside. Unfortunately for the thief, the woman was serving home detention, with a bracelet on her ankle. What he stole was a tracking device with a built-in satellite transmitter that began to signal when it was more than 100 feet from the bracelet. The thief and his stolen machine weren't hard to locate.

Then there was the guy who walked into a corner store, put a $20 bill on the counter and asked for change. When the clerk opened the till, the man drew a gun and demanded all the cash in the register. He got it—but it was only about $15, and he forgot to retrieve his $20 bill. Yes, these are real stories.

One hardly has to emphasize that crime is a serious matter. And it is made all the more serious by many of the efforts made to reduce it. While it may seem to some voters and right-wing politicians that "getting tough" on crime is the best way to stem it, other Canadians point to evidence that suggests this assumption only makes things worse. For example, Quebec courts are less than half as likely to sentence young offenders to prison than are courts in Ontario. Yet youth crime in that province is less than half of what it is in Ontario, including violent crime. The Surgeon General in the United States argues that treating young offenders as adults is a terrible mistake, leading to more criminal behaviour, not less.

The United States is a good example of how "getting tough on crime" can go shockingly wrong. The self-styled "home of the free" has the highest proportion of its population behind bars of any country in the world. The U.S. incarcerates more of its population than do China or Russia, or Iraq under Saddam Hussein. An American is six times as likely as a Canadian to be behind bars. Are Americans innately six times more criminal than Canadians, or has a judicial system with different priorities created a bulge of criminality? Whatever the answer, it seems clear that getting tough does little to make people nicer.

- **Ratio of young offenders in Ontario who are sentenced to those in Quebec: 2.16 to 1**
- **Rate by which an American is more likely than a Canadian to be in prison, expressed as a percentage: 490**
- **Ratio of those who have faith in their local police to those who believe they are corrupt: 2 to 1**

So We Asked You What You Think . . .

In April 2004, we did a survey to try to find out what you think about some of these crime-related issues, and some that are closely related. It produced some interesting results that indicate that Canadians are still pretty divided on how to treat criminals.

Punishment

Let's start with young offenders. Our survey found that most Canadians do want *some* young offenders treated as adults by the courts. Depending "on the circumstances and nature of the crime," 74% of you want an assessment made on a case-by-case basis. A minority of Canadians (18%) say that *all* young offenders should be treated as adults, and a smaller minority (8%) say that *none* of them should be.

Are boot camps more likely or less likely to make young offenders commit future crimes? Well, the Mike Harris government of Ontario seemed to hit a chord on this one, because nearly half of Canadians (49%) do believe that boot camps produce positive results. Just 5% say they believe boot camps will make young people *more* likely to re-offend, while 31% figure they aren't likely to make much difference, with 15% unsure.

Canadians appear to be split pretty well dead even on whether we should be stuffing our jails with more people, American-style. Approximately half our respondents (48%) thought we should, and approximately half (46%) thought we shouldn't.

Canadians are no longer split on the use of the death penalty. Our recent polls show that support for the death penalty in Canada has been dying off dramatically over the years. Our November 2004 survey showed 42% agreeing that capital punishment should be reintroduced and 56% saying that it shouldn't. That is the first poll to show a majority of Canadians *against* capital punishment since we have been doing them.

Support for capital punishment

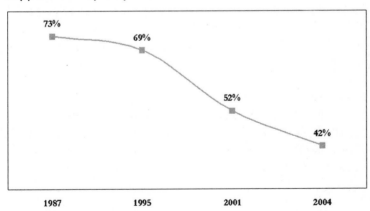

73%   69%   52%   42%

1987   1995   2001   2004

Handguns and Crime

Canadians used to be proud that handguns weren't nearly as prevalent in our cities as they have always been in the United States. But handgun crimes are up in Canada, and police say there are a lot more of them around now. We asked whether people who commit crimes involving handguns should face an automatic minimum sentence of ten years in jail. Quite a few of our respondents agreed (58%), but a sizable minority disagreed (41%).

Smoking Up

A majority of Canadians (55%) believe that smoking marijuana should not be a criminal offence, while four in ten (42%) believe that it should be. That represents a shift toward a more liberal outlook over the past decade or two. When we asked that question in 1987, 39% felt that marijuana possession should be decriminalized.

Nearly two-thirds (63%) of Canadians say they would support the issuing of tickets and fines to those caught in possession of under 15 grams of marijuana instead of charging them with a crime, which, if they are convicted, results in a criminal record. Just over one-third (35%) oppose a change to current penalties.

Men are more likely to hold the view that smoking marijuana should not be a criminal offence (61%, versus 36% who think it should), while women are split on the issue.

University graduates (61%) are more likely than are those without a university degree (53%) to believe that smoking marijuana should not be a criminal offence. Not surprisingly, younger adult Canadians (71%) are more likely than either middle-aged (63%) or older (55%) Canadians to be in favour of decriminalization.

At any rate, decriminalized marijuana seems inevitable. Get ready for the sweet smell of cannabis—and the red-faced reaction of the United States.

Percentage increase in those who believe smoking marijuana should be decriminalized, between 1987 and the present: 41
Ratio of men to women who think marijuana should be decriminalized: 1.25 to 1

We're Not Sure about the Supreme Court

There has been a lot in the news about the Supreme Court of Canada over the past few years, as Canadians debate whether the court has wrested too much decision-making power from elected politicians under the Canadian Charter of Rights and Freedoms, and whether appointments to the court—currently made by the prime minister of the day—should receive more scrutiny, either from Parliament or in other ways.

We found that most Canadians respect and approve of the performance of the Supreme Court. Seven in ten respondents (70%) say they approve of the actions of the Supreme Court, and a whopping 89% say they respect Supreme Court justices.

While respect runs high, there is a widespread perception—by 84% of Canadians—that decisions made by the Supreme Court are influenced to some degree by partisan politics.

But We Like the Charter

Nearly three-quarters (74%) of Canadians believe that their individual rights and freedoms are better protected today than before the Charter of Rights and Freedoms was enacted in 1982. Canadians most associate the Charter with the protection of the rights of all Canadians (72%) and not just the rights of certain groups, such as accused criminals (8%), or with the enforcement of equality rights of women or minorities (7%).

Seven in ten (70%) say that they feel more comfortable entrusting their individual rights and freedoms to judicial interpretation of the Charter than leaving protection of these rights up to politicians in Parliament and provincial legislatures (21%).

At some point, your freedom is going to bump up against someone else's. Your right to a quiet Sunday afternoon is going to clash with someone's right to work in his yard; your need to stop your car at the curb is going to conflict with someone else's need to use that lane. Ultimately, your safety may depend on the abrogation of someone's right to freedom, just as someone else's freedom may depend on the suspension of your freedom as you perform jury duty. Our freedom is not even close to being absolute, and the civil society is the one that acknowledges that and is willing to abide by the greater good. If there is one thing that Canadians can be proud of, it may be this.

Justice

Capital Punishment

In 1995, 69% of Canadians supported the death penalty compared to 73% in 1987. Now, only 42% support capital punishment—down 27 percentage points since 1995. And the demographic trend suggests that support for the death penalty is going to continue to dwindle.

Those between the ages of 18 and 34 (60%) are most likely to oppose the death penalty. But it would seem that the traditional generational gap on this issue has closed; those aged 35 to 54 (52%) and those over the age of 55 (59%) now make up majorities as well. For more on Canadians' views on capital punishment in contrast with Americans', take a look in the "Americans" chapter.

Wrongful Convictions

Canadians are very concerned about justice. Though cases of wrongful conviction are extremely rare, they are clearly something that Canadians feel strongly about. Two out of three Canadians believe that reported cases of wrongful conviction show that Canada's justice system should increase its efforts to deal with people who claim they have been wrongfully convicted. An overwhelming majority of Canadians (94%) believe that those wrongfully convicted should receive compensation.

Who thinks the justice system should do more to deal with those who claim to be wrongfully convicted?

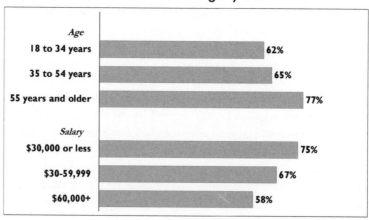

Age	
18 to 34 years	62%
35 to 54 years	65%
55 years and older	77%
Salary	
$30,000 or less	75%
$30-59,999	67%
$60,000+	58%

Province with the highest level of support of the death
penalty: Alberta
Province with the least support: Quebec
Region that feels most strongly that the justice system should
do more to deal with those who claim to be wrongfully
convicted: Atlantic Canada (76%)
Province that feels least strongly: Alberta (54%)
Chances a Canadian with a high school education or less
thinks the justice system should be examined: 8 in 10
That a Canadian with a university education thinks so: 6 in 10

And Rights

Three-quarters (74%) of Canadians believe that their individual
rights and freedoms are better protected today than before the
Charter of Rights and Freedoms was enacted in 1982.

Region of Canada most likely to be satisfied with the
Charter: Atlantic provinces
Least likely: Alberta
Chances that a young Canadian feels this way: 8 in 10
That an older Canadian does: 7 in 10
Likelihood that an Albertan believes that the Charter of Rights
and Freedoms is most associated with the rights of criminals
and accused criminals: 1 in 5
Ratio of Albertans to Atlantic Canadians who hold this
view: 9 to 1

Who Should Protect Our Rights

While some politicians have complained about the increased role of
the courts in Canadian life since the enactment of the Charter of
Rights and Freedoms, a majority of Canadians do not appear to
share this concern. In fact, seven in ten Canadians say that they feel
more comfortable entrusting their individual rights and freedoms to
judicial interpretation of the Charter than leaving protection of these
rights up to politicians in Parliament and provincial legislatures.

Albertans are the least likely to trust the courts. Interestingly,
Saskatchewan and Manitoba, their Prairie neighbours, are the *most*
likely.

The Supreme Court

Seven in ten members of the Canadian public (70%) say that, generally speaking, over the last year or so—a timeframe that includes the controversial Robert Latimer appeal regarding the killing of his daughter—they approve of the actions of the Supreme Court. In addition to high levels of approval, almost nine in ten (89%) say they have respect for Supreme Court justices. These figures are in line with the respect the public has for judges in general, with 91% saying they respect judges.

Quebeckers (77%) are most likely to approve of the actions of the Supreme Court over the last year or so, while residents of Saskatchewan/Manitoba (62%) are significantly less likely (Saskatchewan is the province where Robert Latimer resides).

The approval rating of the Supreme Court generally increases with education and income. University graduates (78%) are more likely than those with less than a high school education (59%) to approve of the highest court's decisions over the last year or so. Canadians with a household income of $30,000 or more (74%) are more likely than lower-income households (65%) to approve.

As noted earlier, while respect and approval run high, there is a widespread perception across the country (84%) that the decisions made by the Supreme Court are influenced to some degree by partisan politics. Half (50%) say the court's decisions are "sometimes influenced" by partisan politics, while 18% say that "partisan politics almost always plays a role in Supreme Court decisions." One in ten (10%) think the Supreme Court is "completely independent of partisan politics."

When the public is asked to identify in their own words which one decision made by the Supreme Court over the last few years stands out most in their minds, the largest number (15%) say the Robert Latimer decision—the case of the father who killed his daughter. The next most frequently mentioned cases are Quebec Referendum/Clarity Bill/Bill C-20 (4%) and a number of specific decisions, including rulings related to same-sex benefits/gay rights (3%), Aboriginal fishing rights/Burnt Church, N.B. (3%) and pornography/child pornography (3%).

A majority of Canadians (59%) say they oppose the Supreme Court's decision to uphold Robert Latimer's mandatory minimum sentence of ten years in prison.

Province most likely to oppose a Supreme Court
decision: Quebec
Least likely: Alberta
Percentage difference between university graduates and
those with less than a high school education who approve
of the Supreme Court of Canada's decisions: 19
Percentage by which lower-income earners (<$30,000) are
more likely than higher-income earners ($60,000+) to be
concerned that they may not receive a fair trial: 16

Marijuana Laws

Canadians appear to back the changes to marijuana possession laws floated by the federal government. When asked in general, a majority of those in the country believe that smoking marijuana should not be a criminal offence, while four in ten believe it should be. When this question was asked of Canadians in the fall of 1997, a slight majority (51%) held the view that smoking marijuana should not be a criminal offence, while ten years earlier (September 1987), just 39% held this position. In every category, we found that the more education you have, the more likely you are to support decriminalization.

And we're increasingly cool with possession. Asked directly about the rumoured changes to marijuana possession laws, two-thirds (63%) of Canadians say they would support the issuing of tickets and fines to those caught in possession of under 15 grams of marijuana instead of charging them with a crime, which if convicted, results in a criminal record (should they be convicted).

Even though Canadians support decriminalization, half of us (53%) feel the new possession laws will make it harder for police to fight the drug trade, 51% believe it will increase demand for marijuana and 51% feel it will induce teenagers to take up smoking pot. Clearly, we have some contradictions on what we want versus what could be.

Rate by which a high school dropout is more likely than a
university graduate to believe that decriminalizing marijuana
will lead to an increase in crime: 50%
Province whose residents are most likely to feel that smoking
marijuana should not be a criminal offence: *not* British
Columbia but Quebec

Province whose residents are most likely to feel smoking
marijuana should be a criminal offence: Alberta
Percentage increase since 1987 in those who believe that
smoking marijuana should be decriminalized: 41

Pellet Guns

After a number of recent incidents involving pellet guns, including
a drive-by shooting in which a six-year-old was hit in the eye, a
majority of Canadians (55%) believe that pellet guns are dangerous
and should be banned outright. As a fallback position, 70% agree
with the view that pellet guns should be treated like other guns, in
that you should need a licence to own and use one.

There is a strong divide on this question between those who live
in urban and rural areas of the country. Significantly more urban
Canadians (58%) agree with this proposition than do rural
Canadians (44%).

Rate by which someone from Manitoba or Saskatchewan is
more likely than someone from Quebec or Ontario to
oppose a ban on pellet guns: 2 to 1
Rate by which a man is more likely than a woman to oppose
an outright ban: 2 to 1
Ratio of urban to rural Canadians who believe pellet guns
should be banned: 10 to 9

The Fight against Terrorism

Canadians are a sophisticated lot. Although they understand that
their freedom is curtailed by the rights of others, many seem to feel
strongly that there has to be a justifiable reason to forfeit any of
their rights. Almost half of Canadians (45%) agree that police and
security forces in Canada are now going too far in using anti-
terrorism powers. Notably, a majority don't.

Five in ten in British Columbia (51%) and in Quebec (50%)
agree that police and security forces have gone too far. Just under
half in Atlantic Canada (45%) and Saskatchewan/Manitoba (45%)
agree with them, while four in ten in Ontario (42%) and Alberta
(36%) feel this way.

Older Canadians more likely to think the police have "gone too far"

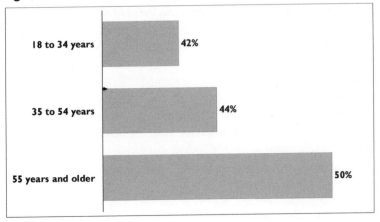

18 to 34 years	42%
35 to 54 years	44%
55 years and older	50%

Many feel that once you're suspected of terrorism, all bets are off when it comes to being treated fairly. Fully four in ten worry that they would not get a fair hearing if they were to be detained by police or security services in Canada and were wrongly suspected of terrorism activities.

- **Residents of Quebec (47%) and Saskatchewan/Manitoba (47%) are the most inclined to worry about receiving a fair trial should they be wrongly suspected of terrorism activities, followed by Albertans (39%), British Columbians (38%), Ontarians (37%) and Atlantic Canadians (36%).**
- **The older the respondents are, the more likely they are to worry that they may not receive a fair trial (aged 18–34, 37%; 35–54, 42%; and 55+, 44%).**
- **Exactly three-quarters give an emphatic "no" when asked if they are prepared to see our police and security forces get more power to fight terrorism—specifically, the power to tap their phones, open their mail or read personal e-mails without their ever knowing it.**

Percentage difference between B.C. residents and Alberta residents who think the police and security forces have gone too far in using anti-terrorism powers: 42
Percentage of Canadians who agree that the government should be allowed to keep evidence secret in court cases against people they think are risks to national security: 51

Reporting on Crime

A free press is integral to a free society, but Canadians appear split over the question of whether confidentiality of sources is sacrosanct. Over half (54%) do not believe that police should be able to search the homes of journalists for leaked documents and confidential sources regarding national security investigations.

Sole province where the majority of residents think the police should be able to search journalists' homes: Alberta
Percentage of Canadians with less than a high school education who think that police should be able to search journalists' homes: 58
Percentage of Canadians with university educations who think so: 36

Identity Theft

It seems that modern ways of doing business are leaving Canadians a little bit anxious. Three-quarters of Canadian adults (75%) say they are concerned about identity theft. Indeed, when asked how likely they would be to provide their personal or account information if contacted by a bank or retailer they frequently deal with, only 14% said they would. Only 7% of Canadians are not at all concerned by identity theft.

The survey then went on to ask Canadians, "How well informed would you say you are in how to prevent becoming a victim of identity theft?" One-fifth (20%) judged themselves to be very well informed. However, half (50%) said they were only somewhat well informed, with another 21% saying "not too well informed" and 9% "not at all informed." These findings suggest that Canadians are quite rightly cautious and concerned about the issue but not necessarily informed about prevention.

"In your opinion, what specific steps or actions should people take to prevent becoming victim to identify theft?"

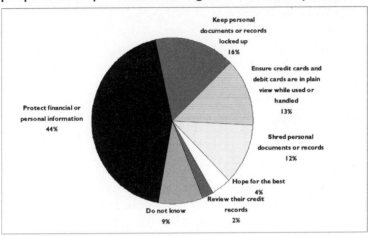

Keep personal documents or records locked up
16%

Ensure credit cards and debit cards are in plain view while used or handled
13%

Protect financial or personal information
44%

Shred personal documents or records
12%

Hope for the best
4%

Review their credit records
2%

Do not know
9%

When Canadians were read a list and then asked whose responsibility it is to protect people from identity theft, the most frequently mentioned response was "individuals such as yourself" (by 92%). While a large majority of Canadians felt it was up to individuals to protect themselves from identity theft, other institutions were also cited by majorities. These included credit card companies (by 83%), other financial institutions such as banks (84%), credit bureaus (71%), retailers (70%) and governments (68%).

Percentage of Canadians who identify crime as the most important problem in their community: 22
Percentage who belive crime has risen over the past 5 years: 59
Province whose residents are most afraid of being a victim of crime: British Columbia
Gender most afraid of being a victim: male

Health Care

Health care is this government's number one priority. We will come to an agreement with the provinces, because we must. We will implement a long-term plan, because we must. And because we must, we will provide a fix for a generation.

—Prime Minister Paul Martin, April 16, 2004

CANADIANS ARE OFTEN confused with Americans when they travel the world, and the two countries have far more similarities than differences. But if there is one difference that Canadians cherish, it is the two countries' approaches to health care. It is not an exaggeration to say that, with the possible exceptions of gun control and foreign policy, no issue differentiates the social philosophies of Canada and the United States the way health care does.

Canada's national health care system was introduced in 1968, six years after Saskatchewan Premier Tommy Douglas precipitated a doctors' strike by introducing medical insurance at the provincial level in Saskatchewan. Former U.S. president Bill Clinton failed to rally sufficient political support to introduce a national U.S. public health care system early in his first term in office, and American health care remains largely in private hands.

Escalating costs and legitimate complaints about people waiting too long for treatment have sullied the Canadian system's reputation in recent years, and there has been a continuing national debate as to how to improve the system. But the U.S. system—which on a per capita basis costs 50% more than any other system in the world—has even more dramatic problems. These begin with the chilling spectre of 44 million Americans without medical coverage and with the billions of dollars squandered on litigation between insurers and ailing Americans.

If that appears unjust to most Canadians, more injustice looms. As Hillary Rodham Clinton pointed out in the *New York Times Magazine* on April 18, 2004, if private U.S. medical insurers gain access to genetic predispositions of individual Americans, they are likely to deny coverage to people with genetic defects the way they now deny coverage to people deemed to have had a pre-existing medical problem. This, she points out, "threatens to turn the most susceptible patients into the most vulnerable." In other words, those with the greatest chance of getting sick would have the least chance of being covered.

Canada's problems are to some degree about a sense of entitlement—the entitlement to timely treatment—but they are also about escalating costs associated with expensive drugs, new technologies and an aging population. Federal and provincial governments are scrambling to determine how to grapple with these costs.

Politicians are confronted with figuring out how to fix the system without abandoning its principles and without bankrupting the country. Our surveys show that Canadians have no intention of abandoning universal public medical coverage, no matter how many challenges it faces. And the fact is, despite the horror stories and claims that the system is falling apart, most Canadians give the current system a decent passing grade: B.

How Dissatisfied Are We with Our Overloaded Health Care System?

Canadians are mixed in their opinions when asked to grade the accessibility of health care services in their own communities. They are most positive about access to their family doctor and to walk-in clinics and about access for children and seniors (at least five in ten assign a B grade or better).

Here is the biggest gripe: When asked about access to medical specialists and diagnostic equipment, the majority assign a C grade or worse. This is clearly a major problem, because when medical specialists and diagnostic equipment are important to treatment, the diagnosis is often likely to be more serious.

An Even Bigger Gripe

Did we just say that lack of access to medical specialists and diagnostic equipment was the biggest gripe? Well, there are people with even better grounds for complaint; 24% of Canadians have been a victim of some kind of medical mistake.

Among those who say they know of a medical mistake, here's what went wrong

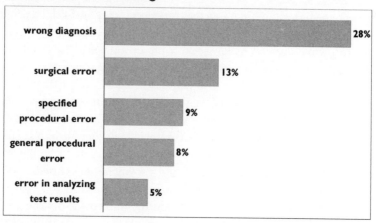

wrong diagnosis	28%
surgical error	13%
specified procedural error	9%
general procedural error	8%
error in analyzing test results	5%

But Whom Should We Blame?

Percentage of Canadians who blame medical errors on government cutbacks: 31
Percentage of victims who do: 6

Long-Term Sustainable Funding

When Prime Minister Paul Martin took office, one of his first promises was that his government would commit to a sustained increase in national health care funding if he could reach an agreement with the provinces on the essentials of an improved system. We found that 82% of Canadians, when asked to rate the importance of long-term sustained funding, ranked that priority between 7 and 10 on a scale of 1 to 10. So the Liberals' 2004 $18-billion injection of cash was in sync with public expectations, but little more than a short-term fix.

So Where Do We Want the Health Care Money Spent?

We gave respondents a list of potential spending priorities and asked them to make choices. We discovered that nearly two-thirds (63%) of Canadians believe that reducing waiting lists for diagnostic services like MRIs and CAT scans should be a top priority for more health care spending.

Number two on the list would be a new national home care program (49%), followed by more efficient methods for providing primary health care services (44%), investing in prevention services to make Canadians in general healthier (42%), creating a new national pharmacare program (33%), freeing up more money for nurses (31%) and spending more money on doctors (18%).

One thing's for sure: Canadians are sick of waiting. Seventy-two per cent of Canadians think the country needs a national system to measure and report waiting times. Moreover, 88% say that Canadians have a right to know how long they can expect to wait for needed treatments.

Canadians are also concerned about a shortage of nurses. More than eight in ten (83%) say that a shortage of nurses makes the health care system more vulnerable to future threats to human health such as SARS or West Nile virus. After the 2003 SARS crisis in Toronto, nearly two-thirds of respondents (64%) told us that their appreciation of the importance of nurses in the health system had increased. Nearly nine out of ten Canadians (88%) support the proposition that the federal government should set up a fund to assist the provinces in educating, hiring and retaining more nurses.

Bottom line: More than six out of every ten respondents (61%) told us that the federal government should implement the Romanow report's recommendations even if it means that their taxes go up a bit.

Overall Quality of the Health Care System

We've all heard the shrill reports of the demise of the Canadian health care system, usually in an editorial or think-tank piece committed to privatization. We are treated to endless pronouncements on how fed up we are and how passionately we want change. But here's the thing: Canadians continue to assign the overall quality of the health care system a fairly positive rating. At least six in ten Canadians give the health care system a B grade or better in terms of overall quality (63%), choice of health services (62%) and their most recent interaction with the system (68%).

But dispite the B–average report card, when Canadians are asked to think about whether Canada's health care system today is better or worse overall than it was ten years ago, a slim majority (54%) say that the overall care the system provides is worse. That means that slightly less than half say that today's health care system provides *better* care than it did ten years ago. Though hardly cause for celebration, these numbers don't exactly herald a crisis of discontent.

Long-Term Sustainable Funding Needed

It is nothing short of amazing that anyone would try to turn health care into a political hot potato. Fully eight in ten Canadians (82%) agree that we need long-term sustainable funding to improve the health care system in Canada. Only 3% disagree. Here's the rub: we agree on the premise, but disagree on the means.

What do you think is the most important thing that can be done to improve the health care system in Canada?

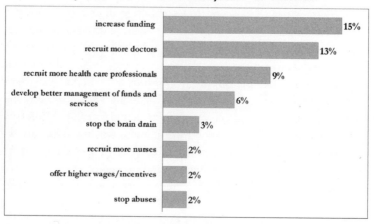

increase funding	15%
recruit more doctors	13%
recruit more health care professionals	9%
develop better management of funds and services	6%
stop the brain drain	3%
recruit more nurses	2%
offer higher wages/incentives	2%
stop abuses	2%

Government Performance

Another note to politicians: Canadians remain negative when asked to assess government performance on the health care file. Only 5% give the federal government's performance in dealing with health care in Canada a very positive rating (that is, an A); over six times as many (32%) give the federal government's performance in this area a failing grade. The rest of Canadians huddle in the middle. But be careful: when you're in a minority government, you have to get your report card signed by all your parents. Similarly only 8% think their provincial government is doing a very good job in dealing with health care in their province, while fully 32% give their provincial government a failing grade.

Percentage of Albertans who think health care has improved over the past decade: 57

Percentage of British Columbians who do: 34

Percentage of Canadians who indicate we wouldn't have to raise taxes to improve health care if we just did a better job of spending the money that's already allocated: 88

Percentage who believe more money for doctors should be a top health care priority: 18

Percentage who say more money for nurses should be a top health care priority: 31

Romanow, O Romanow ...

Eight in ten Canadians (82%) approve of the recommendation of the Romanow Report that the federal government spend an additional $15 billion on health care over the next three years. While Canadians may not have got what they want, at least politicians listened and put some cash on the table at the 2004 Health Care Summit. This ringing endorsement came even though it was been made clear to respondents that if the federal government were to follow this recommendation, it would mean that the projected federal budget surplus for this period would be spent almost exclusively on improving health care services in Canada.

Chances that an NDP supporter endorses the Romanow plan: 9 in 10

Chances that an Alliance supporter does: 7.5 in 10

Percentage of those who support the plan who would like to see the entire federal surplus spent on health care: 52

Percentage of Canadians who say the federal government should implement the Romanow Report recommendations even if it means that their taxes go up a little: 61

Percentage of NDP supporters who say so: 76

Percentage of Bloc/Alliance supporters who do: 51

Rate by which an older Canadian is more likely than a younger Canadian to be familiar with the report: 2 to 1

Credibility on Health Care

Professional organization most trusted by nurses when
talking about health care: nurses
Least trusted by nurses: major business
Percentage of Canadians who trust doctors' associations: 86
Percentage who trust the prime minister: 57

So, What Are the Priorities?

What is Canada's foremost health care priority?

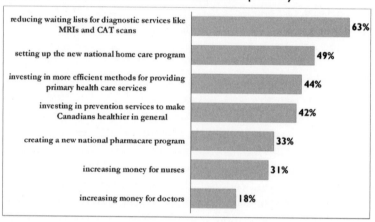

reducing waiting lists for diagnostic services like MRIs and CAT scans — 63%

setting up the new national home care program — 49%

investing in more efficient methods for providing primary health care services — 44%

investing in prevention services to make Canadians healthier in general — 42%

creating a new national pharmacare program — 33%

increasing money for nurses — 31%

increasing money for doctors — 18%

Asked to choose which specific area should be the *single* top spending priority, the ranking remains generally the same—reduced waiting lists (27%), a national home care program (15%), prevention services (15%), more efficient methods for primary health care (13%), a national pharmacare program (7%), more money for nurses (5%) and finally more money for doctors (4%).

Percentage of Canadians who are personally responsible
for taking care of elderly members of their family (driving
them to doctors' appointments, making arrangements for
medical or other services, and doing things they are no
longer able to do themselves): 32.
Percentage of Canadians who believe that more money for
nurses should be the nation's top priority: 5

Percentage who believe more money for doctors should be: 4

Rate by which Atlantic Canadians are more likely than
Albertans to support increased wages for doctors: 2 to 1

Rank of retaining, recruiting and educating nurses as a priority
facing their provincial government: 1st

Rank of reducing provincial tax: 2nd

Ratio of those who favour supporting nurses to those who
favour cutting provincial taxes: 2 to 1

Rank of cutting corporate tax: 5th

Ratio of those who favour hiring more nurses to those who
favour cutting corporate tax: 11 to 1

Health Care Funding: Assessing Federal and Provincial Positions

When the prime minister and the premiers sit down to decide on health care funding options, Canadians appear to say yes to both opposing positions. While these findings appear to be contradictory—support going to federal and provincial leaders who have differing positions—it would appear that there may be another message that has emerged: both sides make arguments that have some punch, but at the end of the day, trust puts the premiers ahead on points. Canadians lean toward the view of the premiers and the provinces (51%) over that of the prime minister and the federal government (42%). Five per cent say they support neither position over the other.

This point is further illustrated by the majority (56%) of Canadians who disagree that they "trust the prime minister and the federal government more than the premiers and their governments to make the right decisions about where health care dollars should be spent."

However, trust in the provincial governments' position on health care funding is not without some skepticism. Six in ten (62%) agree with the view that "the premiers are asking for more money than they actually need to solve their health care problems. They should be dealing with waste and inefficiency in their own provincial health care systems since that is causing the most problems." This seems to be something about which Canadians are of two minds.

Rate by which a Manitoban is more likely than an Ontarian to
disagree that they trust the PM and the federal government
more than the premiers and provincial governments on
health care: 50%
Percentage of Canadians who say federal funding should come
with no strings attached: 67
Percentage who say the federal government needs more
control: 62
Rate by which an Albertan is more likely than a Manitoban to
trust his or her provincial government: 2 to 1
Rate by which older Canadians are more likely than younger
Canadians to say they trust neither their provincial
government nor the federal government: 3 to 1

If You Become Critically Ill Now, Can You Cover Your Needs?

Only half (54%) of Canadians say they are confident that they will
have sufficient money or funds to cover their expenses if they
became critically ill. Forty-five per cent indicate that they will not
have the money to cover such expenses.

Upper-income Canadians are 67% more likely than lower-
income Canadians to think they would have enough to cover their
expenses if they became critically ill.

Canadians Worry about These Things . . .

Eight in ten Canadians (79%) indicate that they worry that they or
someone in their family might become critically ill. Only 21% say
they are not worried about this happening.

Rate by which a younger Canadian is more likely than an
older Canadian to worry that they or a family member
will fall critically ill: 21%
Rank of maintaining one's current lifestyle among concerns
associated with the cost of illness: 1st
Rank of supporting one's family: 3rd

Brave New World

Canadians seem to be less concerned with the religious implications
of medical technology than are Americans. Six in ten Canadians

(61%) approve the creation of cloned human embryos for the sole purpose of collecting stem cells to be used in research.

University-educated Canadians are 35% more likely than high school dropouts to support stem-cell research, and 42% more likely than lower-income Canadians.

Three-quarters (76%) of Canadians also approve of the use of unused extra human embryos (originally created for the purpose of in-vitro fertilization but left unused by a couple) for stem-cell research, as long as consent is obtained from the original couple involved.

How Prepared Is the System for an Epidemic?

Some illness comes naturally, some with age, or injury, or the change of seasons. But some threats are new and are exacerbated by the newness of global culture.

Percentage of Canadians who believe the health care system is unprepared for an outbreak of SARS, West Nile virus or mad-cow disease: 62
Percentage who believe that a shortage of nurses makes the health care system more vulnerable to future threats to human health such as SARS or West Nile virus: 83
Rate by which a university graduate is more likely than a high school dropout to believe this: 66
Percentage of Canadians who say they personally realize the importance of nurses to the health care system more now than they did before the outbreaks: 64
Percentage of Canadians who believe there is a shortage of public health nurses—nurses who provide immunization, educate the public on disease prevention and investigate disease carriers: 83
Percentage of Canadians who indicate that their provincial government must retain more full-time nurses' positions as well as hire more nurses to meet future health care emergencies: 94

Trade-Offs

Percentage of Canadians who would choose their employee health benefit package over an extra $2,000 in cash per year: 81

Over an extra $5,000 in cash: 70
Over an extra $8,000 in cash: 65

Two-Tier Health

While Canadians hold their public healthcare dear, they feel the same way about their own health. Slightly more than half of Canadians (56%) agree that "if the public healthcare system cannot meet the healthcare needs of myself or my family in a timely fashion I should be allowed to pay out of my own pocket to get faster diagnosis or treatment from a private healthcare facility if available" (26% "somewhat agree," 30% "strongly agree"). Four in ten Canadians (43%) disagree with this statement. The remaining 1% of Canadians "don't know" whether they agree or disagree with this statement.

Further, two thirds of Canadians (64%) agree with the premiers' position that "the best way to reduce waiting lists is to create a national pharmacare program, because it will reduce provincial spending on drugs, and allow them to spend this money on reducing waiting lists in a way that is appropriate for each province."

Province most likely to agree with either statement: Quebec
Province least likely: Ontario

However, three-quarters of Canadians (74%) approve of the federal government's desire to direct "any increased healthcare funding to reducing waiting lists instead of a new national pharmacare program." Clearly, some Canadians want it both ways.

Ratio of support for the provinces to that for the federal government: 47:45

And Finally

Politicians, take note: even as we debate the way toward a sustainable health care system, Canadians know what they want—the very best care. Eighty-five percent agree that "as a Canadian [they are] entitled to the best possible health care, regardless of the cost to the government."

Stress

There is more to life than increasing its speed.

—Mahatma Gandhi (1869–1948)

MYTHILY S. EMIGRATED to Canada four years ago to start a family. She left a country ravaged by civil war, a country in which terror lurks anywhere near the likely sites of clashes between government and revolutionary troops.

She came to a country known around the world as a haven from war—good old Canada. She came to a land where we behave toward one another with as much civility as anywhere in the world—with the exception of hockey games, of course, and those can be avoided. What a relief our lifestyle must be for people like Mythily S.

And yet, when CTV interviewed Ms. S. in September 2002 in connection with a study that had just been released, it wasn't exactly the peaceful nature of Canadian society that had made the strongest impression. It was the intense new anxiety she was trying to come to grips with in her new homeland.

In Canada, she told the interviewer, "Everything is moving very fast. In [my country], everything is peaceful—except the war. Everything here gives us so much stress."

Morton Beiser, a researcher who worked on the study "Stress Common among Immigrants," said that "the fact is, when immigrants come to Canada, on the whole their health is better than the Canadian average—and then their health deteriorates."

There are a variety of likely reasons—the stresses involved with such a major move, the relatively low incomes that many immigrants earn when they arrive, less exercise in their new environment, understanding new values and so on. But part of the problem is just the bald fact that Canada—once a rural backwater—has become a largely urban, high-stress society, in which anybody not operating at a frenetic pace is often seen as lazy and unmotivated.

North America: Life in the Pressure Cooker

Immigrants aren't the only ones feeling the squeeze. CTV also interviewed Norta Spinks, a leading consultant on workplace stress: "We've seen an alarming increase in the amount of stress leaves that people are on. It's one of the fastest-growing short-term disabilities . . . that employers are now having to look at. The toll is measured in growing absenteeism, disability claims, high turnover, and drug-plan costs spiralling out of control, growing an average of 16% a year."

Peter Hausdorf, an industrial psychology expert, said some Canadians are in denial: many of his clients "seem reluctant to deal with the fact that the issue is the amount of work . . . What they'd rather do is focus on other aspects. So we'll have fitness facilities to deal with stress, we'll provide additional resources for health care. These are good things, but they're not dealing with the core issue, which is the volume of work."

Our surveys show that the level of stress in modern Canadian society is spilling out a lot of negatives. People are finding themselves less healthy, less convinced that their family relationships are getting the attention they deserve, less satisfied with their sex lives and generally more cynical about the value of their existence. One in five Canadians has contemplated suicide due to stress, and stress is clearly a major contributor to people's feelings that they are unable to cope.

Got Time on Your Hands?

There are, of course, other Canadians who feel they have too much time on their hands. But it isn't happening much these days, at least to many of us, aside from those who are unemployed or retired. Only 7% of respondents to one of our polls complained that they had too much free time in their life, and not surprisingly most were older Canadians.

Once you've put in enough time, there's a lot more breathing room: 55% of Canadians between 19 and 54 feel squeezed for personal time, compared to 25% of respondents over 54.

But things are getting worse. Fully 74% of Canadians feel they have less free time now than they did five years ago.

The rich, of course, are busy, busy, busy: 58% of Canadians with personal incomes above $60,000 feel they don't have enough free time, compared to 36% of those with incomes below $30,000. A combination of factors—including unemployment—undoubtedly contributes to that gap, but it still serves as a reminder than money can't buy everything.

What we've learned from many Canadians' complaints about lack of time is that work takes priority over everything. We complain that work is damaging our relationships, but seldom that our relationships are impinging on our work.

What Is Making People So Stressed?

One factor is that a lot of people are buckling under the pressure of too much work. Work is the big stress button for 43% of Canadians. Of course, work brings us money, but never enough. We discovered that money (that is, managing finances) is the second most stressful factor in Canadians' lives, at 39%.

So more work raises stress, as does less money. That is, neither working less nor working more is likely to reduce your stress.

Hey, maybe the famous economist Joseph Schumpeter was right. Schumpeter (1883–1950), though no socialist, described capitalism as the most destructive force the world has ever known, arguing that by its very nature it "creates, educates and subsidizes a vested interest in social unrest." Not to mention *personal* unrest—sometimes known as stress.

One-tenth of Canadians say they have no stress in their lives. They are the blessed.

Stress: Bad for People but Good for Production?

A bit of stress is not bad for everyone. In fact, many Canadians seem to respond well to the whip. More than three in ten employed Canadians (31%) say that stress has had a positive impact on the quality of work they do, and just under one-quarter say stress has had a positive impact on their relations with co-workers.

But not everyone works well under pressure. Just under one-quarter of respondents (23%) say that stress has a negative impact on their quality of work, and 19% say it has a negative impact on their relations with co-workers.

Nearly half our respondents (47%) think that their co-workers sometimes talk about how stressed they are just to impress them.

Imagine. We're living in a society in which many people regard a high stress level as a badge of honour.

But we shouldn't joke too much about stress. It hurts us. Stress is a drag on productivity and a drain on Canadians' health. We're taking time off work, suffering physical symptoms, seeking therapy and letting our most important relations fall into disuse.

However, we seem to have the solutions at our disposal. Canadians have their strategies for beating stress, and most of them involve family, exercise and time for reflection. We know what we need.

And most of us also believe we need an additional public-holiday long weekend—some day we'll catch up to the Europeans, who seem to have unlimited vacations. Apart from helping our mental health and family relationships, an additional long weekend would be a boon for the beer industry. Beer is the preferred beverage to enjoy on a long weekend. Cheers.

Canadians and Stress

Chances that a Canadian feels that life is beyond control: 4 in 10

Percentage of Canadians who feel the world is changing too quickly: 40

Province whose residents are most likely to feel this way: Quebec

Least likely: Saskatchewan/Manitoba

Percentage of Canadians who agree that there has been a time in their life when they've been under so much stress that they've wanted to commit suicide: 17

Number of percentage points by which a woman is more likely to agree with this view: 33

Number of percentage points by which a lower-income Canadian is more likely to agree than an upper-income Canadian: 70

Percentage of Canadians who do not believe that it is a sign of personal weakness to seek professional help to deal with stress: 85

Likelihood that a Canadian will think it is not a sign of personal weakness to seek professional help to deal with stress, by education level

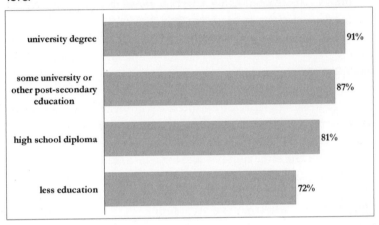

university degree	91%
some university or other post-secondary education	87%
high school diploma	81%
less education	72%

Work and Finances Top Causes of Stress

As indicated previously, it's not hard to determine the leading causes of stress in Canadians' lives: their job (43%) and their finances (39%) are the most cited.

Younger (52%) and middle-aged (50%) Canadians are twice as likely as older Canadians (24%) to say that the main source of stress in their lives is their job, while older Canadians (15%) are more likely to cite their health as a cause of stress than are middle-aged (7%) or younger (2%) Canadians.

Difference between the percentage of middle-income earners and the percentage of upper-income earners who cite finances as a main cause of stress: 1
Factor by which an upper-income Canadian is more likely than a lower-income Canadian to claim that work is the main source of stress: 2
Factor by which a woman is more likely than a man to suffer stress from having too much to do or too little time: 6

Pressure

Not all stress is applied by the boss or the clock. Two-thirds of Canadians (67%) indicate that they put too much pressure on *themselves*. Middle-aged (73%) and younger (71%) Canadians are more likely to agree with this view than are older Canadians (55%).

Province whose residents are most likely to feel they put too much pressure on themselves: Ontario
Least likely: Saskatchewan/Manitoba

Can't Sleep?

Sleep patterns and personal health are the areas that Canadians say are the most negatively affected by the stress in their lives, followed by relations at home or with other family members and on their sex lives. The wealthier you are, the more your sleep and health are affected by stress. About the same number see stress on relations with friends as having a negative effect (21%) as see it having a positive effect (24%).

What suffers when you're stressed?

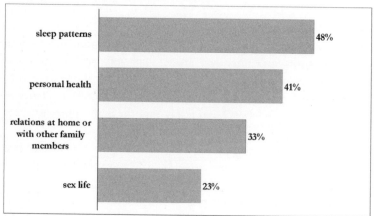

- sleep patterns — 48%
- personal health — 41%
- relations at home or with other family members — 33%
- sex life — 23%

Percentage of Canadians who would prefer a good night's sleep to good sex: 58
Percentage of Canadian women who would prefer a good night's sleep to good sex: 72
Province whose residents' sleep is most affected by stress: Ontario

Province whose residents' health is most affected by
stress: Alberta
Region whose residents' health and sleep suffer least:
Atlantic Canada

Stress and the Workplace

Three in ten employed Canadians (31%) say that the stress in their
lives has had a positive impact on the "quality of work they do at
work," while one-quarter (24%) say stress has a positive impact on
their relations with co-workers. This compares to 23% who indicate
that stress has had a negative impact on their quality of work on the
job and 19% who say the same about their relations with co-
workers.

Percentage of Canadians who think high levels of stress
at work mean you're involved in something important: 48
Odds by which a Quebecker is more likely than an Albertan
to believe that stress has a positive effect on his or her
work: 2 to 1
Percentage of Canadians who have "felt so much stress at
times at work that they have done or seriously thought about
doing things to get back at their boss or co-workers in some
way": 13
Percentage of Canadians who report feeling stress over
unchecked phone or e-mail messages: 18

And It's Getting Worse

When comparing the current amount of free time in their life to five
years ago, four in ten Canadians (41%) say they have less free time,
almost one-quarter (24%) indicating that they have a lot less.

And the more you make, the worse it gets: that's the reward for
your hard work. Of those with an annual household income of
$60,000 or more, almost half (48%) say they have less free time
than five years ago, compared with 42% of those with incomes
between $30,000 and $59,999 and 36% of those with incomes
under $30,000.

Rank of stress, estrangement from friends and family, and
exhaustion as the effects of diminishing free time: 1, 2, 3

When Stress Hits

The afternoon is the most stressful time period for many Canadians.

Time of day Canadians find most stressful

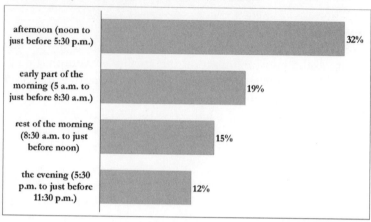

Canadians in upper-income households (28%) are more likely than those in middle- (16%) or lower-income (16%) households to cite job- or work-related reasons for feeling stressed at a particular time in the day.

Percentage of Canadian women who suffer stress over getting children ready or picking them up: 14
Percentage of Canadian men who suffer the same stress: 4

How We React to a post–9/11 world

Twenty-five per cent of Canadian adults indicate that world events are stressful and overwhelming. Four per cent of the adult population indicate they have actually visited their doctor or a professional counsellor to help them cope with how they feel about the threat of terrorism and war, and to deal with both physical and anxiety symptoms. Quebeckers (7%) are more likely than those in other regions to have done so.

Those in Quebec (30%) appear to feel the most overwhelmed by world events, while those in Saskatchewan and Manitoba (15%) appear to be the least overwhelmed.

Percentage of Canadians who indicate that they are more anxious and irritable specifically because of the uncertainty caused by the threat of terrorism and the war on terrorism: 35

Chances that a Canadian adult reports having had trouble sleeping at night because of worry about this conflict: 1 in 7

Factor by which Canadians in households with incomes of less than $30,000 are more likely than Canadians from households with incomes of more than $60,000 to be experiencing troubles sleeping due to worry over the conflict: 2.3

Chances that a Canadian family physician is completely satisfied with the available medication to treat depression and anxiety: 1 in 10

How Do We Beat Stress?

Percentage difference between university graduates and those who have not finished high school who exercise to relieve stress: 33

Odds that a woman is more likely than a man to read to relieve stress: 2 to 1

What Canadians do to beat stress

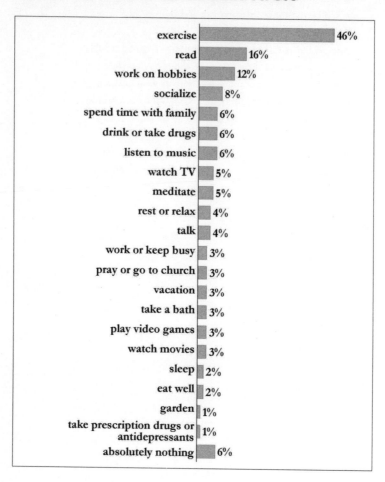

exercise	46%
read	16%
work on hobbies	12%
socialize	8%
spend time with family	6%
drink or take drugs	6%
listen to music	6%
watch TV	5%
meditate	5%
rest or relax	4%
talk	4%
work or keep busy	3%
pray or go to church	3%
vacation	3%
take a bath	3%
play video games	3%
watch movies	3%
sleep	2%
eat well	2%
garden	1%
take prescription drugs or antidepressants	1%
absolutely nothing	6%

A New Public Holiday

In order to increase the amount of free time in people's lives, more than three-quarters of Canadians (77%) support the introduction of "one new public holiday during the spring or summer months in addition to the existing public holidays." Amazingly, 20% of Canadians oppose it.

Support for a new public holiday across Canada

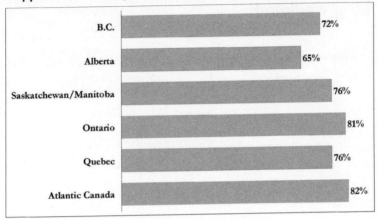

B.C.	72%
Alberta	65%
Saskatchewan/Manitoba	76%
Ontario	81%
Quebec	76%
Atlantic Canada	82%

And What Do Canadians Do with Their Free Time?

Province where you're most likely to relax by dining
out: Quebec
Province where you're most likely to relax by
fishing: Alberta
Province where you're most likely to relax by hanging out
with family and friends: Manitoba/Saskatchewan
Province where you're most likely to relax by doing crafts:
British Columbia

What would Canadians do with another long weekend?

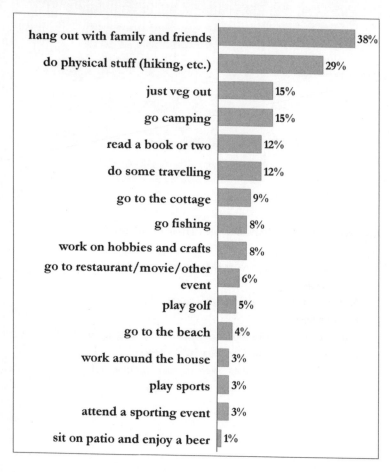

hang out with family and friends	38%
do physical stuff (hiking, etc.)	29%
just veg out	15%
go camping	15%
read a book or two	12%
do some travelling	12%
go to the cottage	9%
go fishing	8%
work on hobbies and crafts	8%
go to restaurant/movie/other event	6%
play golf	5%
go to the beach	4%
work around the house	3%
play sports	3%
attend a sporting event	3%
sit on patio and enjoy a beer	1%

Someone to Hang With

What famous living person would Canadians most like to spend time with on a long weekend? Given the choice on our survey, off the top of their heads, 5% chose "a family member" such as a spouse or a parent—primarily driven by respondents in Quebec (10%).

Next on the list of open-ended choices was then-prime minister Jean Chrétien (4%), who was most likely to be chosen by those in Ontario (5%) and Quebec (5%). Wayne Gretzky (3% overall) was the preference of Saskatchewan/Manitoba (7%), while Celine Dion (3% overall) was the most likely to get an invitation in Quebec (6%). Mel Gibson (2% overall) was the envy of Alberta (6%), whereas Julia Roberts (2%) was offered invitations everywhere except in Atlantic Canada.

The number one guest for youth aged 19–24 was Julia Roberts (7%), whereas those aged 25–34 split between family (5%) and Wayne Gretzky (5%). Family (5%) topped the list for the 35–54 group, whereas the prime minister was most preferred by those 55 and up (7%).

From a gender perspective, the most preferred invite by men went to a family member (6%), compared to women at 4%. Women obviously had a hard time choosing: a family member was tied with Celine Dion (4%) and Mel Gibson (4%).

Stereotypes Confirmed

Favourite Canadian beverage: beer
Province with highest percentage of Pepsi-drinkers: Quebec
Province with highest percentage of wine-drinkers: Quebec
Region with highest percentage of tea-drinkers: Atlantic Canada

Trust and Respect

Before you trust a man, eat a peck of salt with him.

—Ancient proverb

Who has time to eat a peck of salt with anybody these days? A peck is half a bushel—more than 36 litres—and would no doubt take a long time to eat in one sitting.

All the same, it is impossible to exaggerate the importance of trust. Imagine a world in which trust is universal: how would the workplace change if bosses and workers trusted each other? How would marriage change? Business? Law? Advertising? How would politics change if politicians could be trusted? The point is that every facet of human life is corroded by suspicion; a trusting world would undoubtedly be a better one.

Unfortunately, many humans richly deserve the suspicion with which they view each other. Their capacity for deceit and betrayal and violence, to say nothing of shoplifting, fraudulent bookkeeping, false advertising, legal caviling, pool sharking and the failure to return library books in a timely fashion, seems limitless. It's a wonder we trust at all.

Caveat Emptor in the People Bazaar

In the 1950s, young North Americans and Europeans pretty well knew their place. Then, in the 1960s, significant numbers of them publicly rebelled in a short-lived movement against "the establishment." And while capitalism hasn't come close to being overthrown over subsequent decades, there has been an increasing erosion of deference to traditional institutions and people in power. This erosion is endemic to all age groups.

It isn't just politicians and lawyers who are taking the hit—most people have expected these groups to play loose with the truth for many centuries now, and there has always been a healthy measure of skepticism about them. But how about CEOs, journalists, bankers, judges, clerics, royalty, police officers and other authority figures of the past? They're increasingly being looked at sideways in today's world. Enough of them have blotted their copy books that many Canadians don't necessarily take them at their word anymore.

Our List of Liars

When Canadians want to know the truth on a major issue, the last place they expect to hear it is from an elected politician. After politicians, Canadians' liars' brigade is led by lawyers, corporate executives and union leaders.

At the other end of the scale, firefighters rank number one as the hottest in trust. And while patients may be going to the Web more often to check out the validity of their doctors' diagnoses, in relative terms doctors still have a considerable measure of respect in our society, as do nurses, pharmacists and airline pilots. Then again, these are people we very much *want* to trust, aren't they?

Here are the distrusted, in order of distrust

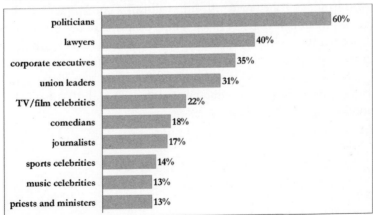

politicians	60%
lawyers	40%
corporate executives	35%
union leaders	31%
TV/film celebrities	22%
comedians	18%
journalists	17%
sports celebrities	14%
music celebrities	13%
priests and ministers	13%

And What About Each Other?

Of course another question arises. This one we haven't measured yet, but how trustworthy are we, individually, as Canadians? As our cynicism about our leaders and institutions has grown, have our own characters eroded as well?

Globe and Mail columnist Judith Timson mooted the question, "How much does telling the truth really matter as a value anymore?" Timson noted that more than one post-mortem analysis of the Martha Stewart case had argued that Stewart had "just lied" (rather than cheated), as if that really shouldn't be a big deal. She quoted Dr. Margaret Somerville, an ethicist at McGill University: "What we've got to worry about here is a culture of deception . . . Our moral intuition has been dulled down."

Food for thought.

Less Likely to Lie . . .

The list of those "very likely to lie" continues with film and television celebrities (22%), comedians (18%), journalists (17%), sports celebrities (14%), music celebrities (13%) and priests and ministers (13%). In general, residents of Alberta are more likely than those in other regions to say that celebrities (film/TV, 32%; sports, 18%; music, 18%) are very likely to lie in the media.

Despite some high-profile cases of suspicious police behaviour in places like Toronto, Edmonton and Saskatoon, the men in blue come out not as badly as the journalists who cover them. Only 8% of Canadians believe that police officers are "very likely to lie." On the other hand, that they made the list at all isn't a good sign. Ditto for doctors (6%) and teachers (5%). These people may not hit double digits, but they're way ahead of people who don't show up much at all in the responses. People like war heroes, philanthropists and pollsters.

Seventeen per cent say that police officers are "not likely at all" to lie, 22% indicate that same view of doctors and 20% hold this opinion regarding teachers.

Perspective: **Canadians are**
- **three times more likely to believe a journalist than they are a politician**
- **two and a half times more likely to believe a sports celebrity than they are an executive**
- **twice as likely to believe a comedian as they are a lawyer**

Rate by which a Quebecker is less likely than an Albertan to say that politicians "are very likely to lie": one-half
Rate by which Albertans are more likely than Atlantic Canadians to assume a lawyer is lying: 2 to 1
Percentage of British Columbians who think corporate executives are very likely to lie: 48
Ratio of Albertans to their neighbours in Saskatchewan/Manitoba who believe journalists are very likely to lie: 2 to 1
Percentage of Quebeckers who believe priests and ministers are very likely to lie: 28
Percentage of Canadians who trust politicians: 9
Percentage of Canadians who trust used-car salespeople: 10

So, Whom *Do* We Trust?

Firefighters (94%), pharmacists (91%), nurses (87%), doctors (85%) and airline pilots (81%) are given top trust marks by Canadians. This is in comparison to local politicians (14%), car salespeople (10%) and national politicians (9%) who are at the bottom of the list. Barely above local politicians and tied with union leaders for fourth place among those least trusted by Canadians: corporate executives. Note: 42% trust pollsters—11 points higher than journalists and 16 points lower than daycare workers. Not a bad place to middle out.

What Industries Do We Trust?

When examining which industries Canadians trust the most, it is the medical research industry (62%), the tourism industry (57%) and national retail/department stores (56%) that top the list. At the bottom is the tobacco industry (8%), the oil industry (17%) and the advertising industry (17%).

Industries we trust (or don't)

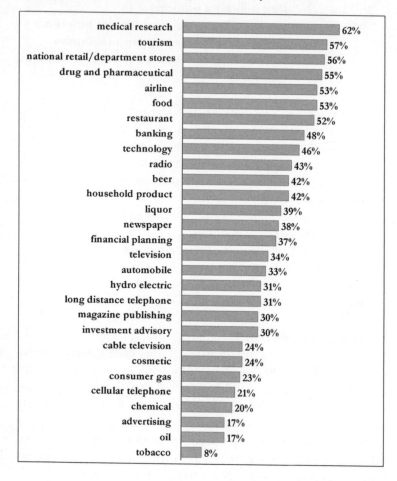

Industry	Percentage
medical research	62%
tourism	57%
national retail/department stores	56%
drug and pharmaceutical	55%
airline	53%
food	53%
restaurant	52%
banking	48%
technology	46%
radio	43%
beer	42%
household product	42%
liquor	39%
newspaper	38%
financial planning	37%
television	34%
automobile	33%
hydro electric	31%
long distance telephone	31%
magazine publishing	30%
investment advisory	30%
cable television	24%
cosmetic	24%
consumer gas	23%
cellular telephone	21%
chemical	20%
advertising	17%
oil	17%
tobacco	8%

Rank of honesty among attributes most important to
Canadians' appraisals of professionals and associations: 1
Rank of education: 8

Vocations we trust (or don't)

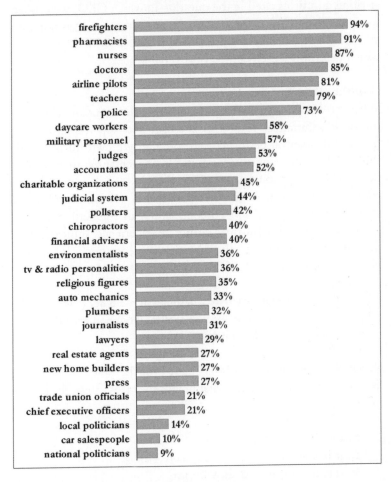

firefighters	94%
pharmacists	91%
nurses	87%
doctors	85%
airline pilots	81%
teachers	79%
police	73%
daycare workers	58%
military personnel	57%
judges	53%
accountants	52%
charitable organizations	45%
judicial system	44%
pollsters	42%
chiropractors	40%
financial advisers	40%
environmentalists	36%
tv & radio personalities	36%
religious figures	35%
auto mechanics	33%
plumbers	32%
journalists	31%
lawyers	29%
real estate agents	27%
new home builders	27%
press	27%
trade union officials	21%
chief executive officers	21%
local politicians	14%
car salespeople	10%
national politicians	9%

Whom and What Do CEOs Respect?

RBC Financial Group (the Royal Bank) is the most admired and respected corporation in Canada as selected by Canadian CEOs. The 10th annual survey, released January 2005, measures nine specific categories; CEOs are able to write in whom they thought was the most admired and respected in each category.

For the overall honour roll scoring, a system was used that gave companies three points for each time they were the first mention in a given performance category (there were eight performance categories), two points for each second-place showing and one point for a third-place mention. An additional three points were attributed to firms cited in the question in which CEOs were asked to name their choice for the single most respected corporation overall. The final tally for each firm is the sum of these points, which determines each company's overall score.

How They Decide

When asked why they had selected a particular company overall as the most admired or respected, the aggregate top responses were "successful/financial performance/profitability/growth/turnaround" (50%), "human resources/good staff/management/employee relations" (17%), "innovative/creative" (16%), "social responsibility/community involvement/corporate citizenship" (16%), "shareholder/investment value" (14%) and "corporate governance/leadership" (12%).

CEOs, reflecting on their corporate experience, indicated that the following attribute was the "first that comes to mind" when they hear that a company or CEO is respected:

- **Honesty/trustworthiness/credibility (53%)**
- **Financial success/profitability/good growth (14%)**
- **Leadership (12%)**

What Brands Do Canadians Trust Most?

When Canadians were asked what brands they trust most, the leaders in each category were:

Major retailer: (tie) Wal-Mart, Sears
Large household appliance: (tie) Kenmore, Maytag
Small kitchen appliance: Black & Decker
Do-it-yourself store: Home Depot
Paint: Benjamin Moore
Personal computer: (tie) IBM, Dell
Credit card: VISA
Bank/trust company: (tie) TD Canada Trust, RBC Financial Group
Food manufacturer: Kraft
Breakfast cereal: Kellogg's
Soup: Campbell's
Flour: Robin Hood

Margarine: Becel

Pet food: (tie) Iams, Purina

Toothpaste: Crest

Shampoo: (tie) Head & Shoulders, Pantene, Herbal Essences

Paper towel: Bounty

Laundry detergent: Tide

Automatic dishwasher detergent: Cascade

Dishwashing liquid: (tie) Palmolive, Sunlight

All-purpose household cleaner: Mr. Clean

Vitamins: (tie) Jamieson, Centrum

Cough/cold remedy: (tie) Benylin, Buckley's

Stomach ailment remedy: Pepto-Bismol

Headache/pain reliever: Tylenol

Children's diapers: Pampers

Hair colouring product: (tie) Clairol, L'Oreal

Hand/body lotion: Vaseline

Facial skin care: Oil of Olay

Feminine hygiene product: (tie) Always, Tampax

Cosmetics: (tie) Avon, Cover Girl

Passenger car manufacturer: General Motors

Pickup truck manufacturer: Ford

Minivan manufacturer: (tie) Chrysler, Ford

Automobile tire manufacturer: (tie) Michelin, Goodyear

And on the Ultimate Liars' Day (April Fool's Day), What Do Canadians Think?

Out of a list of four possible choices, the largest number of Canadians say they would be most likely to play a practical joke on their friends (36%) on April Fool's Day. It may also be a day of marital discord, as spouses (32%) run a close second in popularity as targets for pranks. Meanwhile one-quarter (26%) say their co-workers are their most likely target.

Of six practical jokes tested, the largest number of Canadians (32%) think gluing someone's coffee cup to their desk or table would be the funniest, followed by the classic prank of filling a sugar bowl with salt (18%). Close behind, 17% of Canadians think it would be funny to send a married woman roses with a card from "Hernando" thanking her for a great night.

Percentage of Canadians who think that "putting dog droppings in a bag on someone's doorstep" is funny: 3

Would *You* Wear a Name Tag?

In the spirit of April Fool's, the Comedy Network and Ipsos-Reid played a lighthearted joke of their own by asking Canadians if they would support a new law introduced by "Thomas Fullry, the Federal Minister for Urban Harmony" that encourages Canadians living in major cities to wear a name tag.

In all, one-tenth of adult Canadians (10%) took the bait, saying that they would support the law, and more than twice as many (22%) said that if the law were passed they would wear their name tag at least some of the time. That means 1.2 million adult Canadians say they would wear their tag "all the time!"

Rate by which younger Canadians are more likely than older Canadians to support the name-tag law: 3 to 1

Some of Us Won't be Fooled

Percentage of Canadians who believe that extraterrestrials visit the earth on a "regular basis": 20
Percentage who believe the Loch Ness monster exists: 19
Percentage who believe that NASA "faked the moon landings": 10
Percentage who believe that breaking a mirror brings seven years of bad luck: 7
Percentage who think Elvis Presley is still alive: 3

That's right. More Canadians believe in the Loch Ness monster than believe in their politicians.

The Internet

The Internet is so big, so powerful and pointless that for some people it is a complete substitute for life.

—Andrew Brown

IN JUST ONE short decade, the Internet has profoundly changed the way we Canadians communicate, look for information and— did we forget anything? Oh, yes, amuse ourselves.

Canadians are wired. No, *really* wired. The 2003–2004 edition of the World Competitiveness yearbook ranks Canada first in use of the Internet in general and over high-speed broadband in particular. Fully 78% of adult Canadians have Internet access. (Canada was well out front of the second-place Japan and third-place United States for use of broadband.)

Technologically, Canadians sizzle. CANARIE, Canada's advanced Internet development organization, runs CA*net 4, the longest, fastest and most advanced fibre-optic research and education network in the world. Government, industry and educational institutions use it to innovate in exciting new fields that include distance learning, telemedicine, bioinformatics, virtual-reality modelling and real-time multimedia streaming.

Have we mentioned that the hometown of the Blackberry— that famous little portable device that has so enhanced national fitness by strengthening our long-neglected thumbs—is Waterloo, Ontario? We have now.

Rank of Canada in the world in terms of Internet use: 1st
Rank of the United States: 2nd

So, what are online Canadians doing online?

Sending and receiving email: 93%

Checking the weather: 65%

Sending joke emails: 58%

Looking at job postings: 55%

Conducting online banking transactions: 53%

Comparison shopping: 51%

Instant messaging: 50%

Checking movie show times and reviews: 47%

Receiving viruses through email: 44%

Listening to a radio station over the internet: 43%

Participating in chat rooms: 39%

Using the Internet for personal reasons at work: 38%

Checking lottery results: 36%

Downloading music or MP3 files: 32%

Playing an online game: 25%

Visiting pornographic Web sites: 25%

Posting a resume: 22%

Buying or selling stocks or investments on line: 13%

Bidding on an item at an auction site: 13%

Taking a course directly on line: 10%

Making Internet telephone calls: 9%

Selling an item at an auction site: 4%

Gambling: 3%

Earning a degree/diploma/certificate online: 2%

Why Leave Home?

The Internet and the World Wide Web have changed Canadians'
relationships with their governments. Income-tax refunds come
back much more quickly when you file electronically, so people
are flocking to their computers to do that. Bonus: if your
adding and subtracting are out of whack, your computer will tell
you that.

Competition Bureau chief, Konrad von Finkenstein, ruled in
April 2004 that downloading and sharing music files on peer-to-peer

programs does not violate Canadian copyright laws. Five days later, Bruce Stockfish, director of copyright policy at the Heritage Department, said that Canada's Copyright Act is ill equipped for the Internet age and needs amendments that would clarify when file-sharing of music is a copyright violation. Perhaps, he says, we need a "making available right," under which only copyright holders would be legally permitted to make their music available over the Web, in the same way they have rights when it is played over the radio.

In many Canadian cities, you can go to the Web to pay a parking ticket. In Vancouver, you can find out if any streets are closed, look at your house from an overhead map and pinpoint where the water main enters your property.

But Nothing's Perfect

Oh, yes, there are problems. Plenty of them. Spam, for instance. When half your e-mail messages are uninvited and unwanted, that's a problem.

Then there's pornography. When your six-year old daughter goes to a site called Anne of Green Gables and gets a eyeful of smut, that's a problem.

Then there's addiction. When your spouse, who used to qualify as a passable conversationalist, now spends his or her evenings welded to a computer screen, you may have a problem. And when the Atlantic Lottery Corp. plans to take gambling online, that could end up being a real problem for some.

And then there's that copyright issue—millions of music lovers still downloading songs via share sites on the Internet. For nothing. Some recording artists don't mind—they say it builds fan loyalty and attendance at live performances. Some mind very much. One thing we can be sure of: file-sharing is not going away.

Of course, the Web attracts the charlatans and mountebanks you'll find everywhere else. Consider Moira Greenslade, a 33-year-old British woman who went to jail after offering up her unborn baby for adoption over the Web, pocketing $6,000 from not one, but two of the three couples who responded. She was making a deal with the third couple when she got caught. And no, she didn't have triplets.

Let's look at some of the numbers that reflect Canadians' attitudes toward the Internet and that monster shopping mall, the Web.

Damn Spam

Canadians are fed up with spam. One of our surveys showed that the average Canadian e-mailer receives 134 e-mails a week, with about half (52%) being spam. That percentage had doubled in a year.

From the viewpoint of legitimate firms who have recipients' permission to send marketing messages, the influx of spam is cause for concern. "The increased volume of spam means permission-based e-mail marketers have to work harder and smarter," says Carrie Harrison of Forge Marketing. "Marketers must become familiar with spam filters. They must understand how to minimize the number of warning bells they set off when writing, designing and deploying permission-based e-mails to avoid their e-mails being dismissed as spam."

Surfing for Bargains on the Ground and in the Air

Canadians are increasingly turning to the Web to help purchase vehicles and homes, compare prices on smaller items or do online banking. Fully 63% of online Canadians report that they have used the Web to research vehicles, while 51% have checked out real estate options. Nearly half (49%) of Canadian onliners use the Web for comparison shopping generally, and 53% do their banking online.

Wheels

When it comes to doing vehicle searches, we have to remember that most Canadians aren't in the market every year, or even every couple of years. So the Web's new impact in this industry becomes more impressive when we narrow it down to people who have recently purchased a vehicle, whether they used the Web to research prices, features, availability or other factors. Fully 80% do. This industry has clearly been transformed.

Survey results show that well over one-third of online Canadians (38%) report purchasing a new (16%) or used (22%) car in the past two years.

The primary advantages of using the Internet as a vehicle-purchasing resource are related to having greater access to information.

- **Topping the list is the advantage of being able to easily shop and compare vehicle prices (42%).**
- **The second biggest advantage is that the Internet is a good source of information for features, specifications, colours and so on (31%).**

- Another advantage, according to some, is not having to deal with salespeople to get this kind of information. Just over one-quarter (28%) of those using the Internet as a vehicle-buying resource list this as an advantage.
- Only 7% of Canadian car shoppers cite "not being able to talk to a salesperson" online as a disadvantage.

Advantages of Using the Internet as a Vehicle-Buying Resource/Tool	
Advantages	Percentage of those who have searched for vehicle information online (n=686)
Ability to shop and compare vehicles/prices	42%
Good source of information	31%
Don't have to deal with salespeople	28%
Saves time	13%
Accessibility	10%
Convenience	6%
Shop any time	4%
Access to a lot of choices/models	4%
Other	6%
Nothing/don't know	4%

- One-third of those who have used the Internet as a vehicle-buying resource list the inability to touch the car and kick the tires as a disadvantage.
- Another 9% say the biggest disadvantage is that they can't take the vehicle for a test drive, while 8% worry that the information online may not be current.

For the most part, when people do venture online for information about their new car or truck, they tend to have very positive experiences. In fact, 87% of those who look for vehicles online agree that the Internet allows them to look at more vehicles than they otherwise would be able to look at.

In addition, 82% say that the Internet has met their expectations as an information resource for vehicles, while 81% say they would recommend the Internet as a vehicle-buying resource to others.

Homes

The real estate industry has also been transformed. One of our recent surveys showed that 85% of Canadians who have purchased a home in the past two years have scanned the Web to look for information. Of those who used the Web, 78% say it played a significant role in the purchase experience (51% saying somewhat significant, 27% very significant). Eighty-three per cent say that the Web allowed them to look at more houses, 65% say it saved them time in the house-hunting process and 57% say it made it easier to find the property they wanted. Overall, almost three-quarters (73%) say that the Internet met their expectations as a house-hunting resource.

The use of the Internet as a housing information resource is not limited to those purchasing a home. It is a useful tool for those who are only looking and dreaming. Even among those who have not purchased a home in the past two years and do not intend to do so over the next two years, 42% have used the Internet to gather information about purchasing a new home.

The Internet has distinct advantages in assisting Canadians with their real estate information gathering. One in four online Canadians using it cites viewing a whole range of properties without leaving home as an advantage, with another 15% listing the benefit of easy access to home information. In addition, 23% list the ability to comparison shop as an advantage. On another note, some people prefer to avoid dealing with an agent: 18% say being able to avoid dealing with an agent when looking for information is an advantage.

The Internet does have limitations as a house-hunting resource. The information available is seen as limited and incomplete (19% list this as a disadvantage). In addition, 16% say that they cannot see enough details or get a feel for a house, while 12% see the inability to ask questions as a disadvantage.

In some areas of the country, the selection can be quite limited, and one in ten online house hunters lists this as a disadvantage. In addition, while some Internet users may not enjoy dealing with a realtor, the realtor still plays a very important role. Online Canadians see the realtor as someone with more experience and knowledge who better knows markets and processes. In fact, 38% of people list this as an advantage of using a realtor in the house-hunting process, with 19% seeing the personal service that the realtor provides as an advantage.

Travel

Travel agents aren't enjoying life nearly as much as they used to, as more and more Canadians turn to the Web to book flights and accommodations online. It's only been happening for a few years, but the writing is on the wall—one survey we did in 2003 showed that 36% of Canadian adults with Internet access had gone to the Web to book some element of a trip, whether it be flights, hotels, car rentals or entertainment. The percentage had doubled in two and a half years (31% in June 2002 and 18% in September 2000).

Travel is one of the few e-commerce categories that Canadians have embraced wholeheartedly.

- **The Internet is the primary source of information for planning upcoming travel by 35% of online Canadians, more than double the proportion who consider travel agents (14%) or family and friends (14%) to be the primary source.**
- **While the incidence of booking travel online is on the increase, the number of trips being booked online has dropped, likely due to the various world events that have hampered the travel industry, such as the outbreak of SARS and the war in Iraq. Among those who have booked travel online, the average number of bookings has decreased from 4.1 in 2002 to 2.8 in 2003.**

Despite the increase in the number of people booking travel directly online, the percentage of Canadians with Internet access who are using the Internet to research travel online is relatively flat compared to 2002. Currently, 56% of adults with Internet access have used the Internet to research travel online, slightly lower than 59% in June 2002.

More good news for online travel sites: the vast majority of Internet-using Canadians say they will likely use the Internet to research a trip or vacation in the future (87%). Additionally, over half (55%) say they will likely use the Internet to book travel directly online in the future.

Among those who have booked travel online, percentage decline in the average number of bookings between 2002 and 2003: 32

Ratio of those who consider the Internet their primary source of travel information to those who rely on travel agents: 2.5 to 1

Pleased to Meet You, Invisible Guy

Is the Internet the great social equalizer? In real life, people who aren't shy or homely or too young or too old or too *something* tend to make friends a lot faster than us ordinary folk. On the Internet, who knows?

Our research found that 42% of Canadian adults with access to the Internet have participated in live online chat sessions. We chat, and we play—32% of respondents told us that they have taken part in computer games with other people online. Six per cent—1 out of every 17 Canadians—say they have used online dating services. A whopping 64% of Canadians have chatted online, and 50% have taken part in online games.

But really, that's just the tip of the iceberg. It's easy to say that's just games, or that's just porn, or hockey scores, or chit-chat. Or joke e-mails. Or downloading music. Or working from home. Or whatever. Add it all up, though, and you've got a new way of life, one there's no going back from. And keep in mind: Canada has the biggest per capita online population in the world. We're inventing this stuff as we go along.

What We Think of This New Technology

Somewhere along the way, we all bought into the idea of the Internet. Almost all Canadians (97%) believe that computer technology and the Internet are key to Canada's ability to compete in the global economy in the future.

Percentage of Canadians who believe that computers are used too much in high school: 7

Percentage of Canadians who believe that computers are used too much in university: 7

Percentage of Canadians who believe the government should provide more funding for computer education in schools: 90

Percentage who believe that private-sector companies should be invited into schools to provide computer education: 78

Spam Accounts for Half of All E-mails Received

As we said, the volume of e-mail that Canadian Internet users receive has grown to startling levels, driven by spam and unsolicited commercial e-mail. The study *Email Marketing 2004: Being Heard above the Noise* found that, on average, Canadian Internet users currently receive 197 e-mails each week.

- **The average Canadian Internet user receives 134 unsolicited e-mails per week.**
- **Over the course of a year, online Canadians are flooded with an average of 6,968 junk e-mails.**
- **While two-thirds of Canadians adamantly refuse to open unsolicited e-mails, those who continue to open these e-mails perpetuate spamming practices.**
- **Despite the bad reputation of spam, over one-third (35%) of online Canadians say they have opened spam in the past week.**
- **The average number of spam e-mails opened in a typical week has increased from five in 2002 to seven this past year.**

Percentage increase in the amount of spam received
weekly by the average Canadian since 2003: 109
Percentage of e-mail that is spam: 68
Percentage increase in spam from 2003 to 2004: 60
Percentage of spam opened out of curiosity: 60
Percentage opened because the user "thought it was a
legitimate e-mail": 40

It's Not Spam If You Sign Up for It

Legitimate forms of commercial e-mail are also on the rise. Over
three-quarters (77%) of Canadian Internet users say they have registered with a website to receive e-mail. More striking, however, is the
success of this approach: more than half of those who have ever registered to receive an e-mail say they have then gone on to enter an
advertiser's contest (60%) or visited the advertiser's web page (53%).

Percentage of those unwilling to provide their e-mail address
when requested who give fear of receiving spam as the
reason: 70%
Percentage of Canadians willing to provide their e-mail address
to retailers, websites and other companies when requested: 57
Average number of websites a Canadian registers with to
receive commercial e-mail: 8.1

Swarms of E-mail Cause Us to Be Less Efficient

While Canadians do not yet appear to be ready to live without e-mail,
concerns are becoming apparent. Many feel the swarm of e-mail is
beginning to diminish their effectiveness.

Increase since 2003 in the number of e-mail messages the
average Canadian receives in a week: 74
Percentage of Canadians in 2002 who felt that e-mail made
them more efficient at work: 85
Percentage who feel the same way today: 54
Odds that an e-mail from a colleague is irrelevant: 50/50
Odds that a colleague wishes you had called rather than
e-mailed: 50/50
Percentage of Canadians who dread going on vacation because
of the volume of e-mail they will face upon return: 34

Getting Together

Online Canadians, especially young online Canadians, are turning to the Internet as a way to meet new friends and stay in touch with old ones. Seven in ten online Canadians have used the Internet for social interaction. This includes such activities as taking part in online chat, playing games with other people, using the Internet to contact someone they've lost touch with, participating in forums or bulletin board discussions, using online personals or dating services, and taking part in an online telephone call. Younger online Canadians are especially likely to use the Internet in their social lives. In fact, 82% of those 18 to 34 have taken part in some form of online social activity.

We found that 42% of Canadian adults who have Internet access have participated in live, online chat sessions, the most common way to interact with other people online outside of e-mail. And not only are many online Canadians using the Internet to meet new people, many are using the power of the Internet to reach people from their past. More than one-third of online Canadians (35%) say they have used the Internet to contact someone they had lost touch with.

What are Canadians doing online?

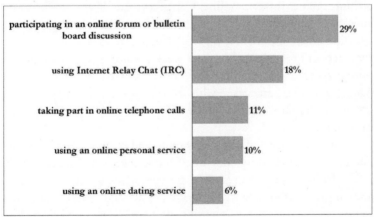

Better than a Blind Date?

Almost one-quarter of online Canadians (24%) have actually met a person offline whom they first came to know online. This figure is significantly higher (41%) for 18- to 34-year-olds. An intriguing aspect of the online social scene in Canada is that in some ways the Internet is perceived to have been more successful than a more traditional way of meeting people: the blind date.

A full 14% of online Canadians have actually dated someone they first met online. In the majority of cases, the most recent person dated exceeded (39%) or met (29%) expectations. At the same time, 30% of online Canadians have never been on a blind date. Of these people, just 21% say that the most recent person they dated exceeded their expectations; only 28% said the person met their expectations.

Rate by which a Canadian 18–34 is more likely to have played an online game than someone over 55: 2 to 1
Percentage of Canadians who say that the Internet plays an "important" role in their social lives: 43
Percentage of online Canadians who plan their schedules around their online activities: 10
Percentage who cancel offline activities to accommodate online commitments: 6

Internet Security

Despite assurances from the online community that making transactions online is safe, online Canadians are likely to be more concerned about Internet security than they were a year ago.

The study found that 32% of Canadian adults who use the Internet for at least one hour per week are more concerned about online security than a year ago, versus only 13% who are less concerned. The percentage who say they are more concerned has increased dramatically from June 2001, when 18% said they were more concerned.

The overall level of concern is high, and poses a significant barrier to the further development of e-commerce in Canada. Only 42% of Canadian online adults have ever made a purchase online, and of those who haven't, security (49%) and privacy concerns (34%) are the top barriers mentioned on an open-ended basis. The vast majority of Canadian Internet users (82%) also say they are concerned about Internet security in general, and 47% indicate that they are very concerned.

Based on these facts, it is not surprising that 84% of online

Canadians say they are concerned about giving personal information online, with 49% saying they are very concerned.

The extent of the public's concern about credit card security and privacy indicates that even the most basic assumptions that we take for granted in the offline world are brought into question online. When asked how concerned they are with various aspects of submitting personal information online, Canadians indicate that they are most concerned with the security of databases that house credit card numbers (60% are very concerned), followed by 58% who say they are very concerned about their credit card information being used for non-authorized transactions once it is in the database of the retailer. Fifty-seven per cent say they are very concerned about their credit card information being intercepted in transit while they are making an online purchase. Forty-seven per cent say they are very concerned with sites that they visit being able to access information that is stored on their computer. Thirty-nine per cent say they are very concerned about discrepancies between themselves and an online company being dealt with in a fair and reasonable way.

Catching Criminals in Cyberspace? Not Likely ...
A fulsome majority (72%) believe that online criminals have less of a chance of being caught than a criminal in the real world. Half of Canadians (49%) say they are less likely to do business through websites because of concern that they could be the victims of criminal activity.

Will It Get Worse?
It would appear that Canadians are evenly split as to whether or not the situation will get more serious (47%), while almost as many (48%) believe that businesses will come up with better ways to protect themselves.

Percentage increase in those who say their concerns about security have increased: 77
Percentage of Canadian Internet users who have suffered a security breach online: 35
Percentage who had in 2000: 21
Percentage who had in 1999: 18

Ready to Use Your Computer as a Phone?

Voice over Internet Protocol (VoIP) technology faces an uphill battle in the short term. While VoIP technology has received considerable attention in recent months, consumer awareness, current usage and interest in using VoIP technology remains low.

Only one in four (23%) online Canadians is aware of the term VoIP, and only one in five has heard of IP telephony. Additionally, among those who say they are aware of VoIP or of IP telephony, only 13% claim to understand "a great deal" about the technology, compared to 52% who say they understand the basics and 35% who say they have heard the name only.

Percentage of Canadian households currently using VoIP: 1

Teens and the Internet

Teens, who once could not be pried off the family telephone, are turning instead to the Internet. Home phone and instant messaging are virtually tied as teens' favoured means of communication, at 45% and 44% respectively. More interestingly, email and cellphones are almost off the radar as the preferred method of chatting. Only 6 of teens report that email is their favourite way to communicate with friends and only 4% reported that they prefer their personal cellphone.

Based on a list of 18 online activities, sending and receiving email (73% do so at least a few times per week) and using instant messaging (70%) far exceed the list of other online activities by a significant margin.

Teens also engage in many other social activities, such as playing online games against friends (28%) or strangers (23%), posting to online forums (11%) or visiting web logs or "blogs" (10%).

Participation in other, non-social online activities—such as doing research for school projects (45% do at least a few times per week), downloading music (29%), visiting news and information sites (23%), looking for movie reviews/show times (15%), uploading photos (15%), or listening to online radio (12%)—are still popular, but far less common.

On the other hand, what adults do online doesn't even register among teens; while at least half of adults engage in comparison-shopping, clicking online advertising, online banking, and e-commerce, almost no teens do these activities.

A caution to parents: 14% of teens report having met in person with someone they originally met online, a number that increases to 20% among those between 15 and 17 years of age.

Finding a Job

The Internet has provided us with a new way to be unemployed. Online Canadians are going online to find a job and to stay on top of the job market. The study found that 60% of online Canadians in the workforce have used the Internet for a job search. This translates into nearly 8.5 million Canadians, up from the 7.6 million reported in the first quarter of 2002.

When it comes to specific job-search activities, 55% of Canadian adults with an Internet connection have looked at job postings online. This translates to 43% of the entire adult Canadian population. Although not as popular as looking at job listings, many Canadians are not averse to posting their résumés at job sites. In fact, 22% of those with Internet access—17% of Canadians as a whole—have posted a résumé online. Both of these activities are more popular among people 18 to 34 years of age as well as with those who have a university degree.

However, online job hunters do not think that online job hunting is a perfect tool. There are distinct limitations to using the Internet for job-search activities, the primary disadvantage being that it is impersonal—no personal contact is possible. As such, it can be difficult to stand out from the crowd. More than one-quarter (28%) of people who have used the Internet to help search for a job list "no personal contact" as a disadvantage. Other disadvantages mentioned are that job postings typically have incomplete information (8%), that many positions are not listed online (8%) and that many other people are using the online approach to job hunting, leading to a much more competitive marketplace (6%).

Province whose residents are most likely to have used the Internet to find a job: Ontario
Increase since 2002 in the number of Canadians who have used the Web for a job search: 900,000
Percentage of Canadians who've used the Internet to post a résumé: 22
Percentage who've visited a porn site: 25

Environment and Energy

"Scratch a Canadian and you find a phony pioneer," I used to say to myself in warning. But all the same it is true, I think, that we are not yet totally alienated from physical earth, and let us only pray that we do not become so.

—Margaret Laurence, *Maclean's,* December 1972

CANADA ENTERED THE twentieth century as a backwoods society and emerged as a very urbanized nation. Four out of five Canadians now live in cities, most of them strung out along our southern border. Nevertheless, the rural, untamed regions of Canada remain at the heart of the country's self-image.

The rivers, the woods, the plains, the mountains, the glaciers and all those loons, polar bears, caribou, beavers, grizzlies and human adventurers that populate them are at the core of our national mythology. Canada's vast spaces are as essential to us as the urban economic hubs that most of us live in.

How well are we protecting this vast heritage? Some say we're not doing a bad job. We have, after all, set aside 38 national parks and park reserves covering more than 222,000 square kilometres, with five more covering another 73,000 square kilometres in the works.

Unlike the United States, we have signed the Kyoto Accord, which commits Canada to reducing greenhouse gas emissions to a level 6% below the 1990 level by 2012. That amounts to reducing the damaging emissions that come from our vehicles, space heaters and other comforts by 7.5 tonnes per Canadian. While industries and power plants will be called upon for the bulk of emission reduction, at least one of those tonnes is going to have to emerge from behavioural changes among individual Canadians if the goal is to be met.

Can we make these kinds of adjustments? How much do we really care? People pay lip service to protecting our environment, but sad stories are always popping up suggesting that when push comes to shove, other priorities get in the way of our concerns about environmental degradation.

The Standing Senate Committee on Energy, the Environment and Natural Resources issued a report in the spring of 2004 that concluded that the federal government is going to have to come up with both financial incentives and stronger penalties on excessive pollution if Canada is to meet its Kyoto targets.

With Canadians seemingly lukewarm about the importance of taking action to counter environmental degradation, it will be interesting to see whether governments will muster the kind of political will that will be required to introduce these kinds of measures.

With energy pricing and supply very much on people's minds these days, substainability of our environment and resources are inextricably linked.

So What Are Our Environmental Concerns?
Canadians believe that the following environmental concerns should be addresses by our leaders today:

Water pollution: 42%
Air pollution: 31%
Garbage disposal: 18%
Forestry and clear-cutting: 16%
Recycling: 13%
Energy: 7%

Canadians: The Green and the Beige

While there are occasional dissenters, international scientists are pretty well unanimous that global warming is a serious problem and that humans are contributing to that problem. We found that despite widespread coverage of this issue in the media, Canadians are not entirely convinced.

When It's Hot, It's Hot Everywhere

While there is no regional difference in how Canadians perceived 2004's hot weather conditions, there are some notable demographic differences.

- **Canadians between 18 and 34 are 19% more likely than those over 55 to say that hot weather is "part of a trend toward increased global warming."**
- **Half of Canadians over 55 say that hot weather is "just an example of a very hot summer that Canada experiences every once in a while."**
- **Canadian women are 13% more likely than men to associate hot weather with increased global warming.**

When it comes to issues concerning global warming, half (53%) of Canadians say that overall, the federal government is doing a poor (38%) or very poor (15%) job, while 37% say the government is doing a good (35%) or very good (2%) job. One-tenth (10%) of Canadians say they "don't know" how the government is doing on global warming. Canadians are also equally split when it comes to their provincial governments. Half (54%) rate their provincial government's job performance on global warming as poor (38%) or very poor (16%), while 35% rate their government as good (32%) or very good (3%). Again, one-tenth (11%) say they "don't know" how their provincial government is performing on the issue. Among Canadians, criticism of the federal government and their individual provincial governments on this issue increases with both education and income.

Provinces where people are least satisfied with the federal government (poor/very poor): Alberta (63%), Ontario (62%) and B.C. (60%)

Provinces where people are least satisfied with their provincial governments: Ontario (64%) and Saskatchewan/Manitoba (63%)

Province where people are most satisfied with their provincial government's efforts (good/very good): Quebec (46%)

Ratio of university graduates to those with a high school education or less who rate the performance of both levels of government on the environment as "poor/very poor": 3 to 2

Ratio of those with a household income of over $60,000 to those with one of under $30,000 to rate the governments' performance as "poor/very poor": 4.5 to 3

Dealing with Vehicle Emissions

Where do our greenhouse gas emissions come from?

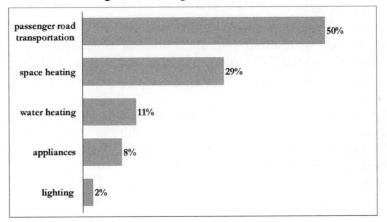

We presented two scenarios for reducing automotive emissions to respondents:

1. That taxes be increased to improve public transit.
2. That the use of vehicles be restricted after a public pollution warning.

Initiative (1) was supported by 37%, while 62% (42% strongly) opposed it.

The second proposed initiative, to restrict the use of cars whenever a poor air-quality warning has been declared, was supported by 58%, versus 48% who were in opposition.

Regions most likely to oppose tax increases to improve transit: the Prairie provinces and Atlantic Canada
Province most likely to support it: B.C.
Regions most likely to support restricted use of cars: Quebec (74%) and Atlantic Canada (63%)
Least likely: Ontario (49%)

Going to the Car Wash

Six in ten Canadians (59%) believe that washing a car by hand in the driveway is more environmentally friendly than using a commercial car wash (chosen by 38%). Three per cent respond that they "don't know."

However, when households that own or lease a car (as 81% of Canadian households do) are asked how the car is washed most often, a majority (53%) report using a commercial car wash. Just under half (46%) report that their car is most often washed by hand in the driveway.

Canadian households with a car indicate that during a typical year, their cars are washed on average three times per month. Ontarians with cars wash them on average twice as often as British Columbians.

Household Concerns

What are Canadians planning to do to be more environmentally responsible?

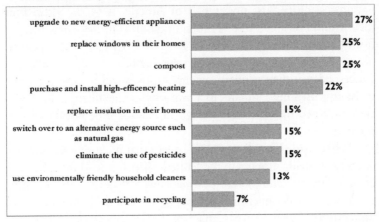

upgrade to new energy-efficient appliances	27%
replace windows in their homes	25%
compost	25%
purchase and install high-efficency heating	22%
replace insulation in their homes	15%
switch over to an alternative energy source such as natural gas	15%
eliminate the use of pesticides	15%
use environmentally friendly household cleaners	13%
participate in recycling	7%

Virtually all Canadians (97%) agree with the statement, "Canada should adopt a comprehensive national water policy that recognizes clean drinking water as a basic human right," with 84% strongly agreeing (13% somewhat agreeing). Only 3% of Canadians disagree with this statement, and 1% "don't know."

Do We Have the Energy?
Public concern about energy shortages is widespread in both Canada and the United States.

Key findings indicate that two-thirds of both Canadians (66%) and Americans (67%) say that they are concerned about being person- ally affected by electricity shortages over the next five years. Virtually the same number of Canadians (65%) are also concerned about gasoline shortages over the next five years, and this climbs to three-quarters (76%) among Americans. Further, half of Canadians (51%) and two- thirds of Americans (66%) say they are concerned about shortages of natural gas or home heating oil over the next five years.

Despite these concerns, six in ten Canadians (61%) and Americans (60%) believe that governments and the energy industry are exaggerating about energy shortages to support their political or financial goals.

The poll also sought feedback on a range of issues related to the North American energy marketplace. Nearly three-quarters (74%) of Americans believe that energy supplied by Canada can play an important part in providing the United States with long-term national security. Just under half of Americans (46%) agree that they would be willing to pay more for gasoline if they knew it came from Canada and not the Middle East. Security concerns appear to play a part in these sentiments. A majority of Americans (78%) are concerned that their country's energy supplies will be targets for terrorist attacks. This compares to a minority of Canadians (44%) who are concerned that Canada's energy supplies will be targets for terrorist attacks.

While many Canadians (42%) believe that increasing the amount of energy Canada supplies to the United States is a good thing because of the economic and job-creation benefits, a majority (56%) believe that doing so will undermine the long-term national independence of the country. Seven in ten Canadians (70%) are already concerned about foreign ownership of Canada's energy resources.

Canadians and Americans show limited knowledge of Canada's energy reserves. Across three true/false questions posed in each country, Americans and Canadians scored only a single correct answer on an overall basis.

Who knew that…?

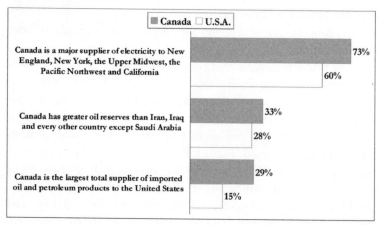

PetroCanada: It Should Be Ours

Three-quarters (73%) of Canadians agree with the statement, "The Canadian federal government should not sell all its shares in PetroCanada as recently announced, but rather it should continue to have part ownership of PetroCanada because it is important to maintain Canadian ownership and influence to ensure Canada's energy security in the future."

- **Atlantic Canadians (80%) are the most likely to agree that the federal government should not sell all of its shares in PetroCanada and should continue to have part ownership of PetroCanada. Least likely are residents of Saskatchewan/Manitoba (68%) and Alberta (68%).**
- **Canadian adults aged 18–34 are more likely than adults aged 35 and older to agree with this statement (80% versus 70%).**
- **Women are significantly more likely than men to agree (85% versus 60%).**
- **Canadians living in rural areas are more likely than those living in urban areas to agree (80% versus 71%).**
- **Those Canadians without a university degree are more likely than those who have a university degree to agree (77% versus 63%).**
- **As annual household income level climbs, the level of agreement with this statement abates (less than $30,000, 85%; $30,000–$59,999, 77%; $60,000+, 62%).**

The Impact of Higher Gas Prices

Most Canadians (68%) believe that the recent rises in gas prices are permanent, with 31% believing the "current prices are here to stay" and 37% believing "prices will get even higher." Higher gas prices are having an impact on Canadians' spending habits: two-thirds (65%) say that the recent price increases in gas have "caused financial cutbacks in other spending that they would normally do for themselves and their family" (20% "a lot," 29% "some," 16% "a little").

Ratio of Canadians who live in rural areas to urban
dwellers who are likely to believe that these higher
gas prices have caused them to make financial cutbacks
on family spending: 6 to 5
Ratio of those with annual household incomes of less than
$30,000 to those with annual household incomes over
$60,000 to believe this: 4 to 3
Ratio of those without a university degree to those with a
university degree who believe that higher gas prices are
causing them to make cutbacks: 3 to 2.2

But What Is Causing Them?
When Canadians are asked to consider from a list of five possible
reasons they think is most responsible for higher gas station prices,
no clear culprit emerges.

What do Canadians think causes the prices to rise at the pumps?

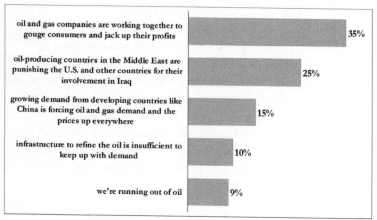

Part of Canada whose residents are the most likely
to believe that "oil and gas companies are working
together to gouge consumers and jack up their
profits": Quebec
Least likely: Atlantic Canada
Region whose residents are the most inclined to believe that
"oil-producing countries in the Middle East are punishing the

U.S. and other countries for their involvement in Iraq":
Atlantic Canada
Least likely: Alberta
Ratio of women to men who are likely to believe this: 3 to 2

The Lights Are On ... or Are They?

As the first anniversary of the August 2003 blackout—which darkened much of Ontario and the eastern United States—approached, fewer than half of Ontarians (43%) believed Canada's electricity supply was sufficient to meet present and future needs.

Nationwide, confidence that Canada's electricity supply is sufficient to meet present and future needs has declined by 12 points among Canadian adults, from 71% in April 2002 to 59% this year.

In response to Canada's growing demand for electricity, 61% of Ontarians and 56% of Canadians nationwide believe that Canada's energy future should include a mix of many sources of electricity—including nuclear energy—rather than focusing on environmentally friendly sources of power. Moreover, fully 88% of Ontarians and 75% of Canadians nationwide believe that nuclear power will be part of Canada's energy mix in the future. In light of this, 67% of Ontarians and 57% of respondents nationwide support upgrading and modernizing Canada's nuclear facilities. In addition, half of Ontarians (50%) and 37% of respondents nationwide support building new nuclear facilities.

Change in support for nuclear energy among Canadian adults in general between April 2002 and August 2004: 0 (at 49%) Among Ontarians: 7 points (from 57% to 64%)

Religion

Which is it. Is man one of God's blunders, or God one of man's?

—the irreverent Friedrich Nietzsche (1844–1900)

The soul recovers radical innocence
And learns at last that it is self-delighting,
Self-appeasing, self-affrighting,
And that it's own sweet will is heaven's will.

—a more reverent William Butler Yeats (1865–1939)

NIETZSCHE AND YEATS are both dead. Nietzsche was a poor candidate for heaven, Yeats a far more likely one. Yeats clearly believed. Nietzsche shook his head at the idea that any sane person could believe. Two very bright people, disagreeing about perhaps the most fundamental issue going.

Of Course, We *Want* to Believe . . .

When we're polling about religion, we have to concede one thing: the believers have an incentive to believe; the non-believers don't. It's Pascal's wager: we have everything to gain and (almost) nothing to lose by faith. Perhaps this is why belief seems to increase with age.

So we concede that little incentives—such as the prospect of eternal life—may nudge people toward voting yes. But even that kind of incentive isn't likely to turn people into outright liars. So when 84% of Canadians tell us that they believe in God, we take them at their word. And when 14% of Canadians say that they do not believe in God—well, these people clearly aren't trying to put something over on us, are they?

Six believers for every one non-believer. That may surprise some people, given that our society is constantly depicted as being extremely secular, its values distorted by the voracious pursuit of money and brand names. Nevertheless, most Canadians clearly believe that the temporal hasn't snuffed out the spiritual—at least not in their case.

Even more noteworthy than the six-to-one ratio is how few Canadians are sitting on the fence. As pollsters, we're used to getting a sizable minority of people saying "don't know," but only 2% of Canadians call themselves agnostics. Despite the complexity of the issue, there isn't much hemming and hawing going on here.

Change is Afoot, But Canada is Still a Christian Nation

So Canadians believe in God. But which God do they believe in? Well, for the vast majority of Canadians, the answer is the Trinity: Father, Son and Holy Ghost. The number of people who believe in Allah, Krishna, Vishnu and other gods is minute by comparison.

Statistics Canada's census tells us that eight in ten Canadians (77%) are Christians and that the population of Christians grew slowly between 1991 and 2001. But that figure does not tell the whole story.

There has also been a 44% increase in the number of people who say they have no religious affiliation, and a remarkable 72% boost in the number of non-Christian Canadians in the decade ending in 2001. Muslims in particular have shown explosive growth (128%) over this time period, while the numbers of Buddhists, Hindus and Sikhs has multiplied somewhere in the range of 80–90%. In contrast, the number of Jewish Canadians grew just 3% over ten years.

All told, however, these non-Christian groups represent a very minute portion of the population. Just 2% of all Canadians are Muslim, 1% are Jewish and roughly only half a percent each are Hindu, Sikh or Buddhist.

So when we do our polling, we find so many Christians and so few Canadians of other faiths that our surveys must invariably focus on Christian beliefs and behaviours—as you will see in the pages that follow.

Loving Him* from a Distance

If the church, synagogue or mosque is God's house, we Canadians aren't dropping in on Him nearly as often as we used to. Only one in five of us attends a place of worship on a weekly basis. Another 13% attend about once a month, which brings us to one-third of the population. Nineteen per cent go a few times a year, and 11% show up once a year or so. No wonder they're selling off churches.

Given these numbers, it isn't surprising that eight in ten Canadians (81%) agree that "you don't need to go to church to be a good Christian." That number clearly includes a lot of Christians: more than three quarters (77%) of Canadians identify themselves with a Christian church.

We've privatized religion. Although 77% of Canadians identify with a specific church, 70% of those who call themselves Christians agree that "my private beliefs about Christianity are more important than what is taught by any church."

Not Dropping Out, but Not Dropping In

So, what's happening here? The decline in church attendance would suggest that we are a much more secular society than we used to be. But there are those who argue that this isn't true.

First, the numbers. In 1949 belief in God was nearly universal in Canada—95% believed. So that number is down, but slipping from 95% to 84% over 55 years isn't exactly what you'd call the bottom falling out of the market, is it?

However, let's look at average, every-week church attendance in Canada in 1946—67%—and the current figure, the aforementioned 20%. This suggests that many Canadians aren't taking their religion seriously. Not only that, but the Americans have turned the tables on us.

In the late 1940s, Canadian church attendance was over 60%, while U.S. attendance was closer to 40%. Now U.S. attendance is still around 40%, while ours is half that.

Some of the Canadian decline stems from a precipitous decline in church attendance in Quebec during the Quiet Revolution of the

*We're going with the traditional, patriarchal language here.

1960s. Quebeckers, once devoted churchgoers, still have the highest ratio of believers in the country, at 85%, but they have the lowest ratio of church attendance: 15%. In fact, Quebec is now facing an architectural and historical crisis—what to do with magnificent cathedrals and parish churches that aren't attracting enough of the devoted to pay for their upkeep?

Can we legitimately say that Canada is a nation of believers when church attendance is at such a low ebb? In his book *Restless Gods: The Renaissance of Religion in Canada*, sociologist Reginald Bibby pooh-poohs the dual theses that modern societies necessarily become secularized and that even people who remain spiritual are picking and choosing from a marketplace of new religious options that are replacing traditional religions. *Au contraire*, says Bibby. In fact, his studies show that 42% of Canadians are Catholic, 19% are traditional Protestant, 8% are fundamentalist Protestant, 20% are non-believers and only 6% divide up among all other religions.

The Church Lady

Remember the Church Lady, the moralistic scold that Dana Carvey made popular on the TV show *Saturday Night Live*? In the 1980s, the Church Lady would whirl into her "superiority dance" whenever she felt she had scored a point over a less pious person.

Well, there is still a strong element of the Church Lady within Canadian churchgoers. Remember we said that 81% of Canadians don't think you have to go to church to be a good Christian? Well, among regular churchgoers, 50% think you *do* have to attend regularly to be a good Christian, while 49% think not.

So, maybe you do, maybe you don't. But the vast majority of Canadians identify with a religion, and a lot of them don't think they don't have to join with others every week to prove their credentials. For many Canadians, religion has become a private thing. But, despite popular perceptions, it hasn't gone away.

• **Weekly church attenders were divided on this question: half (49%) agreed, and half (50%) disagreed. The remaining 1% had no opinion or were unable to answer. This belief in the value of private faith seems to drive church attendance (or the lack thereof).**

- **Those who attend church regularly are charitable to those who do not. Eight in ten (79%) of those who attend once a month or more agreed that church attendance was not a requirement of being a "good Christian," as did 89% of those who attend a few times a year.**
- **Seven in ten (70%) agree that, "My private beliefs about Christianity are more important than what is taught by any church." Weekly attenders of religious services were less likely to agree with this statement. Even so, a clear majority of weekly attenders (62%) agree with the proposition.**

A Nation of Believers

Forget the notion that religion is a divisive issue: belief in God is one thing most Canadians agree on. Still, there are strong regional differences. The Atlantic provinces show the highest level of belief in God (93%), while residents of British Columbia (75%) show the lowest level.

Underscoring the large numbers of Canadians who believe in God, many Canadians (67%) agree with the statement "my religious faith is very important to my day-to-day life," largely unchanged since 1993, when 66% of Canadians agreed with this statement.

Many Canadians (69%) believe in the central theme of Easter, namely, that through the life, death and resurrection of Jesus, God provided a way for the forgiveness of their sins.

Province the residents of which are least likely to believe in forgiveness: Quebec
Most likely: Atlantic provinces

Belief in other articles of faith is also strong. Two-thirds of Canadians (66%) believe that "the Bible is the inspired word or God" (up from 65% in 1993 and 1996). Belief that the Bible is the inspired word of God is highest in Atlantic Canada (79%) and Saskatchewan/Manitoba (78%) and lowest in B.C. (53%).

Percentage change since 1996 in the number of Canadians who believe in the Easter doctrine of the forgiveness of sins: +6

Percentage of Canadians whose belief in God has increased over the years: 27

Percentage whose belief has diminished: 13

Likelihood that a Canadian believes that "Satan, the devil, is active in the world today": 1 in 2

Region where you're most likely to believe the devil is active: Atlantic Canada

Least likely: Quebec

Percentage of Quebeckers who believe the devil is active: 36

Percentage of Quebec Catholics who do: 34

Percentage change since 1993 in the number of Canadians who believe in the devil: +7

Percentage of Canadians who believe in the existence of angels: 61

Who believe in out-of-body experiences: 43

Who believe in past-life regression: 29

Who believe in "channelling, or the ability to communicate with the dead": 27

Believing and Belonging

While the vast majority of Canadians believe in God, just one in five (20%) attends church on a weekly basis. The largely privatized nature of faith in Canada today is also apparent in the finding that 70% agree with the statement, "my private beliefs about Christianity are more important than what is taught by any church."

As noted above, just one in five Canadians attends church, synagogue, mosque or temple once a week or more. Only an additional 13% attend at least once a month. Another three in ten attend occasionally (other than on special occasions such as weddings, funerals or baptisms), with 19% going a few times a year and 11% passing through the portals of a place of praise once a year or so. One-third (36%) did not attend religious services in the past year.

Those aged 55+ were much more likely to attend weekly (31%) than those aged 35 to 54 (17%) or age 18 to 34 (15%). Though B.C. is the least religious province, it has a higher percentage of regular church-goers than does Quebec, the most religious province (18% versus 15%).

Since the Second World War, church attendance has plummeted while belief in God has remained stable. Belief in God was near universal (95%) in 1949 and declined somewhat until 1978, when it stabilized at just under nine in ten (88%), a figure not statistically different from our most recent finding of 84%. Church attendance, however, plummeted precipitously—especially during the late sixties and early seventies—before levelling out in the mid-eighties. In 1946, a high of two-thirds (67%) reported attending church in the past seven days. Attendance then slid quickly downhill during the tumultuous years between 1965 (55%) and 1980 (35%), before levelling out between 1989 (29%) and 1999 (28%).

Percentage of Canadians who pray daily: 45
Percentage increase between the age groups 18–34 and 55+ in the likelihood that a Canadian will attend church regularly: 100
Rank of Quebec among the provinces with the highest number of believers: 1
Rank of Quebec among the provinces with the lowest percentage of regular churchgoers: 1
Likelihood that a Canadian who believes in God actually goes to church: 1 in 4

Pope John Paul II

Catholics have something other denominations lack: a celebrity leader. Overall, 71% of Canadians approve of the Pope's performance as a spiritual leader. Canadian Roman Catholics are even more approving (81%). Canadians' current approval ratings of the Pope as a spiritual leader are slightly higher than they were in April 2000 (66%).

- **Young people like the Pope. Canadians 18 to 34 (76%) are more likely to express approval of the Pope as a spiritual leader than Canadians 55 and older (66%).**
- **Eight in ten Canadians say that John Paul II can be described as "sincere" (86%), "honest" (84%), "forgiving" (82%), and "humble" (83%), as well as "a peacemaker" (79%) and a "force for good in the world" (79%).**
- **Not surprisingly, Roman Catholics are more likely to describe the Pope as "sincere" (92% versus 83% of non-Catholics), "honest" (91% versus 81%), "forgiving" (86% versus 79%),**

"humble" (89% versus 76%), "a peacemaker" (88% versus 74%) and a "force for good in the world" (87% versus 74%) than non-Catholics.

- **Residents of Quebec (89%) are more likely to believe that "humble" describes John Paul II than are residents of British Columbia (72%).**

Not only Catholics approve of the Pope as a spiritual leader

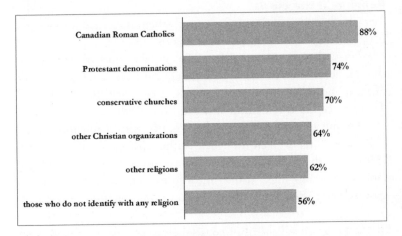

At the same time, a majority describe the pontiff as "conservative" (83%), a "rigid theologian" (61%) and "not open to new ideas" (60%). Canadians are divided on whether or not the Pope is "practical" (50%). In addition, half of Canadians (48%) describe him as "judgmental," though fewer would go so far as to say he is "intolerant" (38%). We can only conclude that 20% of the people who like the Pope do so *because* he is not open to new ideas.

There is statistically no difference between Roman Catholics and non-Catholics in describing Pope John Paul II as "conservative" (84% versus 82%), a "rigid theologian" (62% versus 61%), and "not open to new ideas" (59% versus 60%).

As for agreement with the Pope's pronouncements on topics such as philosophy, abortion, birth control and evangelism, Canadians are now split, with 47% agreeing with the Pope's pronouncements, while just as many—46%—disagree. However, this represents a slight increase in agreement from the 43% recorded in July 2002.

Canadians with a high school education (80%) are significantly more likely than those with a post-secondary education or some university (68%) or a university degree (67%) to express approval.

While there are no significant differences between regions on this question, Canadians in rural parts of the country (53%) are significantly more likely to express agreement than are those in urban areas (45%). Canadians in urban areas (48%) are significantly more likely than those in rural areas (40%) to disagree with the Pope's pronouncements.

Religion in the News

Two-thirds (63%) of those who attend religious services on a weekly basis believe that "the media does a poor job of covering faith and religion and that this area does not get the kind of coverage it should." Further, half (50%) of these regular attendees feel the topic of faith and religion receives "less media coverage than it should." These perceptions remain unchanged from 1998.

Among those Canadians who identify with a religious group (75%), 55% report that they look to the religious media for information on their own specific religious group. Four in ten (40%) look to the religious media for information on other religious groups, while 45% look to the secular or non-religious media.

Factor by which Canadians who feel there is too little religion on TV outnumber those who feel there is too little sport: 5.5 to 1

Harry Potter in Canada

Religious groups have taken time off from protesting sex and violence in order to address another threat: the wizard Harry Potter. More than four in ten Canadian non-magical households (44%) have read at least one of J. K. Rowling's Harry Potter books—of Canadian adults, at least 19% (approximately 4,500,000).

Province with the highest per capita readership of the books: British Columbia.
Odds that a Canadian believes that "the Harry Potter books should be banned from school libraries because they glorify witchcraft": 1 in 6
Percentage of Canadians who believe in "witchcraft and spells": 18

Percentage of Canadian readers who identify with the evil
Lord Voldemort: 1

Other Leaders

Six in ten (59%) Canadians think religious leaders are a force for good in society.

- Though 59% of Canadians believe that religious leaders are a force for good in society, only 2% believe that politicans should be influenced by them.
- Though they are the least religious people in Canada, residents of B.C. are more likely than the generally more religious residents of Quebec and Atlantic Canada to feel that "religious leaders are a force for good in society."
- The majority of Canadians (62%) believe that "religious communities are a force for good in society," while one-quarter (25%) feel that "religious communities tend to contribute to intolerance and mistrust." One in ten Canadians (11%) take neither of these two viewpoints, and 3% state that they don't know.

Those most likely to feel that "religious leaders are a force for good in society"

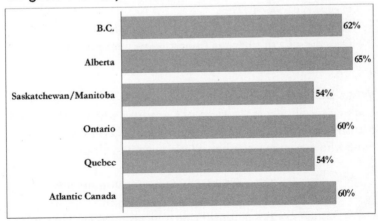

Region	
B.C.	62%
Alberta	65%
Saskatchewan/Manitoba	54%
Ontario	60%
Quebec	54%
Atlantic Canada	60%

Telling Politicians What to Do

As the issues of same-sex marriage and gay rights heated up around the world, the Pope and the Catholic Church waded into the debate with an official document that called on all Catholic legislators around the world to vote against any legislation that would recognize "gay marriage." However, six in ten Canadians (59%) oppose the Catholic Church and other religious groups issuing directives to politicians on how they should vote on public policy issues. In fact, a plurality of Canadians (44%) strongly opposes such directives.

Asked specifically on what basis politicians should decide their vote on same-sex marriage, a majority (54%) feel that votes should be cast according to the wishes of a politician's constituents. This compares to 39% who feel that a vote on this issue should be based on a politician's own conscience. In further evidence of a backlash against the Church, just 1 in 20 (6%) feels that on the same-sex marriage issue, a politician should vote according to his or her religious leader's edict.

One in ten Canadians who oppose gay marriage say that politicians should vote as religious leaders direct them, while four in ten believe that any vote should be cast according to the politician's own beliefs. It seems that these is a much more robust separation of church and state in Canada than in the U.S. "Values" and religion are not the same thing.

> Percentage of Canadians who think the Pope is "a force of good in the world": 79
> Percentage who think legislators should listen to him: 6
> Odds that a Canadian Roman Catholic believes that politicians should heed directives from the Pope: 50/50

What Believers Believe

Looking specifically at the views of Canadians who believe in God, partially believe in God or are unsure in their belief (and excluding those who explicitly state they do not believe in God):

- **77% say God is an impersonal spiritual force, while 17% view God as a person.**
- **75% indicate "God is an ever-present force in my life."**

- 78% agree that "God is the one who created you, but left you with free will."
- 81% feel that "faith gives my life more meaning."
- 61% say the religious texts of their own faith should be understood as "allegories or myths to guide human behaviour," while 44% say that their religious texts "should be taken literally."
- One in ten (13%) believes that "God punishes through illness such as AIDS, misfortune or natural disasters such as floods or earthquakes."

Between Faiths

Three-quarters (74%) of Canadians believe that interfaith dialogue would have a "positive impact" on their community. As education level climbs, the proportion who believe that interfaith dialogue would have a positive impact on their community rises (63% among those with less than a high school education, 70% among those with a completed high school education, 74% among those with some university or a college diploma and 82% among those with a university degree).

Percentage difference between B.C. and the Atlantic provinces among those who say that their religious faith is important to their daily lives: 20
Likelihood that a Canadian believes that "the world would be a better place if everyone shared my religious beliefs": 4 in 10
Chances that a Canadian woman is interested in carolling on Christmas Day: 1 in 4

Everyday Life

DAY, *n*. A period of twenty-four hours, mostly misspent. This period is divided into two parts, the day proper and the night, or day improper— the former devoted to sins of business, the latter consecrated to the other sort. These two kinds of social activity overlap.

—Ambrose Bierce, *The Devil's Dictionary*

Day-to-Day Irritants

It's clear that Canadians are hard up for irritants. The thing that rubs us the wrong way most—traffic (at 42%)—is well chosen. But after that?

Number two on the list is "someone reading over their shoulders." Oh, mercy. Yes, it seems that irritates 18% of Canadians. Atlantic Canadians are particularly vulnerable to this phobia. It is the main annoyance of 29% of them—and they don't even have subways.

No. 3: people who crack their knuckles. Yup, 16% of people loathe knuckle-crackers, with Atlantic Canadians again leading the way at 31%. Women, at 31% across the country, loathe knuckle-cracking far more than men, at 10%, which makes sense when you consider who does the most cracking (and dragging) of knuckles.

No. 4: getting sand in your bathing suit. That's right, 11% of Canadians hate getting sand in their bathing suits. And British Columbians, with their balmy weather when it isn't raining, lead all provinces in this complaint at 15% (even though Wreck Beach, perhaps their best-known beach, is a nudist beach, so go figure what the problem with sand in your bathing suit is there).

No. 5: socks with sandals. They drive Quebeckers particularly nuts, at 14%, but barely raise an eyebrow in fashionable Atlantic Canada, at 2%.

The Frizzies

Far worse than sand in the suit is a bad hair day, as one in five Canadians is likely to tell you. Fully 20% of Canadians are unhappy with their hair. For those who are unhappy, length (26%), colour (23%) and texture (21%) are the main complaints. Texture includes a delicate balance of straight and curly, an age-old fret.

Length, the most troubling problem, does not include baldness. Baldness has its own category—19% mention a desire to stem hair loss. Women (24%) are more likely than men (15%) to be unhappy about their hair. Who would have guessed?

British Columbians are least likely to be unhappy with it, at 16%. Only 13% of British Columbian women wish to change their hair colour, whereas 46% of women in Manitoba and Saskatchewan would like to.

One more thing. If Canadian women had to choose between a hair brush (or comb) and makeup for a day, 70% would go without makeup.

Days Off

We asked a lot of people in ten different countries—Canada, the United States, Brazil, France, Germany, the U.K., Russia, China, India and Japan—about various ways they would like to spend a day off. Getting to vote on and rank each option, it turns out that Canadians are world leaders in a number of categories.

How would you respond if you had the day off and were offered these three options?

1. Staying home and relaxing
2. Visiting friends and relatives
3. Going shopping

Canadians finished second only to the stressed-out Americans in finding "staying home and relaxing," an appealing option. A huge majority of Americans (93%) found that idea either very appealing or somewhat appealing, and we were right behind them (90%). The French were the least likely to enjoy the idea of just knocking around the house for a day.

On the second option, the French led the field in liking the idea of visiting friends and relatives, at 94%. But—get this—Canadians were again second, at 92%. In fact, in terms of those who found this idea *very* appealing, Canadians were no. 1, at 57%.

So we Canadians like to cocoon, and we like to visit friends and relatives. We're great introverts, and we're great extroverts. But it turns out we're mediocre shoppers. Finally, the Japanese (75%), those from India (74%), the Brazilians (71%), the Americans (61%) and the Brits (57%) all led the Canadians (55%) in their craving to spend their day off shopping. Evidently, we are the least shallow and acquisitive.

Puttering around the Kitchen

Further, we asked respondents from those same ten countries whether they found it somewhat or very appealing, if they had the day off, to "cook a nice meal."

Well, here we go again: Canadians finished at the top of the heap, nosing out the Americans 75% to 74%, and also edging them out in terms of which nationalities found this idea *very* appealing (38% to 37%). Far behind, in third place, were the British; 64% found the idea somewhat or very appealing. Only the Japanese failed to muster at least a majority on this question—just 45% of Japanese respondents were willing to say that this idea was at least somewhat appealing, and only 13% of them found it very appealing.

Clearly, North Americans like to cook. And it isn't such a gender thing anymore: in Canada and the United States, only slightly more women than men (76% to 71%) found the cooking option appealing.

Canadian men are in for some credit. They are more likely than men in other countries to cook the main meal of the household on a fairly regular basis—57% every other day or every day, compared to 51% of Filipino men, 47% of British men, 44% of American men and 42% of French and urban Chinese men—and, more drastically, compared to 9% of kitchen-wary Japanese men.

A Nation of Jocks

Okay, you're not going to believe this. Not only are we great introverts, great extroverts and great cooks, we are also a nation of athletes.

The numbers speak for themselves. We also asked respondents in the same ten countries whether they would prefer, on a day off, to be "playing sports or exercising" or "going to a sports event."

Canada finished ahead of every other country in their love of activity, with 77% of Canadian respondents saying it would be either "very appealing" or "somewhat appealing" to play a sport or exercise during that day off. Canadians also led in the percentage (43%) who found the idea very appealing. The French were second, with 73% finding the idea either very or somewhat appealing—35% said very appealing.

Perhaps we have discovered why Paul Henderson was able to rise up and score the goal of the century against the Soviets in the final game of that eight-game series in 1972. Was it because Henderson had grown up in a nation of jocks, while poor Vladislav Tretiak, the Russian goalie, had grown up in a land of bystanders?

Fancy this: the Russians finished dead last in our survey, with only 35% finding the idea of playing sports or exercising on a day off somewhat appealing, and a minuscule 11% opting for *very* appealing.

Computer Blahs
On your day off, would you like to

1. Go to a movie?
2. Watch TV?
3. Play with your computer?

On our days off, 74% of Canadians find the idea of going to a movie either somewhat or very appealing, placing us third, behind the Americans and the French. When it comes to watching TV, we drop to 72%—about the middle of the pack.

Who wants to play with the computer on a day off? Only 48% of Canadians find that a somewhat or very appealing idea, second to the Americans at 52%. It may not be a coincidence that these two countries rank first and second—other studies have shown that Americans have the highest per capita level of *access* to computers in the world, with Canadians second. Your chances of wanting to play with your computer are probably better if you have a computer. That's our guess, anyway.

Canadians and Their Hair Cares

Percentage of Canadians currently happy with their hair: 80
Province the residents of which are most likely to be happy
with their hair: British Columbia
Likelihood that a woman in Saskatchewan or Manitoba wishes
to change her hair colour: 1 in 2
Given the choice between a hair brush or makeup, chances
that a Canadian woman would choose the former: 2 to 1

What Canadians Have on Their Bottoms

Percentage of Canadians aged 18 to 34 who do not own a
pair of jeans: 3
Chances that a Canadian owns six or more pairs of
jeans: 1 in 4
Province with the fewest pairs of jeans per capita: Quebec
Percentage of Canadians who buy jeans for their originality: 1

Getting That Long-Distance Feeling

Seven in ten Canadians (71%) say that if it were free, long-distance
telephone calls would be their preferred mode of communicating with
out-of-town friends. This compares to the number who would choose
e-mail (23%), regular mail (3%) or a pager or instant messaging.

Ratio of women to men who use regular mail to contact
out-of-town friends: 4 to 1
Percentage of Canadian males who would buy more beer if
they didn't have to pay for long-distance phone calls: 35
Percentage of Canadian women who would: 11

Time Off

Percentage of Canadians not taking a vacation this
summer: 42
Rate by which an upper-income Canadian is more likely than
a low-income Canadian to take a vacation this summer: 75%
Percentage of Canadian summer vacationers who stay within
their province: 35

Percentage who stay within the country: 79
Percentage of Canadian vacationers who would choose New
Zealand as their most desired destination: 36
Percentage who would choose Winnipeg: 7
Percentage who would choose Kenya: 4
Province whose residents are most likely to choose Thailand as
their most desired destination: Quebec
Rate by which a lower-income Canadian is more likely than an
upper-income Canadian to choose running with the bulls at
Pamplona as the most desired vacation: 66%

Asked to choose which of a series of international delicacies they'd most likely dare try while on vacation, one-quarter of Canadians (25%) who have ever taken a vacation choose "alligator jambalaya in New Orleans," 15% say "haggis in Scotland," 10% say "turtle fritters in the Cayman Islands" and 6% say "sheep's brains in Morocco." On the other hand, 41% say, "I wouldn't try any, get me to the nearest fast food restaurant."

Province the residents of which are the most likely to head
for the nearest fast food restaurant while on vacation:
Manitoba/Saskatchewan
Least likely: British Columbia
Rate by which a high school graduate is more likely than a
university graduate to head for fast food: 67%
Gender most likely to head for fast food: Women
Gender most likely to eat haggis: Men

And Where Do Canadians Go Over the Christmas Holiday Season?
Most stay home. Canada appears to be the most likely destination for trips over the holiday season (33%), while travel to the United States ends up in second spot (12%). Other holiday travel destinations include the Caribbean (8%), Mexico (7%), Europe (3%), Central/South America (2%), Asia (2%) and some other part of the world (5%).

Winter Break
As a vacation destination between January and April, staying in Canada (26%) also leads all other destinations, with the United

States (19%) as second most popular, followed by the Caribbean (10%), Europe (8%), Mexico (7%), Central/South America (3%), Asia (1%) or some other part of the world (7%).

Rate by which an Albertan is more likely than an Ontarian to stay in Canada: 2 to 1
Province whose residents are most likely to stay within their province: Quebec
Whose residents are most likely to travel to the Caribbean: Ontario

Getting Away from It All?

Likelihood that a Canadian will take a cellphone on vacation: 1 in 2
That he or she will take a digital camera: 1 in 3
Likelihood that a Canadian worker on vacation will keep in touch with the office by voice mail, e-mail or calling in for messages: 1 in 3
Province whose residents are least likely to keep in touch: Quebec
Ratio of men who keep in touch with the office to women who do: 2 to 1
Income bracket least likely to keep in touch with work: middle
Likelihood that a Canadian worker does not use all of his or her vacation days: 4 in 10
Likelihood that a Canadian worker says he or she "does not get vacation days": 1 in 10
Province whose residents are most likely to use all their vacation days: Quebec
Rate by which an upper-income Canadian is more likely than a lower-income worker to use all his or her vacation days: 9 to 1
Rate by which a lower-income Canadian is more likely than an upper-income Canadian to say he or she uses no vacation days at all: 12 to 1

Travelling Companions

Given the choice from a list of Canadian personalities who might join them as a guest on their vacation, Canadians are most likely to choose funnyman Jim Carrey (28%, followed by environmentalist and broadcaster David Suzuki (20%). Broadcaster Pamela Wallin (11%), sportscaster Ron MacLean (10%), Montreal Canadiens goaltender José Théodore (8%), singer Roch Voisine (6%) and model Linda Evangelista (4%) also rank as potential vacation guests.

> Rank of David Suzuki among Canadian celebrities Canadians would most like to travel with: 2
> Rank of Jim Carrey: 1
> Rank of José Théodore among celebrities Quebeckers would most likely travel with: 1
> Rate by which women are more likely than men to choose Pamela Wallin: 2 to 1
> Rate by which men are more likely to choose Ron MacLean: 2 to 1
> Rate by which men are more likely to choose Linda Evangelista: 7 to 1

When in Rome ...

Men appear to be more willing to go with local beach custom than women. When men are asked if they were visiting a country where it was normal for men to wear bikini-type swimsuits, such as a Speedo, four in ten Canadian men (41%) say they would go along. In comparison, slightly fewer women (35%) indicate that if they were visiting a country where sunbathing topless was the norm, they would do it.

> Rate by which an Atlantic Canadian man is more likely than a Manitoban or Saskatchewanian to wear a Speedo-style bathing suit on vacation: 2 to 1
> Rate by which a Québécoise is more likely to sunbathe topless on vacation than a woman from Manitoba or Saskatchewan: 2 to 1

Have You Seen a Canadian Film This Year?

On an open-ended basis, three-quarters (73%) of Canadians cannot name a Canadian film that they have seen in the theatre in the past year.

> Rate by which a Quebecker is more likely than other Canadians to have seen a Canadian film in the past year: 150%

It's the Thought That Counts

While more than half of Canadians (57%) are satisfied with their Christmas or holiday gifts, more than one in three (34%) received at least one gift that they didn't like, didn't fit into, or couldn't use during the last holiday season. On average, Canadians received one such gift during the last holiday season.

And what do Canadians typically do with these orphan gifts? Only 23% claim they keep and use "unwanted" gifts. More than one in four (26%) claim they return the gifts, 25% claim they pass the gifts along to someone else and 22% claim they store and put the gifts away.

Chances that a Quebecker is dissatisfied with a Christmas gift: 1 in 10
That an Albertan is: 1 in 2
Rate by which a young Canadian is more likely than an older Canadian to be dissatisfied with a Christmas gift: 2 to 1
Province whose residents are most likely to return an unwanted gift: Alberta
Rate by which an Albertan is more likely than a Quebecker to return a gift: 4 to 1
Percentage of Canadians who "re-gift": 25

This Just In ...

Over eight in ten Canadians say they follow local news (87%), international news (85%) and national news (84%) closely. Two-thirds (67%) follow health and lifestyle news closely, while half closely follow business (50%) and entertainment (50%) news. Just four in ten (42%) indicate that they follow sports news closely.

Rate by which men are more likely than women to follow business news closely: 50%
Rate by which university graduates are more likely than high school graduates to do so: 50%
Region the residents of which are most likely to do so: British Columbia
Least likely: Atlantic Canada

Gardening

Let's assume that gardening is not a solitary endeavour—and keep in mind that we are not talking about nude or contact gardening. We asked Canadians what celebrity they would most like to garden with. Canadian musical superstar Shania Twain (27%) is the top choice, followed by actress Nicole Kidman (17%), lifestyle guru Martha Stewart (17%) and actor George Clooney (14%). One-tenth (11%) say they would like to garden with Canadian gardening expert Mark Cullen, while 2% choose HGTV host Kathy Renwald.

Rate by which men are more likely than women to choose
Shania Twain: 223%
Rate by which women are more likely than men to choose
George Clooney: 400%
Province whose residents are most likely to choose Shania:
British Columbia
Least likely: Ontario

Ninja Gardeners

One in six (16%) Canadians admits to having secretly clipped flowers from a neighbour's or a public garden.

Percentage of Albertans who have harvested secretly: 22
Percentage of Ontarians who have: 14
Gender more likely to steal flowers: female (clearly we're not talking about drunken boyfriends and husbands plucking gifts on the way home)

Competitive Gardeners

Of the two-thirds (66%) of Canadians who have a lawn or garden, one-tenth (10%) say they feel the need to compete with their neighbours for the best garden or greenest lawn. Quebeckers are the least likely to feel the need to compete, residents of Saskatchewan and Manitoba the most.

Gardeners with Bored Spouses

And finally, the study found that one-fifth of Canadians (18%) who have a lawn or garden and have a spouse or partner, would rather spend time in their garden than spend intimate time with their spouse or partner on a sunny Sunday morning.

> Province whose residents are least likely to prefer gardening to a morning snog: Quebec
> Most likely: Atlantic provinces
> Gender most likely to prefer the sunny morn to a lover's arms: female
> Rate by which lower-income Canadians are more likely than upper-income gardeners to do so: 100%

We'd Rather Be Watching TV

Shocking new research reveals that Western civilization has begun its slow descent into barbarism. Television watching is more popular than reading out of a range of leisure activities: 35% of Canadians say they prefer to watch TV, compared to just 25% who claim they prefer to read books.

Two-thirds of Canadians (63%) indicate that they rely mostly on television for accurate news and information, while approximately one in ten opts for radio (13%) or daily newspapers (12%). Seven per cent say they relay on the Internet most.

As for what types of programs Canadians are most likely to surf on television, one-third (33%) say they most frequently watch news programs, followed by documentaries or educational programs (16%), sports (14%), drama (12%) and sitcoms (12%). More on TV later.

As for Those Who Prefer to Read

Canadians seem to set aside the summer months for reading—reading is a summer sport. (Television watching does not seem to be a seasonal pursuit.) But what do we read?

Forty-seven per cent of Canadians tend to read "any kind of book they can get their hands on." Those with more particular preferences choose either "books that are lighter and more entertaining" (25%) or "books that are more challenging and in-depth" (21%).

When it comes to the specific genre of book most preferred in the summer, "non-fiction, such as history books or biographies" tops the list of four, with 44% of Canadians who say this is their preferred genre. One-third of Canadians (32%) prefer to read "mysteries or thrillers," while just one in ten prefers "romance or chick literature" (9%) or "Canadian authors" (8%). Again, one might be inclined to doubt some of these claims, particularly about what Canadians claim they're looking for in a book.

Half (46%) of Canadians say they prefer to read books that make them "escape." Three in ten (31%) want to "laugh," and one-seventh (14%) prefer to read a book that makes them "feel warm and fuzzy."

Percentage of Canadians who "start a new book without finishing the one they were already reading": 58
Percentage who "skip chapters or read ahead": 34
Percentage who "hide or disguise what they're reading from others": 10
Percentage who "pretend they've read the book when they've only seen the movie": 9
Province whose residents are most likely to choose non-fiction: Quebec

Grilling Canadians

Percentage of Canadians who say "barbecue season never ends": 40

A further 23% think barbecue season begins Victoria Day long weekend, and 22% think it begins "the first day the thermometer creeps above 10 degrees." Only 8% of Canadians think the Canada Day long weekend signifies the beginning of barbecue season.

Albertans (57%) are the most likely to say "barbecue season never ends," followed by residents of British Columbia (48%), Ontario (45%) and Atlantic Canada (42%). Residents of Saskatchewan/Manitoba (34%) and Quebec (19%) are significantly less likely to feel this way.

Rate by which an upper-income Canadian is more likely than a lower-income compatriot to believe that barbecue season begins "the first day the thermometer creeps above 10 degrees": 56

- Nearly eight in ten Canadians (78%) own a barbecue, and during the summer months their cooking time is evenly divided between the kitchen (50%) and the backyard or deck (49%).
- Rate by which an upper-income Canadian is more likely than a lower-income Canadian to own a barbecue: 50%
- Seven in ten Canadians with a barbecue (69%) say it is the men in the household who do the barbecuing, and two-thirds (67%) think that, in general, men are better barbecuers.
- Rate by which men are more likely than women to believe they are better barbecuers: 33%
- Given a choice of five celebrities, 45% of Canadians with barbecues say they would want Jim Carrey to host a backyard barbecue for them and their friends. In a distant second place is George Foreman (18%), followed by Gwenyth Paltrow (13%), Jamie Oliver (7%) and Nigella Lawson (3%).
- While 55% of barbecuers say "spending time at the cottage or the beach" is their favourite summer outdoor activity, "barbecuing with friends" is the favourite for 35% of the barbecuing crowd. One-tenth (10%) say their favourite summer outdoor activity is "hanging out on a restaurant or bar patio."

Summertime Hangouts

A majority of Canadians of legal drinking age (71%) plan to get together with friends and family this summer, for one to ten gatherings. Many of these get-togethers may be casual and close to home. In fact, when asked which of four options is their most preferred way to spend a playful evening with friends and family this summer, 54% say "whooping it up at a backyard barbecue." Moreover, when asked which of four activities will bring their family and friends together this summer, 51% say "casual gatherings over the course of summer."

Rank of "an intimate evening picnic dinner for two" on the list of things most appealing to those who want a sensuous evening with someone special: 1
Percentage of Canadians who would choose it: 30
Percentage of Canadians who want nothing more than to "head down to the beach for a night of cuddling and stargazing": 23
Percentage who believe the secret to a great barbecue meal is "a top-notch barbecue": 7

Money

Money, it turned out, was exactly like sex; you thought of nothing else if you didn't have it and thought of other things if you did.

—James Baldwin, American essayist and novelist

Percentage of Canadians who have lost confidence in the stock market: 59

On April 2, 2004, Canadians learned that a man named Raymond Sobeski, a farmer from near Brantford, Ontario, had won $30 million in a Super 7 draw nearly a year earlier—and had left the winning ticket in a safety deposit box while he pondered what to do next.

At first it appeared he was just an incredibly prudent man—he said he had waited because he didn't want to "do anything rash." Then, a few days later, a woman named Nynna Ionson told her story. She said that she and Mr. Sobeski had married in 1998. They slept together at his home, but she always returned to her home during the day. She received divorce papers in January but never signed them.

She said they had slept together at a motel again after he cashed the lottery ticket. Then he told her not to go near the media, but she did. Then he disappeared. For more than a year, Ms. Ionson said, she had lived in poverty with her four children from a previous marriage, without a television or a telephone, hitchhiking to most of the places she needed to go.

If Sobeski had cashed his ticket when he knew he had won, he could have at least given her the $700,000 in interest the $30 million would have earned over the 12 months. But he didn't.

So Let's Say You Win $10 Million

One of our recent polls showed that 41% of Canadians feel that the best description of their financial situation is "getting ahead." But 48% say they are "treading water," and 10% say they are "falling behind." At the moment, it would appear that Raymond is "getting ahead," and Nyanna is "falling behind." Way ahead. And way behind.

But let's talk about *you*. Whichever of the above three categories you fit into, what would you do if you were to win $10 million?

What would you do if you won $10 million?

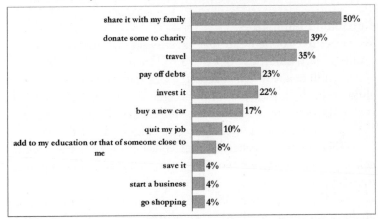

share it with my family	50%
donate some to charity	39%
travel	35%
pay off debts	23%
invest it	22%
buy a new car	17%
quit my job	10%
add to my education or that of someone close to me	8%
save it	4%
start a business	4%
go shopping	4%

When we asked Canadians this question, we got some good news: not one of them said he would stiff his impoverished wife and run off with all the loot.

The largest response we got was "share it with my family," at 50%. The 55+ crowd was most generous in this regard (66%), and the younger set, between 18 and 34, the least generous (40%). Ingrates.

The next biggest response was "donate to charity," at 39%," with female respondents far more ready to do the decent thing (46%) than their male counterparts (32%).

We're not known as a nation of Air Miles collectors for nothing: 35% said they would travel. The homebodies came next: 29% would build a new house. Then came the financial planners: 23% would pay off debts, and 22% would put the money into investments. Quite a few people (17%) mentioned a new car—you can get a lot of Geos with $10 million.

Surprisingly, only 10% mentioned that they would quit their jobs. That fits perfectly with another survey we did. It showed—wait for it—that 10% of Canadians hate their jobs. Another 8% mentioned acquiring further education for themselves or someone close to them. Given current tuition fees, maybe just a few semesters.

Down near the bottom, at 4%, were "save it," "start a business" and "go shopping" (in Dubai?).

So there you are. Raymond does indeed fit in—with the 35% who would travel.

Canadian Millionaires

We did a survey of rich Canadians and found that their demographic profile is very different from that of Canadians as a whole. When you're a millionaire in Canada, there's a 64% chance that there are no children in the house. *Big* savings there. Of course, millionaires do tend to be older: 68% are over 55, and 40% of them are retired. So, in these cases, it's not surprising that the kids have left the nest.

Millionaires are generally well educated: 82% have attended college or university, compared to the overall average in the population—62%.

More than one-third (38%) of Canadian millionaires have postgraduate university credentials, compared to the Canadian average of 9%.

Not surprisingly, money and business mix. Nearly six in ten millionaires (58%) say that someone within the household owns a business. The number of self-employed millionaires (35%) is more than double the rate for the general adult population. So is the percentage of retirees.

Percentage of Canadians who are millionaires: 4
Percentage of Canadian millionaires who are male: 79
Percentage of millionaires who are self-employed: 35
Percentage who are retired: 40

Percentage who are farmers: 4
Percentage of millionaires who think they are wealthy: 26
Ratio of Canadian millionaires with post-graduate degrees to
the national average: 4.2 to 1

Debt

We asked Canadians how concerned they are about being able to manage their current level of debt. "Debt" was defined for respondents as being any credit card balances, lines of credit, loans or mortgages.

Just under one-third (31%) of Canadian adults say they are concerned about managing their current debt levels, with 11% "very concerned" and 20% "somewhat concerned."

There was a big provincial gap here, perhaps reflecting the reality of hard times on the prairies, or perhaps representing attitudes as well. Residents of Saskatchewan and Manitoba are the most likely to be concerned (46%), followed by residents of the Atlantic provinces (41%), while Quebec residents are the least likely to say they are concerned (15%).

Those under the age of 55 are the most likely to be concerned (18- to 34-year-olds are at 36% and 35- to 54-year-olds at 34%), while only 22% of those aged 55 and older are concerned. In fact, 13% of those over 55 state that they have no debt.

As expected, Canadians between the ages of 18 and 34 have the highest debt-to-equity ratio (3.72 in 2002), followed by 35- to 54-year-olds (1.14) and those 55 and older (0.28).

However, debt loads appear to be increasing the fastest among the older groups. Canadians aged 55 and over have seen an increase of 31% in their debt loads since the year 2000, while those between 35 and 54 years old have seen an increase of 25%. The 18- to 34-year-old group has seen an increase of 18% since the year 2000.

Nine in ten Canadians (90%) believe that "paying down debt, such as a mortgage or other loans" is important. In fact, more than three-quarters (77%) say that it is very important. However, just four in ten (39%) of those who feel this is an important goal say they are personally very close to achieving this goal.

Perspective: What You Need to Know

There are some common themes in how Canada's most affluent live their lives. Indeed, if you want be like them you may want to do the following:

1. Forego having children.
2. Get a good education.
3. Be self-employed.
4. Focus on assets, not cash flow.
5. Don't count on an inheritance.
6. Live in Ontario or B.C.
7. Use money as a yardstick for evaluating your own success.
8. Think of yourself as comfortable, not rich.
9. Adopt a "live for the moment attitude," or act like old money. There isn't much in between.
10. Get on the Internet.
11. Don't try to manage your money by yourself; get professional financial advice.
12. Buy insurance.
13. Create a financial plan.
14. Make a comfortable retirement your goal.

The Millionaires' Club

Where Are Your Next-Door Millionaires?

Millionaires are overrepresented in the provinces of Ontario (49% of millionaires versus 38% of the national population) and British Columbia (17% versus 13% of the population). They are under-represented in Quebec (14% versus 25%) and the Atlantic provinces (5% versus 8%). Their representation in the Prairie region is approximately the same as the general population.

Wealthy Attitudes

Percentage of Canadian millionaires who believe that their "money allows [them] to help other people": 89
Percentage who believe "money [to be] a way of measuring how well [they're] doing compared to everyone else": 36
Percentage who agree that their financial success or money

provides them with "a way of measuring [their] own performance to [themselves]": 48

Percentage who believe their money allows them "to show other people that [they] are someone": 16

Percentage who believe that "money allows you to protect your family's future": 84

Percentage who believe it allows you "to do the things you want to do": 88

Percentage who believe that "money gives you power and control over other people": 21

Percentage who believe that people are responsible for their own fortunes: 81

Lifestyles of the Rich but Not So Famous

Two in five (41%) respondents agree that they are "enjoying today without worrying about tomorrow." However, half (50%) say that they consider themselves "more traditional than experimental," and one-quarter (25%) agree that "things are changing too fast these days for them to feel comfortable."

This dichotomy in lifestyles is also indicated by the type of leisure activities that millionaires typically engage in. These activities cut across more sedate pursuits such as reading (25%) and gardening (19%), though a portion are more active, either on the golf course (23%) or the jogging track (12%). Travel (24%), attendance at cultural activities (23%) and entertaining (12%) are also reported by the millionaires as leisure activities. A portion (10%) report that they are active in volunteer or charity work.

Even the Affluent Need Advice

Most affluent Canadians admit they have only an "average" knowledge of investments or ability to handle their own finances. Few of them are willing to listen to family, friends or the grapevine about investment advice. In fact, over eight in ten (85%) Canadians who have more than $250,000 to invest seek advice from financial professionals, and a majority of them (59%) indicate that they don't rely on anyone other than their professional advisers. And the wealthier they are, the more likely they are to rely on professional investment advice. Someone with a million dollars to invest is almost twice as likely to consult an expert as is someone with between $100,000 and $250,000.

Canadians with more than $250,000 to invest report holding mutual funds (86%), stocks (77%), GICs (58%), bonds (44%), investment property (36%), segregated funds (31%) and international assets (28%). The majority of this group (58%) report having less than $25,000 in financial liabilities.

Average Knowledge, Superior Advice
Canada's wealthiest citizens appear to be hungry for more information about their finances: 34% access their investment accounts online, and 33% use the Internet to research investments.

As for the investing preferences of affluent Canadians, at the time of this survey, 51% list mutual funds as the top investment in their portfolios. Individually held stocks are the top investment for 17% of wealthy Canadians. However, the number is significantly higher, at 37%, for people with $1 million in assets.

> Percentage of affluent Canadians who cite a comfortable retirement as their financial goal: 86
> Percentage of Canadian millionaires who do not expect to inherit money: 66

Planning Their Wealth
When it comes to planning for the future, 46% of Canada's most affluent individuals have formal written financial plans, 79% of which were developed with the assistance of a financial adviser. In light of recent market volatility, 86% of affluent Canadians have reviewed their investments and 59% of them have adjusted their investment mix accordingly.

And Speaking of Taxes, Everyone Has a View
Canadians in general, not just the upper tier, don't feel they are receiving fair value for the taxes that they have to pay. In fact, three-quarters (73%) agree—half (49%) strongly—that Canadians are taxed too high in comparison to the services, such as health care, education and economic development, that they receive in return. One-quarter (25%) express the opposite view.

Interestingly, Canadians with household incomes of between $30,000 and $60,000 are more likely than those with incomes of $60,000 or greater to express this view (75% and 70%).

Rank of Alberta among provinces that feel most aggrieved
by the taxman: 2
Rank of Quebec: 1

Financial Goals

Surely there must be a point to all the work we do. And there is: the financial goal that keeps us on the treadmill. Six in ten Canadians strongly agree that "setting financial goals is very important" to them, but just four in ten strongly agree they are "generally very satisfied with [their] ability to achieve financial goals."

So what are Canadians' financial goals? Nine in ten believe that "paying down debt, such as a mortgage or other loans" is important. In fact, three-quarters say that it is very important.

Other goals that are viewed by Canadians to be important include

- **"Making the best choices for my investments" (89%; 62% very important)**
- **"Saving for retirement" (85%; 60% very important)**
- **"Building up a 'nest egg' in case of emergencies" (87%; 55% very important)**
- **"Saving for children's education" (70%; 52% very important)**

Percentage of Canadians who feel financial goals are important who say they are personally very close to achieving this goal: 40

- **Residents of Alberta (65%), Ontario (63%) and British Columbia (63%) are more likely than residents of Atlantic Canada (47%) to agree strongly that they feel "setting financial goals is very important." Canadians with total household financial assets of over $100,000 (71%) are more likely than those with between $30,000 and just under $100,000 (61%) and those with less than $30,000 (55%) in total household financial assets to share this position.**

- **Older Canadians (42%) are more likely to strongly agree they are "generally very satisfied with their ability to achieve their financial goals" than are younger Canadians (32%). This view is also more likely to be held by higher-net-worth households ($100,000+ financial assets, 48%) than by those in the middle range ($30,000 to <$100,000, 38%) or those in the lowest range (28%) of total household financial assets.**
- **Canadians who contribute to their savings and investments on a regular monthly basis are more likely to say they strongly agree that they are satisfied with their ability to achieve their financial goals (42%) than are those who contribute less than once a year (32%).**

So What Are Canadians' Financial Goals? And How Close Are They to Achieving Their Goals?

Younger and middle-aged Canadians are more likely to believe that "paying down debt" (94% for both), "building up a 'nest egg'" (younger, 90%; middle-aged, 89%) and "saving for children's education" (younger, 79%; middle-aged, 72%) are important goals than are older Canadians ("paying down debt," 81%; "building a 'nest egg,'" 82%; "saving for children's education," 58%).

Saving for children's education is more likely to be seen as important by those in the low (73%) and middle (73%) range of total household financial assets than by those in the high range ($100,000+, 61%). Canadians in the high and middle ranges are more likely to view as important "making the best choices for [their] investments" (high, 95%; middle, 93%) and "saving for retirement" (high, 90%; middle, 89%) than those in the low range (investment choices, 84%; "saving for retirement," 82%).

Among those who consider specific goals important, how close are they to achieving them?

- **"Making the best choices for my investments": 29% very close**
- **"Paying down debt": 39% very close**
- **"Saving for retirement": 25% very close**

- **"Building up a 'nest egg' in case of emergencies":**
  31% very close
- **"Saving for children's education": 22% very close**

Regionally, Quebeckers who feel that "building up a 'nest egg' in case of emergencies" is important are more likely to say they are very close to achieving this goal (39%) than are those in Ontario (30%), British Columbia (24%) or Atlantic Canada (23%).

In general, middle-aged and older residents are more likely than their younger counterparts to say they are very close to achieving the goals they view as important. This is also true of those in the high and middle range of total household financial assets compared to their counterparts in the low-range group.

Most important financial goal for Canadians in the low range of financial assets (less than $30,000): paying down debt
Most important financial goal for Canadians in the middle range of financial assets ($30,000–$100,000): saving a nest egg
Percentage increase in the likelihood that an upper-income Canadian will have a written plan, compared to a lower-income compatriot: 127

Canadians' Savings and Investment Habits

Percentage of Canadians who "pay themselves first": 19
Percentage who "always stick to their budget": 16
Percentage who "accomplish the financial goals they set for themselves": 28

For those of us not running a deficit, and for those not spending the surplus each month, there is something to save. Four in ten Canadians say they add to their savings or investments on a regular basis, at least once a month, while 18% indicate they do this on a regular basis several times during the year and 17% say they add to their savings or investments in a yearly lump sum. One-tenth (11%) say they make lump-sum payments to their savings or investments less often than once a year.

Province whose residents are most likely to invest monthly:
Ontario
Rate by which a Quebecker is more likely than an Albertan to
invest once a year: 3 to 1
Rate by which a younger Canadian is more likely than an older
Canadian to invest monthly: 2 to 1

Debt

Ask any economist: there is no economy without debt. By consuming yourself into debt, you're keeping the economy ticking and securing your own job. Credit card balances, lines of credit, loans and mortgages—these are the magic that keep the economy afloat, and you are helping out. But when the bills arrive at the end of the month, you may wonder whether you are up to the task. One-third (31%) of Canadian adults say they are concerned about managing their current debt levels (11% "very concerned" and 20% "somewhat concerned").

Percentage of Canadians who agree that "being in debt scares
me": 62
Percentage who agree with the statement, "I will have a lot
more freedom when all my debt is paid off": 85
Rate by which a resident of Manitoba or Saskatchewan is
more likely than a resident of Quebec to be concerned about
debt: 3 to 1
Rate by which a lower-income Canadian is more likely than an
upper-income Canadian to be concerned about debt: 2 to 1
Percentage of Canadians over the age of 55 who say they have
no debt: 55
Age at which a 25–34-year-old expects to be debt-free: 45.7
Age at which a 45-year-old expects to be debt-free: 56.6
Age at which a 56-year-old expects to be debt-free: 60.2

Debt-to-equity ratio is a general indicator of Canadians' ability to cover their debt. The higher the ratio, the more difficult it would likely be for Canadians to cover their current debt with their current financial assets. According to the Ipsos-Reid Canadian Financial Monitor, the debt-to-equity ratio for Canadian households increased from 0.73 in 2000 to 0.94 in 2002. This increase is largely due to growing levels of debt and to the declining value of financial assets.

But for whom is the debt load the highest? And for whom is it increasing the most? As expected, and based upon October 2004 data, Canadians between the ages of 18 and 34 have the highest debt-to-income ratio (1.47), followed by 35–44 year olds (1.34), 45–54 year olds (1.00), 55–64 year olds (0.92) and then those 65 years of age or over (0.71). However, perhaps counter-intuitively, there are indications that the debt-to-income ratios have increased the most among those in the 55–64 age category. Loans for financing kids at college or university? Borrowing to improve the home before cashing in and cashing out? Taking the cruise now and paying later? All plausible.

Percentage growth in debt/income of all Canadians 2001 to 2004: 4%

Percentage growth in debt/equity of ages 18–34 2001 to 2004: 6%

Percentage growth in debt/income of age 55–64 2001 to 2004: 15%

Is All This Good or Bad?
Over four in ten Canadian adults feel their own financial situation will improve in the upcoming year. That is a remarkable increase from 36% in July 2002 and 29% in April 2001. Only 12% expect their own financial situation to get worse. Like wisdom, pessimism seems to increase with age: Canadians over the age of 55 are less than half as likely as young Canadians to expect things to improve.

Most economically optimistic province: Ontario, tied with Alberta

Most economically pessimistic: British Columbia

Getting Ready to Face the Future
Some day you're going to want to spend all that money you've saved. But how can you be sure it will be there? Only one in eight (12%) Canadians claims to have made lifestyle or retirement planning changes due to recent market volatility or economic uncertainty.

Even those who are expecting things to get worse are not taking immediate action. Only 17% of those who expect that their financial situation will get worse in the upcoming year say they have made lifestyle or retirement planning changes due to market volatility or economic uncertainty.

Here's how panicked Canadians are as a result of economic volatility:

Percentage of Canadians who have delayed retirement: 2
Percentage who have deferred buying a house: 1

Saving for the Kids' Education

Though Canadians may not be particularly worried about their own finanacial futures, they are clearly thinking about their children's. More than eight in ten (85%) Canadians with children under the age of 18 say "increases in tuition and lodging expenses for post-secondary education are a concern for [them]."

- **Increases in post-secondary education expenses are most concerning to parents living in Saskatchewan/Manitoba (95%), followed by Atlantic Canada (93%), Alberta (87%), Ontario (86%) and British Columbia (86%). Quebec parents (74%) are less likely to be concerned.**
- **Parents with only a high school diploma (90%) are more likely to be concerned than parents with a university degree (82%).**

And this is not a minor worry. It could shape the entirety of the next generation. Two in three parents think "the cost of a college or university education is putting it out of reach for [their] children."

- **Atlantic Canadian parents (79%) are most likely to think "the cost of a college or university education is putting it out of reach for [their] children," followed by parents living in Alberta (76%), British Columbia (75%), Ontario (65%) and Saskatchewan/Manitoba (62%). Quebec parents (46%) are the least likely to feel this way.**

- **Parents with a high school diploma or less (79%) are more likely than parents with a college diploma or some university (67%) and parents with a university degree (48%) to agree.**
- **Parents with an annual household income of less than $30,000 (82%) or between $30,000 and $59,000 (74%) are significantly more likely than parents with an annual household income of $60,000 or more (52%) to feel this concern**

Obviously, one way to pay for a child's education is to let him or her pay for it. Another six in ten (61%) parents agree with the statement, "I don't know how my children will be able to pay off their post-secondary education debt."

Percentage of women who feel this way: 68
Percentage of men who do: 54

The Cost of Education

The concerns about the cost of a post-secondary education are put into perspective when parents are asked to estimate how much it will cost for a child in their family to get a college or university education (including tuition fees, housing and other costs). The average dollar cost for a post-secondary education is estimated to be $52,442.30.

- **Parents living in Alberta give the highest estimated cost ($69,028.20), followed by parents living in Saskatchewan/Manitoba ($64,512.80), Ontario ($58,923.80), British Columbia ($55,015.90), and Atlantic Canada ($53,548.70). Parents living in Quebec give a significantly lower estimate ($27,127.40).**
- **Parents with a university degree ($60,399.90) and parents with an annual household income greater than $60,000 ($56,680.80) also give high estimates.**

How much debt do Canadian parents think they can take on to send their kids to college or university?

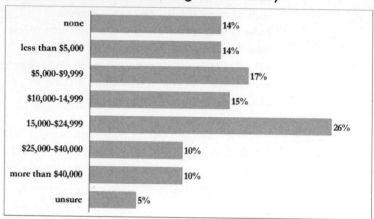

none	14%
less than $5,000	14%
$5,000-$9,999	17%
$10,000-14,999	15%
15,000-$24,999	26%
$25,000-$40,000	10%
more than $40,000	10%
unsure	5%

Investing for Your Kids

Despite the claims of children across the country, parents are actually quite generous to their children. And their tuition will one day be paid for by many a new car or dishwasher or vacation that their parents managed to do without. Four in ten Canadian parents have a registered education savings plan (RESP) for their children's education.

Parents with an annual household income greater than $60,000 (46%) are more likely to have an RESP for their child or children than are parents with an annual household income between $30,000 and $59,000 (34%) and parents with an annual household income of less than $30,000 (19%).

Estimated mean value of all RESPs: $15,558.70
Average number of years that parents who have an RESP have been contributing to it: 6.3
Of those who have opened an RESP, average age of the child for whom it was intended at the time it was opened: 3.5
Rate by which parents with university degrees are more likely than parents with less than a high school diploma to have opened an RESP: 2.5 to 1

Percentage of Canadian parents who have seen, read or heard of the Federal government's Canada Education Savings Grant (which "adds 20% to the first $2,000 in contributions made into an RESP on behalf of an eligible beneficiary each year"): 62

How do Canadian parents share education expenses with their kids?

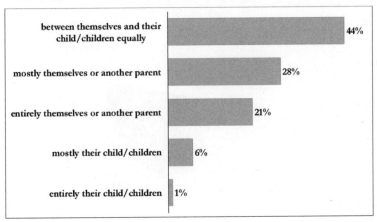

It seems bizarre to put your money in an investment that you expect to fail, but that is precisely what 46% of Canadian investors did last year. Only 54% of those who contributed to an RRSP in 2004 expected a positive rate of return. And that is bullish compared to 2003—a 38% increase. Only four in ten investors expected a positive return that year.

Average rate of return Canadian investors expect in 2004: 6.3%
Average rate of return expected in 2003: 0%

Increased Appetite For Risk
It seems impossible to depress financial expectations for long—optimism appears to be the direct consequence of pessimism. Here's the cycle: you expect little from your investments; you decide to risk more; you expect more. Canadians have increased their appetite for risk significantly—up 10%. One-third say they

are willing to take at least some risk for above-average returns, as opposed to 25% last year.

RRSPs and Retirees

Income sources of retired Canadians under the age of 69

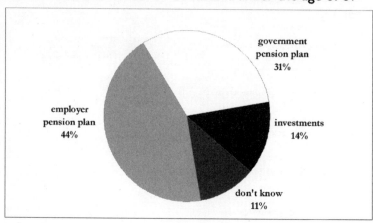

We know we have to save for retirement to supplement other assets, employee pensions, CPP and OAS (of this the television ads leave little doubt). But how much? Obviously, there is no fixed answer. Much will depend on the tastes and habits you've formed over the course of your earning years.

Twenty per cent of Canadian adults expect they would need to personally save $100,000 or less toward their retirement needs, 15% expect to need between $100,000 and $250,000 and over one-third (35%) of Canadians say their expected saving needs are $250,000 or over.

Percentage of retirees over 69 who do not contribute to an RRSP: 79
Percentage of Canadians who do not know how much they think they need to save: 28
Province with the highest expectations of retirement needs: Alberta (24% of adults in Alberta had expectations of $1 million or more)
Province with the lowest expected needs: Quebec

Rate by which a man is more likely than a woman to expect to need more than $250,000: 2 to 1

Keeping Track

How do investors follow investment-related news?

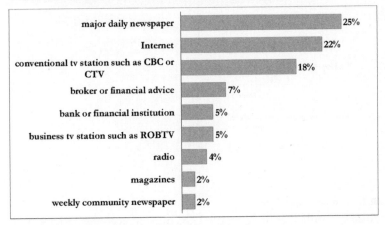

major daily newspaper	25%
Internet	22%
conventional tv station such as CBC or CTV	18%
broker or financial advice	7%
bank or financial institution	5%
business tv station such as ROBTV	5%
radio	4%
magazines	2%
weekly community newspaper	2%

Rate by which an Ontarian is more likely than a Quebecker to follow investments in the newspaper: 2 to 1
Rate by which an Atlantic Canadian is more likely than an Ontarian to follow investments through television: 2 to 1
Rate by which younger investors are more likely than older investors to follow investments on the Internet: 3.5 to 1
Rate by which upper-income investors are more likely than lower-income investors to follow investments on the Internet: 2 to 1

What media do you trust to provide thorough and reliable information concerning economic and investment matters?

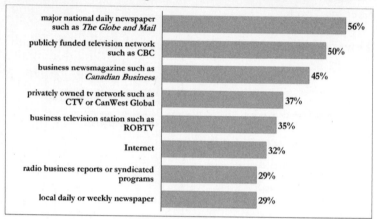

major national daily newspaper such as *The Globe and Mail*	56%
publicly funded television network such as CBC	50%
business newsmagazine such as *Canadian Business*	45%
privately owned tv network such as CTV or CanWest Global	37%
business television station such as ROBTV	35%
Internet	32%
radio business reports or syndicated programs	29%
local daily or weekly newspaper	29%

A Lot to Account For

After a number of high-profile U.S. cases of accounting irregularities, Canadians continue to believe that "Canadian auditing standards are more effective in protecting the public interest than they are in the U.S." (60%, up 6 points from July 2002). Similar numbers agree that when they "hear a company has released its audited financial statements, [they] have confidence that the reported figures are accurate" (60%, compared to 58% in July 2002) and that "Canada's financial regulators do a better job of policing the activities of companies than their American counterparts" (57%, compared to 55% in July 2002).

However, six in ten (59%, compared to 56% in July 2002) say they "have lost confidence in the stock market and would rather put [their] money into other things, such as real estate or gold." As well, an increasing number of Canadians say that "these situations of accounting and financial irregularities don't only affect a few companies and that the problem really is widespread" (59%, up from 51% in July 2002).

Number one response to the question, "what is free in life?": nothing

The Workplace

Liberty is, to the lowest rank of every nation, little more than the choice of working or starving.

—Samuel Johnson

YOUR WORKPLACE MAY be a place of joy or a place of dread. In either case—or in all those cases that rank somewhere in between—it is inevitably a font of strong emotions and vivid memories.

All of us remember our first job. After that, images linger of characters in all those subsequent jobs who could sometimes make the workplace feel like a second home. Or like nine-to-five hell.

Most of us have little stories of what a given job meant to us.

When the Levi Strauss plant closed in Edmonton recently, putting 488 people out of work, Heather Majeau looked down at the last pair of Levis to be shipped out, and then . . . "I felt I had to do something to mark the occasion, so a grabbed a pen and wrote that this was the last pair of jeans to be made at the Edmonton plant."

That's poignant. There are also, of course, funny stories—that time Wanda and Frank were caught stealing a kiss in the broomcloset, that time Jack kicked the photocopier and broke his toe. Well, maybe Jack didn't find it all *that* funny. Nor did Wanda's husband. Oh, well.

The truth is that many Canadian workplaces may be getting to be too stern for even little doses of fun now and then. Think about this: the City of London, Ontario, recently banned practical jokes in the workplace after a stressed worker who was out of town was sent a prank e-mail by his colleagues telling him that a major report had to be finished by April 1. Despite the mention of that magic date, he didn't get the joke. He was so shaken up he ended up on stress leave, finally taking a retirement package.

The Grind

There is certainly nothing funny about these statistics: In 1991, 44% of Canadian workers reported physical and mental stress in the workplace. Ten years later, that number had jumped to 55%.

Linda Duxbury, a business professor at Carleton University in Ottawa who worked on that report, says that only half of Canadians are satisfied with their job, while one-quarter contemplate leaving their current organization at least once a week. The report concludes that the direct costs of absenteeism due to high work–life conflict are approximately $3 billion to $5 billion a year.

Workplace health has become a big issue for business and labour leaders alike. They are responding with a slew of "wellness" programs, healthier food in cafeterias, in-house daycare, gyms, diet programs, flexible hours and sabbaticals.

But those things are all aimed at making it easier to work and don't get at the root problem—workload, says Duxbury. "All these concierge-style services companies are offering, like making your dinner and doing your cleaning, are aimed at making you stay at work and not leave. What good is a flextime policy if you're working a 60-hour week—so you can come in before 6 a.m. and leave after 8 p.m.?"

The Office Cast List

Let's start at the top, with the boss.

What could be worse than spending 40 to 60 hours a week working for someone you hate? Luckily, that's not happening to the vast majority of Canadians. In fact, 88% of Canadians say they are happy with their jobs, which suggests that their boss isn't driving them nuts.

However, 10%—one out of ten—told us they hated their boss, and 11% said they dreaded going to work every day because of their boss. Apparently 1% could not bring themselves to "hate," but "dread" is a pretty strong word too.

There are approximately 16 million people in the Canadian labour force. This survey suggests that about 1.75 million of them go to work every day grinding their teeth, all because of one person: the boss. (We haven't tried this one on people who work at home, the self-employed. We're not into self-loathing here.)

Working Canadians in lower-income houses are more than three times as likely as those in upper-income houses to say that they hate their boss (22% versus 7%). That may be because they're trapped—it seems more likely that upper-income employees would find other options if they were carrying a bag of loathing into work with them every day.

Like the teacher's pet, there is always the colleague who wants to get in good with the boss. We found that 8% of respondents "would be willing to suck up to [their] boss to get ahead in [their] career."

Younger people were more prone to toadying—16% said they do that. For older workers it was a nice, clean 0%. Could it be that these people don't believe that any amount of sucking up is going to rocket them to the top at this point? Or have they simply acquired a measure of dignity in their later years? A bit of both perhaps? Or just plain weariness?

Ratio of young workers to middle-aged workers who suck up to the boss: 2.28 to 1

The Talent Game: Attracting and Retaining Employees

We asked Canadian workers to tell us what employers could do to entice them to stay at one job or go to another job. Not surprisingly, financial incentives were No. 1 on the list.

- **Improved employee benefits such as increased salaries and broader health and dental coverage topped the list at 70%, with workers from Atlantic Canada most financially motivated at 80% and women more financially motivated, at 75%, than men, at 69%.**
- **No. 2 motivator? An extra week of vacation each year, mentioned by 66% of respondents.**
- **Third on the list were peripheral benefits such as sabbaticals, education and health club memberships, mentioned by 57% of respondents.**

- **Profit-sharing or stock options were mentioned by 56%. Entrepreneurial Alberta led the way on this one (68%).**
- **Would you like to work from home at least one day a week? We found that 42% of Canadians would, women (47%) more than men (38%).**
- **37% of respondents said they would like different job responsibilities.**
- **Another 37% wanted fewer hours in their workweek.**
- **Finally, 25% of respondents called for a less formal working environment, with Quebec (29%) and Atlantic Canada (28%) leading the way.**

White-Collar Blues

Thirty-six per cent of Canadians hold white-collar jobs. Since these are the folks who lead Canada's organizations and are in some of the positions many aspire to, we decided to do a survey focused specifically on their motivations and grievances. And we've profiled them even more here because, according to our January 2005 "Most Respected Corporations" survey, they are the priority talent pool target for companies. So head hunters, take note.

White-collar workers indicate that while increased salary may entice someone to a new job, day-to-day tasks and the company mission are key determinants in whether he or she will be content in the position.

Percentage of Canadian workers who work in a white-collar environment: 36

Percentage of white-collar workers who say, "My career is a big part of who I am": 52

Percentage difference between the size of the "young and restless" group of white-collar workers who keep their résumé up to date and the national average: 41

Percentage difference between the size of the "stable and satisfied" group of white-collar workers who keep their résumé up to date and the national average: −3

We found that Canada's white-collar worker population could more or less be divided into four major groups.

1. The Young and the Restless

This may seem like an unlikely starting point, but fully 26% of white-collar workers could be described as "young and restless." They are generally better educated than the larger white-collar worker population, and somewhat younger. They are the most likely to have already changed positions and/or employers, and are the most likely to make another move within the next two years. Their characteristics certainly make them mobile:

- **Confidence in finding alternate employment (78% versus 65% of white-collar workers overall)**
- **Optimism about future career opportunities (76% versus 62%)**
- **Keeping a résumé up to date (75% versus 34%)**
- **Believing there is a maximum time to stay in a job (42% versus 27%)**

2. Stressed Successes

Another 26% of white-collar workers are paying a price for their success. These "stressed successes" are relatively young and already hold senior positions. But the pressures are starting to show. Yes, they are at least "moderately satisfied with their job," but 79% agree that their family and friends resent the number of hours they work.

This group scored highest on

- **Friends and family resenting hours worked (79% versus average 28%)**
- **Career being a "big part of who I am" (67% versus 52%)**
- **Schedule conflicting with responsibilities (59% versus 22%)**
- **Having more to do than they can comfortably handle (51% versus 28%)**
- **Experiencing tension at work (48% versus 27%)**

3. Stable and Satisfied

Twenty-nine per cent of white-collar workers could be summarized as stable and satisfied. They are very happy with their current position. In fact, 69% agree that they are currently working for "the ideal company."

This group tends to be older, more senior and the least likely to make a move.

The stable-and-satisfied group scored lowest on

- **Keeping a résumé up to date (3% versus average 34%)**
- **Being worried about job security (2% versus 18%)**
- **Experiencing tension at work (9% versus 27%)**
- **Having more than they can comfortably handle (11% versus 28%)**
- **Believing there is a maximum time to stay in a job (12% versus 27%)**

4. Anxious Cynics

Nineteen per cent of white-collar workers seem perpetually dissatisfied with work. They tend to be older, have comparatively less education and lower income and have stayed the longest in their current jobs.

This group scored highest on

- **Finding it harder to make ends meet (57% versus average 31%)**
- **Being worried about job security (44% versus 18%)**
- **Working just for the pay (32% versus 12%)**
- **Feeling they could be next in the firing line (16% versus 6%)**

White-Collar Pace of Change

- **Sixteen per cent have changed employers within the last two years; 35% have changed jobs with the same employer in the last two years.**
- **Twenty-seven per cent said they would likely change employers within the next two years; 37% said they would likely change jobs with their current employer in the same period.**
- **Thirty-four per cent keep their résumé up to date because "you never know when you might have to look for a new job."**

Many Canadian white-collar workers are tied to their job beyond 9 to 5.

A study of white-collar workers coast to coast and across a variety of industries finds that they:

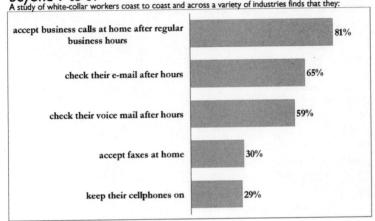

accept business calls at home after regular business hours	81%
check their e-mail after hours	65%
check their voice mail after hours	59%
accept faxes at home	30%
keep their cellphones on	29%

Percentage of Canadians who agree that they have "the type of job that requires me to be available 24 hours a day, 7 days a week": 21

Why Stay? Why Go?

There is a unique relationship between what determines job satisfaction and what another employer could offer to draw a white-collar employee away.

Top five reasons for staying at a job

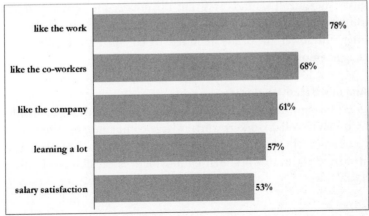

like the work	78%
like the co-workers	68%
like the company	61%
learning a lot	57%
salary satisfaction	53%

Rank of corporate "culture": 8th

The top five most appealing offers that an employer could make to poach white-collar workers

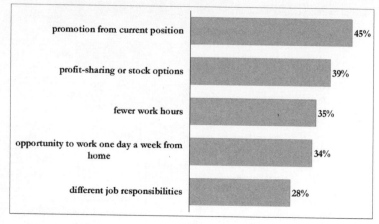

promotion from current position	45%
profit-sharing or stock options	39%
fewer work hours	35%
opportunity to work one day a week from home	34%
different job responsibilities	28%

Rank of a salary increase of 10%: 9th

The Lure of Money

A majority of white-collar workers (62%) would change jobs for less than a 30% salary increase. However, the required salary increase jumps significantly as the degree of uncertainty about the opportunity increases. When asked what salary would be required to prompt a move when the candidate has some uncertainty about the new job, only 35% would change jobs for less than a 30% salary increase. This indicates that the greater the certainty about the job opportunity and the company that can be provided in an offer, the lower the salary required to convince an employee to change employers.

And of a Better Workplace

In exploring what constitutes an ideal employer, although a majority of white-collar workers work at large companies, medium-sized companies of 21 to 50 employees were perceived as the most attractive places to work. Self-employment is the choice of only a hardy few:

- **Self-employed/sole proprietor: 9%**
- **Small company (fewer than 20 employees): 20%**
- **Medium (21–50): 28%**
- **Large (51 to 250): 21%**
- **Very large (more than 250): 21%**

When asked what detracts most from their current job, white-collar workers most frequently choose

- **red tape and bureaucracy: 37%**
- **office politics: 24%**
- **paperwork: 19%**
- **meetings: 15%**
- **gossip: 15%**

In addition, 27% said they experience "a great deal of tension at work" and 22% say their work often conflicts with personal responsibilities.

White and Blue Collar Report Cards

When asked to grade their employers with respect to five work-environment statements, employed Canadians give their employers an overall grade-point-average (G.P.A.) of 2.93, approximately representing a "C+". In fact, a minority of four in ten employed Canadians (38%) provide an overall grade of "A" for their employer in these five areas.

And looking at the individual grades for each of the five areas, just four in ten or fewer employed Canadians give their employers an "A" grade:

1. 42% of employed Canadians give their employer an "A" grade in when it comes to their employer making them feel that "they fit in their work role"
2. 39% give their employer an "A" grade when it comes to their employer making them "feel supported in their role"
3. 38% give their employer an "A" grade when it comes to making them feel "clear in their role"
4. 38% give their employer an "A" grade when it comes to making them feel that they "are valued at their work"

5. 2% give their employer an "A" grade when it comes to making them feel "inspired"

While three in ten (28%) of workers identify themselves as current union members, a further 21% of non-union workers (totals 71%, with 21% of this group or 15% in total) say "they would definitely join a union if given the choice." This suggests that the potential union labour force in the country could, if circumstances exist or permit, grow to 43% of the national workforce (28% of current union members plus 15% of other workers).

Percentage of Canadian workers who say that "without unions, workers would not receive the pay and job security that they deserve": 38
Province the residents of which are most likely to believe this: Quebec

Starting Out: University Students and the Job Market

Seventy-nine per cent of university students say they will enter the workforce immediately after finishing their schooling, and 8 in 10 want careers. The ambitious young scholars are most attracted to "interesting" vocations (81%), not just high-paying occupations (19%), with their sights firmly set on starting annual salaries of $46,145 for undergraduates ($57,301 for graduate students), and with expectations to earn $68,084 within a couple of years ($81,052 for graduate students), $170,004 by 2020 ($177,908 for graduate students) and $264,041 by retirement ($246,306 for graduate students). Many (43%) aspire to be executives at large companies and nearly one in four would prefer to work at a company with more than 500 employees.

University students in general want time to smell the roses. Seven in ten (70%) would prefer to work regular hours for a longer period of time, balancing work–life interests. This preference was clearly favoured over a career with a shorter work period earning a lot more money and with more leisure time afterward (30%). One in four say they are "family focused," with 30% saying they expect to be "married, have two kids and drive a minivan." They want time to enjoy dream homes (45%), travel extensively (45%) and volunteer in the community (43%).

The survey we did provides a compelling blueprint of university students' career intentions and expectations for Canadian employers focused on recruiting and retaining top talent in the New Economy. In short, Canada's university students want it all, and 81% are confident their education will pay off in the long run.

What They Want to Be

- Fifty-three per cent are "very interested" in working temporarily outside of Canada, and 33% are "somewhat interested" in stints elsewhere in the world.
- University students' ranking of career desirability shows they are most interested in becoming entrepreneurs or consultants (40%); lawyers or other professionals (36%); teachers (31%); technology workers (23%); filmmakers, musicians, artists or writers (22%); doctors/physicians (21%); directors of not-for-profit agencies (20%); computer programmers (15%); stockbrokers (13%); politicians (11%) and commissioned salespeople (2%).
- Twenty-four per cent say they will spend five years at their first job; 15% say three years, 15% say two years and 4% say one year; 9% say six to ten years, and just 2% say 31 to 50 years.
- Twenty-two per cent say they will change jobs three times in their careers, 17% say six times and 14% say five times. Two per cent say they may change jobs 11 times or more; 4% say 10 times.

Where They Want to Work

• Twenty-nine per cent would prefer to work for a company with 100 to 500 employees, 31% for a medium-sized company. No one expressed a preference for working for a small company with fewer than 20 employees.

How to look for a job

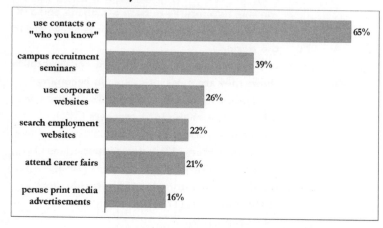

use contacts or "who you know"	65%
campus recruitment seminars	39%
use corporate websites	26%
search employment websites	22%
attend career fairs	21%
peruse print media advertisements	16%

• When choosing a place to work, students place equal importance on organizations that provide opportunities to learn and that support professional development (41%) and on making a choice based on salary (41%). Similarly, a company's vision and mission (32%) and support of work–life balance (32%) ranked as high priorities in selecting a place to work.

• Fifty-one per cent say they want to "experience a variety of tasks and opportunities," 44% say "challenging work responsibilities," 36% say job security, 36% say opportunities for promotion, 18% say "direct responsibility over tasks" and 15% say they want interesting co-workers.

Benefits and Compensation

Seventy-five per cent of students would take a 10% cut in salary in exchange for medical and dental coverage of all basic expenses, 61% of students would accept a 10% pay cut in exchange for employer-paid job training, 57% would take a pay cut for flexible work hours and 56% would take less money in exchange for job security.

Percentage of Canadian university students who believe they will become millionaires: 16

Percentage of Canadian university students who are interested in a career in the public sector: 28

Percentage of students who would rather have an average salary, with an opportunity to earn more through performance or bonuses: 67

Online Job Hunters

Job-searching is now among the most popular online activities of Canadian Internet users. In fact, more Canadians have looked for a job online than have ever banked online, shopped online, comparison shopped or downloaded music. Younger online job-seekers are more likely to have used the Internet in a job search than are older people (73% of those 18–34, compared to only 35% of those 55 years of age or more).

Where They Look

The activity most common among online job hunters is looking for a job at a job-posting website (80%). However, almost two in three people actively using the Internet as a job-hunting tool have also researched a prospective company online (62%), and more than half have sent in a résumé by e-mail (62%).

Of those who admit to searching the Internet for jobs while at work, three-quarters (75%) state they are keeping themselves informed about the job market, while almost one-half (46%) say they are using the Internet access provided by their current employer to find another job.

What They Do

There are a number of Internet job-hunting tools that are not being widely used by job seekers. For example, only 36% of those in the job market have ever posted a résumé online, and only 22% have used information at a job website to help prepare a résumé or cover letter.

Changing Loyalties

One-fifth of Canadian employees (19%) say that, compared to a few years ago, they now feel "more loyal" to their employer, while a similar proportion report feeling "less loyal" (22%). A solid majority (59%) indicate no change in the loyalty they feel toward their employer.

The most significant variation can be seen between private-sector and public-sector employees. Specifically, whereas private-sector employees are split on this question (22% more loyal versus 21% less loyal), their counterparts working in the public sector lean toward feeling less loyal rather than more loyal to their employers today than they did a few years ago (22% versus 15%).

Employer Disloyalty Is Growing

A plurality (39%) of Canadian employees subscribe to the view that their employer "values its employees less today and is now more likely to take job-cutting measures to save money" compared to a few years ago. One-quarter (25%) hold the opposite perception, that their employer "values its employees more today and puts a higher priority on protecting jobs than they used to." One-third (34%) sense no change in their own employer's loyalty over the past few years.

Although Canadian employees are currently still inclined to believe that employer loyalty has diminished in recent years, the proportion holding this view has declined from 53% in our 1995 survey to 39% today. This negative view of employers is particularly common among part-time workers (46%), public-sector employees (45%) and older employees (47%).

Wearing the Union Label

The prospect of joining a labour union is given the thumbs down by one-half of working Canadians. One-quarter (27%) of those surveyed strongly agreed that "if given the choice, I would definitely join a union." Almost twice as many (50%) strongly disagreed with this statement.

Across regional and socio-demographic lines, certain segments of employees are more averse than others to the idea of joining a union if they had the opportunity to do so. These groups include a majority of those in Alberta and Ontario (58% strongly disagreed with the statement), men (54%), older employees (74%) and those in the higher-income bracket (58% of those with a total household income of at least $60,000 annually). Meanwhile, employees from Quebec and Atlantic Canada tended to be more evenly divided on this count.

Interestingly, many employees who already belong to a union would rather not. A narrow majority of current union members expressed strong agreement with the pro-union statement, but one in five (21%) indicated otherwise. On the other hand, a majority of non-union members were satisfied with their current status—six in ten strongly disagreed that they would definitely join a union if they could, versus 18% who said they would prefer to be part of a union.

Frustrations at the Office

Twelve per cent of the Canadian workforce have become so frustrated with the photocopier that they have actually kicked or hit it, with another 30% seriously wanting to do so. Fifty-eight per cent say that they have not wanted to do either. The number of men (13%) and of women (12%) who have kicked or hit the machine is virtually the same. Those who are more affluent (14%) are more likely to have taken on the machine than those earning under $30,000 per year (8%). And those with post-secondary or university education (13%) are more likely to have actually kicked or hit their machine than those with a high school education (10%).

Distance (in kilometres) that the average Canadian walks in one year to go to the printer or photocopier: 40

So, Are We Sharing?

Fully three-quarters of urban Canadian office workers (75%) in six of Canada's leading economic centres say that sharing information with their co-workers has become more important over the last five years. Other office observations include

- **Workers in larger organizations (500 employees or more) spend much more time on average in meetings than those in smaller organizations (less than 50 employees) or medium-sized organizations (50–499 employees)—6.9 hours versus 3.8 and 4.6 hours, respectively.**

- **Montreal workers spend less time each week in meetings (3.8 hours) than their counterparts in other major urban centres (5.7 hours).**
- **Most workers (91%) report that they collaborate with others in their organization on the same documents or electronic files (52% frequently and 39% sometimes).**
- **Collaboration is even more common among workers in larger organizations (60% frequently collaborate versus 42% in smaller organizations and 53% in medium-sized organizations).**

Almost all workers (96%) agree that "fast and easy access to information is a critical part" of their job. Furthermore, more than half (57%) say that the need to work in teams as opposed to working individually has increased over the last five years. Further highlighting the need to share information, one-quarter (26%) of workers say that job sharing in their organization has increased over the same time period.

So, Let's See What You Mean ...

Visuals, such as diagrams, charts and pictures, are an important and growing means of sharing information in the Canadian workplace. Indeed, four in five workers (81%) use such visuals to illustrate their work (39% frequently and 42% sometimes). Furthermore, 42% say that their use of visuals has increased since five years ago. Only 8% say it has decreased.

- **Larger organizations use visuals, such as diagrams, charts or pictures, more frequently (47%) than smaller (30%) or medium-sized organizations (36%).**
- **Moreover, use of visuals in larger organizations has increased more significantly (53%) than in smaller (31%) or medium-sized organizations (41%) over the last five years.**

Work to Live or Live to Work?

Average hours worked per week: 47.5

Workers say that their worklife encroaches upon their personal time and that this trend has worsened over the last five years. For example, half of workers (50%) say that the number of hours they work in total has increased over the past five years.

- **Three in five workers (59%) say they often skip lunch or eat at their desk in order to leave work on time. Moreover, 59% sometimes have to take work home to be able to meet their personal commitments.**
- **Forty-two per cent also say that they try to visit the gym, bank or dentist during working hours so they can get it all done.**
- **More than two-thirds (69%) have to come in early or leave late just to keep up with their workload.**
- **In Calgary and Edmonton, workers are more likely to have to work during evenings or weekends (61%), while Montreal workers are less likely to do so (48%).**
- **Men (60%) are also more likely than women (46%) to do work at home during the evenings or weekends.**

	Total	Region				Gender	
		Toronto/Ottawa	Vancouver	Montreal	Calgary/Edmonton	Male	Female
Proportion of Workers Who Agree with Personal and Professional Lives Management Statements							
I often bring work home to finish in the evening or on the weekend.	55%	57%	53%	48%	61%	60%	46%
I often skip lunch or eat at my desk in order to leave on time.	59%	61%	65%	55%	56%	55%	64%
I sometimes have to take work home with me to be able to meet my personal commitments too.	59%	65%	57%	51%	63%	63%	53%
I try to visit the gym, bank or dentist during working hours so I can get it all done.	42%	40%	44%	39%	45%	45%	37%

How's Your Mobility?

Workers are pursuing flexible hours, working in non-traditional locations and using mobility technology to stay connected. Indeed, three in five (60%) agree that they vary their work schedule from day to day or with their partner simply to get personal or family things done. Moreover, close to half (45%) will work at home if the babysitter is sick or when they are expecting a delivery or a service person.

Technology in the Workplace

Software Experimentation and Learning

When it comes to software, workers like to experiment. Eighty per cent of workers experiment with new features of the software they use at work rather than using the same features and not experimenting. When they want to learn new features in software applications, half just experiment on their own (50%), while one-fifth (19%) ask friends or colleagues, 13% read books or manuals and 12% find online help. Only 6% take a training course to learn more about software applications.

What Your CEO Thinks

While protecting the company from malicious attacks is a low business priority, it is a high IT priority.

- **Three in four CEOs (75%) say that protecting the company's IT systems and the information they contain is a major IT priority.**
- **Ensuring the continuity of operations in case of a security breach is deemed a major IT priority by 66% of CEOs.**
- **Just under half of CEOs (45%) state that their company has been infected by a computer virus in the past year, making computer viruses the most prolific type of security breach. Twenty per cent say they've been hit by outside hacker attacks.**
- **Twenty-two per cent report that they have had computers stolen in the past year.**
- **The incidence of security breaches is higher among companies with more than 50 computers.**
- **Half (51%) of CEOs report that they are using independent consultants for IT security assessments.**
- **Of those CEOs who do use outside consultants, 64% report that they personally review the IT security assessments. This is equivalent to 27% of all respondents.**

Antivirus software (98%) and firewalls (85%) are popular security measures, while policies on acceptable use of computers are the most popular security policies (80%).

- **Almost all medium-sized companies have antivirus software in place (98%), with the incidence of firewalls also high (85%). More than half use centralized single sign-on and access control software (68%) and intrusion detection systems (60%).**
- **Only 22% report using authentication devices.**
- **Among security policies, policies on acceptable use of computers are most popular (in place in four of five companies), with policies on security and access to computers just behind (79%). Two in three CEOs (68%) report that in their company, passwords are changed regularly according to strong policy.**

Fraud in the Workplace

One-fifth (20%) of employed Canadians indicate that they are personally aware of or have been personally involved in fraud in their workplace over the past year. Eight in ten (79%) are not aware of such instances in their workplace during the past year.

- **Employees who work in the services sector (33%) are the most likely to report being aware of fraudulent activities in their workplace, while those in the high-tech and telecommunications sectors (13%) and in health care (13%) are the least likely to report knowledge of these types of activities.**
- **"Taking office items or shoplifting" (41%) is the highest reported type of workplace fraud. "Stealing or taking product or money" (20%), "inflating expense accounts" (16%), "claiming extra hours worked" (13%), "pocketing money from cash sales" (11%), "taking kickbacks from suppliers" (11%) and "creating phony supplier invoices" (4%) are the next highest type of**

workplace fraud witnessed. While "altering the books" is viewed as a major problem in Canada, within their own companies only 1% report personal knowledge of this type of fraud, making it the least reported types of workplace fraud.

- Canadians who are in positions of little or no supervisory responsibility (47%) or are supervisors or middle management (40%) are more likely to know of incidents of office items being taken or shoplifting than mid- to senior-level managers (29%). Those in supervisory to middle management (17%) and middle to upper management (22%) are more likely than those with little or no supervisory responsibility (5%) to indicate knowledge of incidents where extra hours were claimed.
- Women (48%, versus 36% of men) are more likely to indicate knowledge of taking office supplies or shoplifting, while men (24%, versus 13% of women) are more likely to say they know of incidents of stealing or taking products or money.
- Those who were aware of fraud occurring estimated that $1,882.60 was lost to their company monthly. Over a year's time, this level of fraud would result in the loss of $22,591.20 to their employer.

Do We Tell?

While three-quarters (78%) of employed Canadians say they would report on a co-worker stealing from their employer, of those who've had the chance only one third (35%) actually did.

An overwhelming majority (78%) of working Canadians say that if they were aware that one of their co-workers was defrauding their employer by taking goods (valued higher than a pad of paper or a couple of pencils) or money that did not belong to them, they would be likely to report them. This compares to only one-quarter (22%) who say they would be unlikely to report on their co-worker.

Percentage of workers who have detected workplace fraud: 20

Percentage of these who have reported fraud to a supervisor: 35

Percentage of female employees who would report a fraudulent co-worker: 46

Percentage of male employees who would: 29

Rate by which a middle-aged colleague is more likely to report than a younger one: 2 to 1

- **Of the 65% who did not report the workplace fraud that they were aware of, the main reason was that they were concerned about their job (24%) and that they didn't know about the fraud until it was reported (18%). Just under one in ten (8%) indicates that someone else reported the activity.**
- **Mid-level managers who did not personally report fraudulent activities that they were aware of are more likely to indicate that it was because they were concerned with their own personal position (30%). Senior-level managers indicate that they didn't report these activities because they didn't know about them until after they were reported (43%).**
- **When asked if they would be more or less likely to report an incident of fraud if they had to identify themselves, four in ten (41%) indicate they would be less likely. This compares to the three in ten who say it would make them more likely (29%) or that it would not make a difference either way (28%).**

"Cooking the Books" and Pocketing Cash Sales

With the backdrop of recent news coverage of white-collar crime stories and the unravelling of the Enron scandal, when asked to rank on a zero-to-ten-point scale how much of a problem various types of workplace fraud are, according to working Canadians the top problems are "altering the books to make profits or costs look better"

(65%) and "pocketing money from cash sales" (64%). The remaining types of fraud tested include "altering, creating or forging checks issued by your employer" (63%), "inflating expense accounts" (62%), "creating phony supplier invoices" (62%), "taking office items or shoplifting from your employer of items more than minor things like paper and pencils" (54%) and "taking kickbacks from suppliers" (48%).

Percentage of company profits estimated by employed
Canadians to be lost to fraud: 20.4
Estimated average monthly loss: $4,017.50

• **The effect of technology on the ability to commit fraud in the workplace is split almost evenly, with 38% believing that technology makes it easier for employees to commit fraud and 37% believing that it makes it harder to commit fraud. One in four (24%) says that technology doesn't make a difference.**

Ratio of those who say they would report a co-worker who
was stealing from their employer to those who have actually
reported a co-worker: 2.23 to 1

Percentage of Canadian moms and dads who say that parenting
is "more challenging than any job I've ever had": 90

House and Home

**'Mid Pleasures and palaces
though we may roam,
Be it ever so humble
there's no place like home.**

—John Howard Payne (1791–1852)

Percentage decline, between 2003 and 2004, in the number of
Canadians 18 to 24 who are likely to buy a home: 32.5

FOR MOST PEOPLE, home is where the heart is. For many
Canadians, home is also where the wallet is.

A number of forces came together in the early years of the
twenty-first century to make a home a great investment. Real estate
prices soared in most parts of Canada. Travel abroad seemed more
perilous. Baby boomers began to cocoon. The 2000 tumble made
stock investors wary. Interest rates were low, so socking money away
in bank accounts and guaranteed income certificates proved far less
rewarding than it had been in earlier decades.

Click! A light bulb popped on over many Canadians' heads:
"Hey, I can make my money do double duty. I can get it to improve
my surroundings at the same time that I'm getting a better return
on my investment than I could at my bank or brokerage."

That's not a formula for all decades. When interest rates are at
21%, as they were at one point in the 1980s, GICs are where you

want your money. And when the stock market is soaring, as it was in the late 1990s, there *is* a better place than home—that place would be the stock exchange. But home investment has been a juicy formula for mixing a better lifestyle and a better investment portfolio in the early 2000s, and Canadians have been pumping money into their homes at a rate unseen since the Second World War ended.

But this chapter is *not* entirely about money. Just how crass do you think we really are?

Homes are where sentimentality and shrewd investment sense hold hands. At least they have been in recent years. So let's take a look at homes from two angles: first, as the nesting place for Canadians, with all their dreams and foibles; and second, as places in which to invest hard, cold dollars.

Where You Live

CIBC World Markets released a report entitled *Home Is Where the Money Is*. It identified the real estate market as "the sole champion of the current economic cycle." Said Benjamin Tal, senior economist at CIBC World Markets, "Lured by historically low mortgage rates, Canadians have been refinancing their mortgages at a pace never seen before—nearly one in two mortgage holders refinanced between 2002 and 2003."

Not surprisingly, then, we at Ipsos-Reid discovered a great deal of interest when we probed Canadians about the real estate market. One-tenth of Canadians believe that they are very likely to purchase a home within the next two years. Among expectant buyers, people who currently rent lead those who currently own by more than a 2-to-1 margin—20% to 9%. And younger Canadians are more likely than their middle-aged or older counterparts to be planning on buying. Both results make sense: much of the interest is among people who don't yet own their own homes and who don't want to miss out while mortgage interest rates are low.

You Don't Have to Buy to Spend

Among those who are already owners, 28% indicate they are planning renovations over the next year (virtually unchanged from 2003, when 26% said so). Of those who responded a year ago, 39% wanted to upgrade their current living space, 22% wanted to increase living space and 21% just wanted to do some decorating.

Is everybody spiffing up just to sell? Not exactly: a year ago, 27% identified general upkeep/upgrading/bringing it up to modern standards as the reason, 24% cited wanting the place to look better and 22% wanted more living space. Only 4% planned to renovate in anticipation of selling.

Canadians expected to pay less for renovations in 2004 than the year before—$8,850, down from $9,860.

What's the Payoff?

A whopping 86% of Canadians feel that purchasing a house or a condominium is either a good or a very good investment. A small rump of 13% don't believe that. They will be proven right if property values crash.

There hasn't been that much inflation in the Canadian economy generally over the past decade, but our respondents believe that the real estate market will continue to be the exception to the rule. In 2003, when we asked what expectations were for a year hence, 54% said they felt housing prices would be higher, 51% said interest rates would likely rise and 61% said they expected rents to go up.

Buying and Selling Strategies

Most Canadians (55%) think it makes sense to approach home-buying with a little firmness, but with a little flexibility as well. They say they would go into the process with a maximum price in mind but would be willing to bend a bit if they had to.

We found that 51% say they would still be interested in a property if they heard there was a bidding war going on. Canadians are split on this—47% said they would immediately stop inquiring about a home if there was fierce competition.

What Am I Bid?

Just over one-eighth (13%) indicate they've been involved in a bidding war for a property they wanted to purchase. Of those who have been involved in a bidding war, just over half won the bidding.

Of those who lost, a majority say that in hindsight they were relieved that someone outbid them because they would have blown their budget. Four in ten (39%) say they were upset for not having bid higher, since they really wanted the property at any price.

As for the winners in a bidding war, not surprisingly, over eight in ten (84%) say they were pleased because they won and that the house was worth they price they paid.

From a home seller's perspective, Canadians are split on whether to price a home above the average listing price of what similar properties sold for (47%) or to price a home to get multiple bids on the property (47%).

A majority of Canadians (55%) say that if they were to bid on a new home, they'd go in with an idea of a maximum price they'd like to spend, but with some flexibility to pay more if they had to. Four in ten (43%) say they would go into the process with a set maximum that they would be willing to spend and go no higher.

- Quebec is the only region in the country where a minority (39%) say they would go into the process with a maximum price in mind but with some flexibility to pay more if they had to. In fact, a majority (58%) in Quebec say they would go into the process with a set maximum price they would be willing to pay and no more.
- Canadians 18 to 24 years of age (80%) are the most likely to say they would be flexible in their budget, while Canadians 65 and older (37%) are least likely to approach shopping for a new home in this manner.

However, Canadians are split as to whether they want to get involved in a bidding war over a home they like. Just under half (47%) of Canadians said they would immediately stop inquiring about a home if they heard there was a bidding war for the it, while a slight majority (51%) say they would continue to look at the home.

- Regionally, a majority of residents of Saskatchewan/Manitoba (62%), Alberta (57%), Ontario (54%) and Atlantic Canada (53%) say that a bidding war would not stop them from inquiring about a home. However, the story is

different in Quebec, where a majority (56%) say they would quit looking at a home if they knew there was a bidding war for it. British Columbians split evenly (50/50) on this question.
- A majority (59%) of Canadians in communities with populations of 100,000 to 1,000,000 say that a bidding war would not stop them from continuing to look at a home.

One of the reasons for not wanting to get involved in a bidding contest may be that Canadians do not know what to do in the event of competitive bidding on a property. Six in ten say they do not know how to wage bidding war. Bidding accumen seems to increase as you move westward. Residents of Atlantic Canada are least likely to know what to do in a bididng war. British Columbians are most likely.

Setting the Selling Price

From the seller's perspective, Canadians are split on whether to price a home above the average listing price of what similar properties sold for (47%) or to price a home to get multiple bids on the property (47%).

- Canadians between 55 and 64 years of age (54%) are more likely than those 65 and over (38%) to say they would price their home to get multiple bids.
- Regionally, those most likely to say they would price their home to encourage multiple bids are from Quebec (59%) and British Columbia (55%). This compares to the views of residents of Atlantic Canada (35%).
- A majority of Canadians who live in larger communities, those with populations of 500,000 and higher (55%), are more likely to say they would price their home to encourage multiple bids than are those in mid-sized cities, those with populations of between 100,000 and just under 500,000 (41%), or in small communities, with populations of up to 10,000 (40%).

"Oh I Like This One, Darling! Should We Put in a Bid?"

Before putting in a bid on a home, how many properties do Canadians feel they need to see? Three in ten (29%) say that if they liked the first property they looked at, they'd put in an offer. However, the remaining seven in ten (70%) say they would need to visit other homes before putting in an offer on any property.

- Canadians in larger cities with populations of at least 1,000,000 (40%) are the most likely to say they would put in an offer on the first house they saw if they liked it before seeing other properties.
- Regionally, residents of Quebec (35%) are the most likely to say they would put in an offer on the first house they saw if they liked it, while those in Atlantic Canada (20%) are least likely to follow this route.
- Canadians on average say they need to see about 11 properties (mean 10.8) to feel comfortable that they've seen what is available and to make a decision on a purchase.
- Regionally, Quebeckers need to see the least number of homes (mean 6.8) before they feel they have seen what is available, while residents in Atlantic Canada (mean 14.0) say they would need to see more than twice as many as Quebeckers.

The Outcomes of a Bidding War

Just over one in ten Canadians (13%) indicate they have been involved in a bidding war for a property they wanted to purchase.

- Residents of British Columbia (24%) and Saskatchewan/Manitoba (22%) are the most likely to say they have been involved in a bidding war for a property, while those in Atlantic Canada (10%), Alberta (9%) and Quebec (7%) are the least likely.

- Canadians with household incomes of at least $100,000 (22%) are more likely to say they have been involved in a bidding war, followed by those with household incomes of between $50,000 and just under $100,000 (16%). Canadians in lower-income households (9%) are the least likely to say so.
- On average, the property that was the object of the bidding contest went for just over 12% (12.4%) higher than the original asking price according to the Canadians who were involved.

What Do We Want?

- Asked the reasons they are thinking of buying a home, 17% say they are "looking to upgrade," while 13% say it is to "find a suitable home." Other responses include "for equity/stop wasting money on rent" (9%), "an investment" (8%), "better than renting/just to own a home" (8%), "moving to a new city" (7%) and have the "ability to afford the purchase" (7%).
- The kitchen (58%) is the one room Canadians think has the most significance or the biggest impact on potential buyers of a home, followed by the living room (20%). Bedrooms (6%), the den or family room (4%), bathrooms (2%), the front entrance (1%), the basement (1%) and the dining room (1%) are also cited.
- One-tenth (8%) of Canadians say they would be likely to seriously consider purchasing or building a bomb shelter.

Sharing Decision-Making Responsibility

When it comes to purchasing a new or different home, Canadians share the responsibility. Six in ten Canadians (62%) say when it comes to making decisions about purchasing a new or different home, they share the decision-making with someone else. One-third of Canadians (33%) say they are the primary decision-maker when it comes to purchasing a new home; only 4% say that some-one else is the primary decision maker.

Men are more likely than women to say that they are the primary decision-maker (37% versus 30%), while women are more likely than men to say that decisions are shared (65% versus 58%).

Taking on a significant amount of debt is an important decision. Just over half of Canadians (54%) say that when it comes to these matters, they share the decision-making with someone else. Four in ten Canadians (41%) say they are the primary decision-maker, while only 4% say someone else is the primary decision-maker when it comes to decisions about taking on a significant amount of debt.

Women are more likely than men to say that they are the primary decision-maker when it comes to home decorating (65% versus 29%), while men are more likely than women to say that they share the decision-making with someone else (41% versus 32%).

We Like to Live Near Where We Work

Seven in ten Canadians (70%) feel proximity to where they work would be important if they were looking for a new home. However, just half (52%) feel that being close to public transit would be important if they were looking for a new home.

- **This last point is not surprising, given that three in four employed respondents (76%) indicate they most often drive to work, while just one in nine (11%) say they most often take public transit. Four per cent report they do both equally, and the same number report walking to work.**
- **On average, it takes Canadians 22.2 minutes to get to work from home, and, on average, Canadians are willing to look at a new home that is 34.4 minutes commuting time from their jobs.**
- **One in three Canadians (34%) say they would definitely or probably consider purchasing a home that was not exactly what they were looking for in order to be closer to their workplace.**

On the Move

Percentage of Canadians who believe buying a home or condo is a good investment: 86

As indicated, one in ten Canadians (11%) indicate that they are very likely to purchase a home within the next two years. This finding is consistent with the results over the past three years' studies (2003, 13%; 2002, 12%; 2001, 13%).

- **In total, 26% of Canadians (11% very likely, 15% somewhat likely) are likely to buy a house in the next two years, also a consistent finding since 2001.**
- **Canadians living in Alberta (36%) and B.C. (35%) are most likely to intend to purchase over the next two years.**
- **In 2004, current renters (33%) are significantly more likely to want to purchase within the next two years (down from 38% in 2003). Of those who already own a home, 21% are likely to buy a home in the next two years, up slightly from last year (18%).**

Most likely to buy a home in the next two years, by region

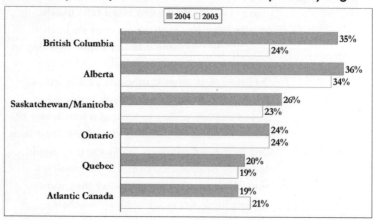

And What Do They Intend to Buy?

A majority (75%) indicate they will buy a detached (66%) or semi-detached (9%) home. One-tenth have their sights set on a townhouse (10%), followed by condominiums (9%), apartments (5%) and lofts (1%).

After a slight dip in 2003, preference for resale homes has returned to 2002 levels (65% in 2002, 60% in 2003, 64% in 2004). Conversely, 33% prefer to buy a brand-new home—down from 38% in 2003 but consistent with results since 1996.

Half (47%) say they will buy a bigger home (down 9 points since 2003), while 33% indicate a preference for the same size of house (up 5 points) and 20% will look for a smaller house (up 4 points).

Who's Not Buying?

Among respondents *not* likely to purchase a home within 24 months' time (75%), one-sixth (17%) say they are planning to purchase a home at some point in the next seven years, while 13% say it is likely to be eight years or longer before they purchase. Seven in ten (69%) indicate that they are not planning to buy a home at any time in the future.

Rate by which a homeowner is more likely than a renter to claim to be satisfied with his or her residence: 8 to 1
Rate by which a renter is more likely to say he or she can't afford to buy a home: 7 to 1

Canadians Prefer Resales

New homes are the choice of four in ten (38%) Canadians who plan to purchase a home within the next seven years, while six in ten (60%) indicate they would likely buy a home on the resale market.

• Younger Canadians (73%) are more likely to say they will be purchasing a larger home than are their middle-aged (42%) or older (26%) counterparts, while those in the older age category (55%) are more likely than their middle-aged (21%) or younger (5%) counterparts to say they will likely purchase a smaller home.

- **Regionally, residents of Quebec (71%) are the most likely to say they would purchase a larger home, while residents of British Columbia (41%) and Atlantic Canada (37%) are the most likely to indicate they would purchase a house of comparable size.**

Future Markets?

When asked to forecast the direction of a number of the factors that affect housing purchase decisions in one year's time, Canadians believe that each will be higher at that point. Six in ten Canadians (61%) believe that the price of rental accommodations will be higher, while 57% believe this to be true of housing prices. Fifty-four per cent believe this will be the case for interest rates as well as mortgage rates (51%).

- **Younger Canadians are more likely to believe that interest rates (61%) and mortgage rates (58%) will be higher one year from now than either their middle-aged (interest rates, 49%; mortgage rates, 49%) or older counterparts (interest rates, 55%; mortgage rates, 48%).**
- **There is no statistical difference between the views of current owners and those of current renters regarding the direction of those factors.**

Mortgages

A majority (54%) of Canadian homeowners report having a mort-gage on their home, down from 56% in our 2003 survey. The average amount still owed is $86,175, up from $70,361 in 2003.

- **Younger (76%) and middle-aged (69%) homeowners were more likely than older Canadian homeowners (23%) to have a mortgage on their home.**
- **Younger and middle-aged homeowners, on average, started with higher original mortgages (younger, $101,055; middle-aged, $104,335) and have a higher average still left to pay (younger, $80,926; middle-aged, $70,125) than their older**

counterparts (original mortgage, $69,391; left to pay, $47,259).

- Quebec (64%) and Alberta (63%) homeowners were the most likely to say they currently have a mortgage, followed by those in British Columbia (59%) and Ontario (56%). Homeowners in Saskatchewan/Manitoba (44%) and Atlantic Canada (42%) are the least likely to have a mortgage on their homes.
- On average, the highest original mortgages are on homes in Ontario ($114,058), while the lowest are found in Saskatchewan/Manitoba ($64,701).
- In 2004, B.C. homeowners had the largest outstanding principal, at $111,280; Ontario had slipped to second place, at $104,139, followed by Alberta ($91,854), Atlantic Canada ($61,221), Quebec ($54,125) and Saskatchewan/Manitoba ($53,348).

One-quarter (24%) of those with a mortgage report that they would consider borrowing against the equity in their home, while 74% say they would not.

- Homeowners with mortgages in Atlantic Canada (33%) and British Columbia (32%) are the most likely to consider this, while those in Quebec (11%) are the least likely.
- Middle-aged homeowners with mortgages (28%) are more likely than their counterparts who are younger (19%) or older (17%) to consider this move.
- Of those who would consider borrowing against their home equity, three-quarters (74%) would contact their primary bank, while one in ten would look to another bank (8%) or to a mortgage broker (9%).

Renovating

Almost three in ten (28%) Canadians indicate that they are planning renovations to their home during the next 12 months, about the same proportion as in 2003 (26%). In the earlier survey, four in ten (39%) of this group indicated that the renovations would involve upgrading or making changes to existing living space (such as redoing the kitchen or bathrooms), while 22% indicated that the renovations would be to increase living space and one-fifth (21%) said it would be mostly decorating.

- **In 2003, middle-aged Canadians (32%) were more likely than either younger (25%) or older (16%) Canadians to say they were planning on renovations to their home during the coming year.**

But It's Not Free

The largest portion of homeowners with a mortgage (45%) plan to spend between $1,000 and just under $5,000 on home renovations or makeovers this year. A further 17% plan to spend less than $1,000, 14% will spend $5,000 to just under $10,000, 5% will spend $10,000 to just under $15,000, and 3% will spend more than $15,000. Of the remaining respondents, 14% plan to spend no money on renovations in the coming year and 1% don't know how much they will spend.

- **Half (50%) of those earning over $60,000 a year plan to spend $1,000 to $5,000 this year on home renovations or makeovers, compared to 44% of those earning between $30,000 and $60,000 and 34% of those earning less than $30,000.**

Room most in need of renovation

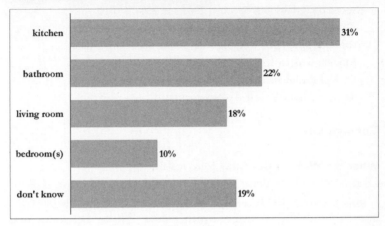

kitchen	31%
bathroom	22%
living room	18%
bedroom(s)	10%
don't know	19%

Rate by which a British Columbian is more likely than a Manitoban or Saskatchewanian to think the kitchen needs renovation: 2 to 1

Rate by which a a Manitoban or Saskatchewanian is more likely than a British Columbian to think the bedroom needs renovation: 2 to 1

What to Reno?

Half (49%) of mortgaged homeowners believe that the one part of their home that would increase overall resale value if it were renovated is their kitchen. One in five (21%) believe that renovated bathroom(s) would increase the resale value, and another one in five (18%) believe that renovating the living room would increase value. A small group (6%) think their bedrooms, if renovated, would increase the resale value of their home. The remaining 7% don't know.

Average amount spent on renovations: $8,850
Decline in the amount Canadian homeowners expected to
spend on renovations between 2003 and 2004: $1,010
Of those who plan to renovate, ratio of those who plan to
spend under $1,000 to those who plan to spend more than
$15,000: 5.67 to 1
Rank of the kitchen on a list of rooms that would most
increase a home's value if renovated: 1st

Cottage Life

When You Want to Get Away from It All

Of the 9% of Canadians who say that they currently own a recreational property, the majority (68%) say that their cottage has been in their family for 10 or more years, while 13% say between 5 and 9 years, 12% say between 2 and 4 years and 7% say less than 2 years.

Few existing cottage owners say that they plan to sell their property in the next three years. Only 5% of respondents (down from 8% last year) said that they are very likely to sell, and 8% said they are somewhat likely to sell (the same as last year). Fifteen per cent of cottage owners report that they are somewhat unlikely to sell (up from 11% last year), and 71% are very unlikely to sell (the same as last year).

Instead, the majority of current cottage owners (81%) report that they plan to bequeath their cottage to a family member. This is of little surprise given that these cottage owners already share their cottages with extended family: 97% of cottage owners report that at least one member of their extended family also uses their cottage. Thirty-three per cent of these say that more than 10 family members use their cottage, 31% say 6 to 10 members share it and 33% say it is used by just 1 to 5 members.

Those Who Have It Are Keeping It

Inventory in the recreational property market in Canada will remain tight in the foreseeable future. Currently, 13% of cottage owners are likely to sell their property, while 6% of Canadians say that they are planning to purchase a cottage or recreational property.

- **Cottage ownership is highest in Saskatchewan/ Manitoba (11%) and Ontario (10%), followed closely by Quebec (8%), Atlantic Canada (8%), British Columbia (6%) and Alberta (6%).**
- **Higher-income households are more likely to own recreational property ($60,000+, 13%) than middle-income ($30,000–$59,000, 8%) and lower-income (less than $30,000, 4%) households.**
- **The likelihood of purchasing a cottage or recreational property in the next three years is highest in Alberta (9%), followed closely by Saskatchewan/Manitoba, Ontario and Atlantic Canada (each at 6%), and Quebec and British Columbia (each at 5%).**

But Family Cottages Can Cause Problems

While the majority (97%) of cottage owners share their cottage with other family, more than one in ten (11%) report that shared use has caused a rift in the family in the past. Even more owners (22%) believe that when they do pass their cottage down to other family members, it is likely to cause strife in the family (10% very likely).

This issue weighs even more heavily on the minds of the 6% of Canadians who say they plan to purchase a cottage in the next three years. One-third (34%) of prospective purchasers say that bequeathing the family cottage will likely cause a rift in their family (16% very likely).

Watching TV

Consistent with other industry reports, a majority (53%) of Canadians say that they are watching "somewhat" (26%) or "much" less (27%) TV than they did five years ago. Another 28% say that they are watching the same amount, while only 19% say that they are watching more.

The reported decline in TV watching over the last five years cuts across most regional and demographic lines, although younger Canadians (65%) are much more likely to say that they are watching less TV than older Canadians (45%).

- **Over half (54%) of those who say that they are watching less TV now than five years ago say that the main reason is that they have other activities to fill their spare time. The other challenge is content. Almost one-third (30%) of these less frequent viewers say that they are watching less because there is nothing on TV that interests them.**
- **Competing activities is identified with higher frequency as the reason for decline in watching TV over the last five years among younger Canadians (66%), the better educated (58%) and higher-income households (60%). Nothing of interest on TV tends to be given as a reason with higher than average frequency among the less educated (33%), lower-income households (35%) and older Canadians (56%).**

What It's For

Most current TV viewers (47%) say that to be informed or educated is the main reason why they watch TV. To be entertained (31%) emerges as the second most frequent reason for watching TV, followed by relaxation (22% "use it as a release from other parts of the day").

Consequently, viewers report that they spend 43% of their TV time in an average week watching personal-interest programming ("personal-interest and learning programs like news, information shows, talk shows, documentaries"), while 35% of this time is spent watching entertainment programs ("entertainment programs like comedies, drama, movies, reality shows"). Of the remainder, 14% is spent watching sports, while 7% is spent watching game shows.

Rate by which a man is more likely to watch sports than is a woman: 3 to 1

What Are the Kids Doing After School?

Six in ten (59%) parents say their children are involved in non-formal extracurricular activities after school, such as piano lessons or a sport. These kids engage in their extra activities two or three times a week on average.

Things our kids do after school

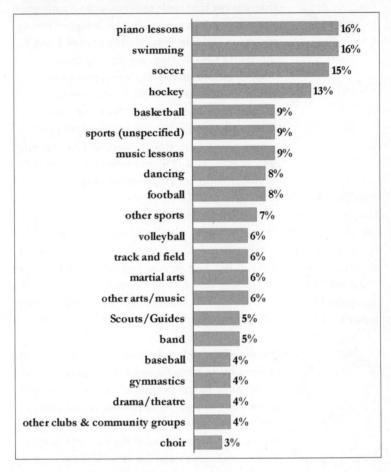

piano lessons	16%
swimming	16%
soccer	15%
hockey	13%
basketball	9%
sports (unspecified)	9%
music lessons	9%
dancing	8%
football	8%
other sports	7%
volleyball	6%
track and field	6%
martial arts	6%
other arts/music	6%
Scouts/Guides	5%
band	5%
baseball	4%
gymnastics	4%
drama/theatre	4%
other clubs & community groups	4%
choir	3%

Formal After-School Programs

One-quarter (26%) of parents of children between the ages of 6 and 17 say that their children are currently enrolled in a formal after-school program that includes a range of structured activities supervised by professionals or an organization.

Average number of after-school sessions per week: 3

- **One-quarter (24%) of parents of children currently enrolled in a formal after-school program say that their children attend a program four or five times per week. This is higher among parents of children between the ages of 6 and 11: one-third (33%) of these parents say their children attend four or five times per week.**
- **The types of formal after-school programs children attend vary widely, the most common involving sports (13%), general daycare (11%), community groups (6%), basketball (6%), dancing (6%), martial arts (5%), homework or study (5%), drama or theatre (5%), or choir (4%).**

Why They Are There

The primary reason parents say that they enrolled their children in a formal after-school program this year is that the "children were interested" (44%). Fewer parents indicated that they chose to enrol their children in an after-school program for child care because they are "at work" (15%), "to keep them busy" (15%), to give them an opportunity to "socialize and spend time with friends" (14%), because "it's good for them/keeps them fit" (9%) or to "help with school curriculum" (5%).

- **Parents with children between the ages of 12 and 17 were more likely to enrol their children in a formal after-school program because "they were interested" compared to parents of children between the ages of 6 and 11 (58% versus 29%).**
- **Parents of children between the ages of 6 and 11 were more likely to enrol their children in a formal after-school program for "childcare/parents are at work" (21% versus 3% for older children).**

Parents who have chosen a formal after-school program say that providing a "safe environment" (71% "very important") and "helping their children gain confidence and self-esteem" (71% "very important") were the most important factors when they decided to enrol them.

Following these two factors are "reinforcing basic social skills such as cooperation, team building and conflict resolution to help youth begin to develop workplace competencies" (63% "very important"), "skill development in sports, arts and culture or languages" (61% "very important"), "keeping them from hanging out with a bad crowd or getting into trouble" (61% "very important"), "participating in structured, organized activities" (54% "very important"), "not being home alone" (48% "very important"), "within my budget" (46% "very important"), "improving their academic achievement through tutoring and homework assistance" (39% "very important") and "computer use and instruction" (21% "very important").

Percentage of mothers who cite "providing a safe environment" as a very important factor: 84
Percentage of fathers who do: 62

Access to After-School Programs

A significant majority (87%) of all parents surveyed believe it is important that parents have access to a formal after-school program in their area, and nearly half (47%) feel that this is "very important." However, just three in ten (30%) believe that these programs are "very accessible" in their area, whereas four in ten (40%) believe that these programs are only "somewhat accessible." Almost one-quarter (22%) indicate that formal after-school programs are "not very accessible" and 3% say they are "not at all accessible." Four per cent say that they "don't know."

- Parents with household incomes between $60,000 and $80,000 are slightly more likely (36%) to say that formal after-school programs are "very accessible" in their area than are parents with household incomes of less than $60,000 (26%).
- Single working parents are slightly more likely to indicate that it is "very important" that parents have access to formal after-school programs in their area than are those from households with two working parents (57% versus 48%).

Early Childhood Education

Canadian parents are split as to whether day-long school programs for three-, four- and five-year-olds are a good thing. Half (47%) agree that these school programs are a good idea (23% agree somewhat, 24% agree completely), while the other half (52%) disagree (27% disagree somewhat, 25% disagree completely). Only a very small portion (1%) say they don't know.

- **Agreement that day-long programs are good varies considerably by region: Ontario (53%), Saskatchewan/Manitoba (53%), Atlantic Canada (50%), Alberta (44%), Quebec (42%), British Columbia (37%).**
- **Disagreement with the idea that day-long programs are good is higher among parents with younger children aged 0 to 5 than among parents with children aged 6 to 17 (51% versus 46%).**

Non-Formal Custodial Arrangements

Fourteen per cent of parents of children between the ages of 6 and 17 say that they have a non-formal custodial arrangement, such as going over to a neighbour's or having an adult watch over the children from after school to dinnertime.

- **24% of parents of children aged 6 to 8 have a non-formal custodial arrangement for their children after school, compared with 15% of parents of children aged 9 to 11, 11% of parents of children aged 12 to 14 and 7% of parents of children aged 15 to 17.**
- **On average, parents who have arranged for someone else to watch over their children say that this occurs two to three times per week.**

Parental Concern

Parents were asked to rate the level of concern they have with respect to their children in a number of different areas. Seven in ten parents (72%) say that they are "very concerned" with their children's "safety." Six in ten (62%) are "very concerned" about their children "hanging out with a bad crowd or getting into trouble," and equally as many are "very concerned" about their children "dropping out of school or not going to university or college" (61%). In addition to safety and staying in school, half of parents surveyed (50%) say that they are "very concerned" about their children "having fun," and just under half (46%) are "very concerned" that their children are "not getting the academic help that they need."

"Being home alone" (34%), "maintaining a balance between structured and free time" (32%) and "being by themselves too much—not interacting with other kids" (30%) are attributes that three in ten parents say that they are "very concerned" about. Half as many parents (15%) are "very concerned" about their children "not doing structured activities in their free time."

- **Parents who have children currently enrolled in a formal after-school program are more likely to indicate being "very concerned" about their children "having fun" than are parents whose children are not enrolled in a formal after-school program (58% versus 35%).**
- **Parents who have children currently enrolled in a formal after-school program are more likely to indicate being "very concerned" about their children "maintaining a balance between structured and free time" than are parents whose children are not enrolled in a formal after-school program (40% versus 21%).**
- **Parents who have children currently enrolled in a formal after-school program are more likely to indicate being "very concerned" about their children "not doing structured activities in their free time" compared to parents whose children are not enrolled in a formal after-school program (25% versus 10%).**

The Issues Children Face Today

Parents were asked for their top-of-mind thoughts on issues facing children and youth in Canada. The quality of education is a top issue for parents, with four in ten (41%) indicating this. The next most frequently mentioned issues are drugs and alcohol (18%), crime and violence (11%), economy and jobs (11%), peer pressure (9%), family stability (divorce, single parents) (7%), poverty (7%) and safety and security (5%).

Education: Meeting Educational Goals

Most Canadian parents are not completely satisfied that the education system is helping their children reach what they deem to be important education goals.

The study, involving 1,000 parents of children aged 8 to 15, found that almost all parents (91%), when given a list of eight educational goals, rated a good understanding of the basics as extremely important. However, only 51% are completely satisfied with their child's progress toward this goal. Three-quarters of parents rated as extremely important the skills to get a good job (77%) or to attend university (76%), developing disciplined study habits (76%) and the ability to work independently (74%). One-half (51%) rated gaining confidence to work alone as extremely important, while fewer (42%) give achieving good grades a top score.

Just over half (51%) of parents are actually satisfied with their child's progress toward the understanding of the basics, and 46% are satisfied that their child is achieving good grades.

Notably, significantly fewer are satisfied with their progress toward other educational goals. Only one-third are satisfied with their child's building of skills for a job (30%) or university (37%). One-quarter (25%) are satisfied that their child is developing good study habits. For these three goals, the proportion who are completely satisfied is less than half the proportion who find the goal extremely important.

- **While parents of boys and girls rate the importance of educational goals similarly, the parents of boys are generally less satisfied with their child's progress towards these goals than are parents of girls.**
- **Parents of children in Quebec are less likely to rate most goals as very important than those in other provinces. They are also less likely to say they are completely satisfied with their child's progress on these goals.**
- **Just over half of parents of children in Ontario (52%), the Prairies (56%) and Atlantic Canada (56%) are relatively satisfied with their children's understanding of the basics. Parents in these**

same regions are relatively satisfied with their child earning good grades (Ontario, 48%; Prairies, 52%; Atlantic Canada, 54%).

Keeping Up in School

While the majority of parents (72%) think their child's school is spending enough time teaching the basics, 44% agree that the curriculum is becoming more difficult to keep up with. Almost two-thirds (64%) of parents believe that children need to stay ahead of their peers and not just keep up. As well, almost three-quarters (72%) agree that individual assistance in the classroom or after school is available for their child.

- **Parents in Ontario are significantly more concerned about the tougher curriculum than parents elsewhere. Fully 59% of them agree that the curriculum is getting tougher, whereas one-quarter of those in B.C. (26%) and one-third of those in the Prairies (29%), Quebec (36%) and Atlantic Canada (35%) feel this way.**
- **Parents in Quebec are more likely than parents in other provinces to agree that additional help in school is available (84%).**
- **Parents whose children are behind are more likely to agree that the curriculum is getting tougher (73%) but less likely to agree that extra help (62%) and a focus on the basics (44%) are in place. While less than one-third (29%) of parents whose children are ahead believe that school standards and curriculum are getting tougher, almost half (48%) of parents whose children are right at grade level feel this way.**
- **Parents of girls are significantly more likely than parents of boys to agree that keeping up is not enough (68% and 61%, respectively) and that it is more difficult to keep up with the evolving curriculum (47% and 41%, respectively).**

Making the Grade

Most parents believe that their child is at (58%) or ahead of (33%) grade level. More boys (10%) than girls (7%) are perceived to be behind grade level, as are those in higher grade levels. Eleven per cent of children in high school are seen as being behind grade level.

Wealthier parents (those with household incomes above $60,000) are more likely to see their child as ahead of grade level (38%), as are those who have a college diploma or university degree (36%).

When it comes to helping their child succeed in school, more than one-third (39%) of parents feel that the best thing they can do to help is encourage their children and offer them support. One-fifth (20%) mention being involved in their child's education, 19% state that helping their child with their work is key, and 8% believe that teaching them positive habits and behaviour is most helpful. Only 2% of parents mention tutoring or supplemental learning.

Are Children Spending Enough Time Doing Homework, or Too Much?

Almost half of Canadian children (46%) are spending 30 minutes to one hour per night on homework. Just over one-quarter (28%) spend 30 minutes or less, while one-quarter (25%) spend one to three hours per night.

- Regionally, those living in the Prairies (32%) tend to spend 30 minutes or less per night on average doing homework, while just over half of those living in Quebec and in B.C. (55% and 53% respectively) spend 30 minutes to one hour. Although almost half of those living in Ontario and in Atlantic Canada spend 30 minutes to one hour on homework (42% and 46%, respectively), children there are significantly more likely to spend between one and three hours per evening doing homework (28% and 33%, respectively).

- Although almost half of boys (48%) and of girls (45%) spend between 30 minutes to one hour, one-third (33%) of boys tend to spend less than 30 minutes, whereas one-third (32%) of girls tend to spend between one and three hours on homework in a night.
- Not surprisingly, the time spent on homework increases with grade level.
- Parents spend time helping out their children as well. Two-thirds (64%) spend 30 minutes or less per evening with their children on schoolwork, while almost one-third (29%) spend 30 minutes to one hour per night. Only 6% spend between one and three hours on average helping their children each night.

It All Comes Out in the Wash

Percentage of Canadian women who don't read washing instruction labels at all: 6

One-third (33%) of Canadian women say doing laundry is the most important household task in their home, second only to cleaning the house (54%). Nearly one in ten (7%) say "weeding/planting the garden," 1% say "mowing the lawn," 1% say "washing the car," and 3% don't think any of these are important. (The remaining 1% don't know.)

In addition, Canadian women estimate that they spend a mean average of 5.6 hours a week doing laundry—that is, sorting, washing, drying, folding and putting clothes away.

Canadian women in the Atlantic region spend significantly more time—8.5 hours—doing laundry than others: British Columbian women spend 5.0 hours, Saskatchewan/Manitoba women 5.1, Quebec women 5.2, Ontario women 5.5 and Alberta women 6.4.

When it comes to handwashing delicate garments, 34% of Canadian women say they *never* do it. The remaining 66% of the Canadian women surveyed responded as follows:

More than once a week: 11%

About once a week: 20%

About once every two to three weeks: 9%

About once a month: 12%

About once every two to three months: 3%

Less often: 10%

Don't know: 1%

Parents' Report Cards

More than nine in ten (92%) Canadian teens give their mom an overall good grade (A or B), with 50% giving her an A. This compares to just two in three (65%) who give dad get an overall good grade, with 29% giving him an A.

The teens were asked to grade their moms' and dads' performance in a number of different areas. It appears that moms excel most in the areas of birthdays (73% given an A), providing a home that is happy and safe (72% given an A), and working hard (72% given an A). Dads also excel most in working hard (61% given an A) and providing a home that is happy and safe (53% given an A), but not to the same extent. In fact, moms beat dads in all areas except driving, where the results are actually quite close (46% dad vs. 41% mom).

Percentage of Canadian mothers considered uncool by their children: 6

Percentage of Canadian fathers who are: 9

Percentage of Canadian mothers who get an A or B for "sex ed.": 54

Percentage of Canadian fathers who do: 25

Personal Health

The health of the people is really the foundation upon which all their happiness and all their powers as a state depend.

—Benjamin Disraeli

AT THE TURN of the twentieth century, Canadians were lucky if they made it to their fiftieth birthday. By the time Statistics Canada started keeping track in the 1920–22 census, the average Canadian man was living until 59, and the average woman until 61. Better, you might say, but still not great.

By 2002, however, we were living it up, up, up. The *CIA World Factbook* says that by 2002 the average Canadian's life expectancy had climbed to 79.6 years—76.2 for men and 83.1 for women.

Hey, we're lagging behind the real oldies (Andorra, 83.5; Macau, 81.7; San Marino, 81.2; Japan, 80.8), but we're in 11th place. The Americans are wallowing in 42nd place at an average of 77.3 years—74.4 for men, 80.1 for women.

Benjamin Disraeli said that a country full of healthy people would be both happy and empowered. Canadians are living a lot longer, so we must be healthier than our forebears, despite all the trans fatty acids. So, according to Disraeli, we should be happier than those who went before us.

And yet our statistics show us the following shocking fact: a majority of Canadians say that they personally think about the possibility of getting a life-threatening illness at least once a month.

That's happy? Going around worrying about being struck down, despite the fact that it's far less likely to happen to the average Canadian than at any point since the beginning of time?

Okay, there's nothing funny about major illnesses. People do get them, and they can be grim. But when do we Canadians start celebrating that we're 11th best in the world at hanging in there and that—unlike those short-lived Americans—we have a national health care system to nourish us along?

Rank of cancer among conditions that most concern
Canadians: 1
Rank of lower back pain: 2

The Benefits of Worrying about Your Health

Many Canadians say they have made lifestyle changes in an effort to reduce their chance of contracting a life-threatening disease. We're eating better, and one third of us say we are exercising more. All the same, fully 27% of Canadians say they are not doing anything at all to reduce their chances of contracting a life-threatening illness.

Now here is something worth considering regarding the 6.9% gap between the average life expectancy of female Canadians and male Canadians: women (57%) are more likely to say they have begun eating better than are men (44%), and more men (30%) are likely to say they are doing nothing to ward off the possibility of life-threatening illness than women to say *they* are (24%). Clearly, the men aren't putting in the effort. As the Greek philosopher Menander (342–292 BC) said, "Health and intellect are the two blessings of life." If men aren't smart enough to live healthily, then it shouldn't be surprising that they're less healthy.

Looking for Alternatives

Beyond eating better, exercising more, having a regular medical checkup and prodding governments to improve the health care system, what other measures are Canadians prepared to take to fend off life-threatening illnesses?

Well, although many medical practitioners do not recommend the use of alternative or non-traditional medicines in treating life-threatening illnesses, if faced with a life-threatening illness, two-thirds of Canadians say they would be likely to investigate and use these medicines even if their doctor was against it.

Ratio of younger to older Canadians who say they would
investigate and use alternative medicines for a life-threatening
illness: 4 to 3
Province whose residents are least likely to turn to alternative
medicine: Quebec

All the Same ...

Canadians trust their medical professionals, and our fear of death is largely balanced by an optimism about science. Most Canadians believe that the spectre that haunts their dreams and their lifestyle choices—cancer—will be eliminated within their lifetimes. And Canadians also follow their doctors' orders to the letter when it comes to prescriptions, at least when their symptoms are not life-threatening. Getting a Canadian to quit smoking in order to cure chronic bronchitis is another matter altogether.

Antibiotics

In 2000, 61% of Canadians reported having been prescribed an oral antibiotic in the past three years. This figure had fallen to 53% in 2002. Among those who have been prescribed an oral antibiotic, 80% report that they always finish their antibiotic prescription, even if they feel better in a couple of days. This figure has increased slightly from 76% in the 2000 study. Further, 47% say their level of knowledge and understanding about antibiotics has increased compared to two years ago.

Percentage of Canadians who mistakenly believe that
antibiotics are useful for treatment of viral infections: 53
Percentage of Canadians who believe antibiotic resistance is a
serious health issue: 84
Percentage who believe it is a serious health issue that could
affect *them*: 24
Percentage decline in Canadians who say they've been
prescribed an oral antibiotic in the last four years: 13.1

Whom Do You Trust?

On an open-ended basis, six in ten Canadians mention pharmacists (60%) or doctors (59%) among the sources of information they rely on specifically for prescription medication and drug information. Doctors (40%) are generally the public's first top-of-mind source for information related to prescription medications, followed by pharmacists (36%). One in ten (10%) Canadians say that they use the Internet or books for information about prescription medication and drug information, while roughly the same proportion rely on family and friends (7%) or the media including magazines (4%), newspapers (3%) and TV (4%).

Whom would you rely on for drug information?

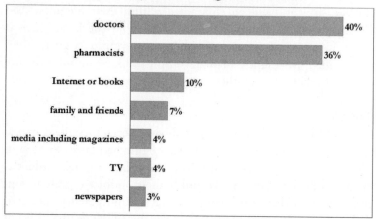

- doctors 40%
- pharmacists 36%
- Internet or books 10%
- family and friends 7%
- media including magazines 4%
- TV 4%
- newspapers 3%

Canadians most likely to rely on doctors for prescriptions:
British Columbians
Canadians most likely to rely on pharmacists:
Atlantic Canadians

"Ask Your Doctor About ..."

Seven in ten Canadians agree that advertising about prescription medications and drugs directly to Canadian consumers should be allowed. Critics of the practice argue that advertising drugs makes patients into consumers and makes decisions about prescriptions more like shopping and less like the traditional doctor-patient relationship, in which decisions are left to the latter's expertise. Those in favour of drug marketing argue that advertising merely gives consumers the ability to make more informed choices. Given that the pharmaceutical industry is huge, enormously profitable and growing, this seems like an issue that will be with us for some time.

Although support for direct-to-consumer advertising (DTCA) is fairly even across the country, it is slightly higher in Ontario (70%) and Saskatchewan/Manitoba (70%) and lower in Quebec (66%), B.C. (66%) and Alberta (62%). The intensity of opposition is higher in Alberta, where 22% strongly disagree, compared to B.C., where 18% strongly disagree, and Quebec, where just 16% strongly disagree.

Chances that a university graduate supports DTCA: 6 in 10
Chances that a high school dropout supports it: 7 in 10
Percentage who think that DTCA should have special regulations beyond what other product or service advertisements have to follow: 69

How to Regulate DTCA

After being read each of the following components of the made-in-Canada solution proposed by the Alliance for Access to Medical Information, the majority of Canadians rate each of the components either "excellent" or "very good." The made-in-Canada solution requires that any direct-to-consumer advertising of prescription medications

- describe for whom the product is appropriate and inappropriate;
- describe the major side effects;
- include a "consult your physician" tagline;
- provide sources for further third-party, unbiased information; and
- be pre-screened and approved by an independent regulatory authority appointed by the government.

As well, the solution would require that the advertisement provide questions for patients to ask their physicians and would require that advertisements for new drugs not run until after a six-month waiting period following Health Canada approval, to allow practising physicians time to learn about the new medication.

The component that finds the most favour with Canadians is describing the major side effects: half (49%) rate this regulation as "excellent" and 28% rate it as "very good." Describing for whom the product is appropriate and inappropriate (44% "excellent" and 29% "very good") follows next. Two-thirds (64%) say including a "consult your physician" tagline is "excellent" (38%) or "very good" (26%). Six in ten (57%) find a six-month period to allow physicians time to familiarize themselves with the new medications "excellent" (34%) or "very good" (23%), and almost as many (58%) say providing sources for third-party, unbiased information is "excellent" (33%) or "very good" (25%).

Cancer Will Be Beaten

Seven in ten Canadians (70%) are confident that, within their lifetime, scientists will find a cure for cancer. Most optimistic in this regard are residents of Quebec (77%) and Canadians aged 18 to 34 (76%). At 60%, residents of Saskatchewan and Manitoba appear comparatively pessimistic.

And Will Be Manageable

More than two-thirds of Canadians (68%) think that, within the next ten years, cancer will become something you treat and live with rather than something you die from. Again, Quebeckers appear to be the national optimists in this regard (at 77%). Older Canadians (77% of those aged 55 and older) are also very likely to share this point of view.

And We Want to Know More

Almost nine in ten Canadians (87%) say they would like to know more about the latest advances in cancer research. This sentiment is most prevalent among residents of Quebec (91%), while residents of B.C., on the other hand (81%), are least likely to want to know more about advances in cancer research.

Whom Has Cancer Touched?

Clearly, this is an issue of real and personal concern to Canadians, with almost nine in ten (87%) reporting that they have friends or family members who have or have had cancer. Given the disease's increasing prevalence with age, it is not surprising to note that Canadians aged 55 or older are most likely to know someone personally who has been diagnosed with cancer (91%).

Percentage-point difference between Quebeckers (most
optimistic) and Saskatchewan/Manitoba residents (least) in
belief that a cancer cure will be found in their lifetime: 17
Percentage of Canadians who say they would be willing to
donate tumour tissue for research: 92
Percentage by which men are more likely than women to say
they are "doing nothing" to reduce their chances of
contracting life-threatening illness: 25
Among those who have had a friend or family member
diagnosed with cancer, ratio of those who say treatment was
"extremely effective" to those who say it was "not very
effective": 2 to 1

Hacking Away

If cancer stalks one end of the spectrum of illnesses, chronic bronchitis, while hardly life-enhancing, is somewhere near the other. Sufferers of chronic bronchitis tend to be current or ex-smokers. In addition to chronic bronchitis, many have heart problems, such as high blood pressure or angina (46%). Most have breathing difficulties when climbing a hill (77%), when accelerating from their "normal pace of walking" (68%) and when "climbing stairs or steps at [their] normal pace" (54%). Many also experience shortness of breath when doing chores at home, such as vacuuming or putting out garbage (39%).

Skepticism about Doctors' Role Is Rife

Only one-third of sufferers say they see their doctor regularly for their cough. Twenty-one per cent say they have consulted a doctor about these persistent coughs in the past but do not do so anymore, and 18% have "never consulted" a doctor. This means that nearly two in five sufferers (39%) do not see a doctor for their bronchitis symptoms.

Complacency appears to be the main reason for never having seen a doctor. Three in ten say they have "just a smoker's cough," 27% say it is "not that bad" and 17% say they have "stopped worrying about it."

Main argument against seeing a doctor for bronchitis: the
perception that their doctor "was not helpful"
Average time (in years) that those with chronic bronchitis
have suffered from it: 9.8

Percentage of coughers who believe doctors are too busy to spend time to really get to know their patient's medical problems: 45

Percentage of chronic bronchitis sufferers who claim to have changed their job largely as a result of their persistent cough: 9

Estimated number of Canadians aged 40 to 75 who suffer from chronic bronchitis: 1,080,000

Amount spent by chronic bronchitis sufferers on over-the-counter remedies in the past 12 months: $30 million

Amount spent by chronic bronchitis sufferers on prescription drugs in the past 12 months: $34 million

Percentage of coughers who say they're not worried because "it's just a smoker's cough": 26

It's One Thing to Advise Smokers to Quit, Quite Another for Them to Comply

Percentage of chronic bronchitis sufferers told to quit smoking by their doctors: 44

Percentage who actually do: 16

Percentage who feel their doctor could have done more for them: 20

Chronic Bronchitis Has an Economic as Well as a Social Cost

The impact on work and lifestyle of chronic bronchitis can be summarized as follows:

	Unable at All on One or More Occasions	Ability Affected on One or More Occasions
Go to work	17%	20%
Carry out daily activities at home	23%	32%
Leave the house	24%	26%
Attend social or family events	21%	26%

Osteoporosis and Men

Although most Canadians are aware of the dangers of osteoporosis in older women, a recent survey suggests that Canadians have a lot to learn about osteoporosis in men. While most understand that men are affected by the condition, half of Canadians mistakenly believe that there are evident signs of osteoporosis that they are able to recognize. Furthermore, three quarters of Canadians vastly underestimate the actual prevalence of osteoporosis in men over the age of 50.

Occurrence of osteoporosis in men over 50: 1 in 8

Chance that a man will be aware of this fact: 1 in 11

Chance that a woman will be: 1 in 20

Percentage of Canadians who believe it affects only women: 27

Gender more likely to know that men can be affected by osteoporosis: women

Gender more likely to know that osteoporosis can be treated: women

Gender more likely to believe erroneously that the likelihood of developing osteoporosis is smaller than that of developing Parkinson's disease: men

Gender more likely to answer "I don't know" to every osteoporosis-related question on the poll: men

High Blood Pressure

In keeping with our ignorance of what threatens us, polls suggest that middle-aged and older Canadians have a lot to learn when it comes to avoiding hypertension. Despite the fact that 89% of Canadians agree that they are responsible for their blood pressure, 74% acknowledge there is a great deal they don't know about the condition.

The survey examined the level of understanding about hypertension among those Canadians whose age alone puts them at a higher risk of developing the condition—for women it is ages 40 and older, and for men ages 50 and older.

Percentage of Canadians within the age group most at risk who have never discussed high blood pressure with their physician: 42

Percentage who mistakenly believe that they can recognize the symptoms of hypertension: 63

Percentage who deem themselves "somewhat" or "very" likely to develop high blood pressure: 42
Percentage of Canadians over the age of 65 who deem themselves likely: 27
Percentage of Canadians who have been diagnosed with high blood pressure: 34

Getting Tested

One-third of Canadians have their blood pressure checked annually—usually at the doctor's office. However, six in ten indicate having a reading done even more frequently: 18% say every six months, 21% say every three months and 20% say every month. Most of those having more frequent readings have been diagnosed with high blood pressure.

Percentage of Canadians who can provide a correctly formatted number when asked for their latest blood-pressure reading: 56
Percentage who can cite 120 over 80 as the normal blood-pressure reading: 26
Percentage who say they have more important things to worry about: 43

Do you think you're at risk for hypertension?

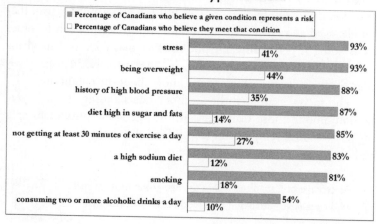

■ Percentage of Canadians who believe a given condition represents a risk
□ Percentage of Canadians who believe they meet that condition

	Risk	Meet
stress	93%	41%
being overweight	93%	44%
history of high blood pressure	88%	35%
diet high in sugar and fats	87%	14%
not getting at least 30 minutes of exercise a day	85%	27%
a high sodium diet	83%	12%
smoking	81%	18%
consuming two or more alcoholic drinks a day	54%	10%

The Pill

According to our most recent poll, young Canadian women (aged 18 to 24) trust the pill for preventing pregnancy—currently used by 53% of those polled—more than any other method of birth control.

Percentage by which a Quebecker is more likely than an Ontarian to be on the pill: 30

Percentage by which a woman from the western provinces is more likely than a Quebecker to say she is not using any birth control at all: 70

Rate by which a Quebecker is more likely than an Albertan to say she is on the pill because she is planning to be sexually active soon: 2 to 1

Average age at which birth control is first used in Canada: 16.4

Percentage of birth-control pill users who are satisfied with their birth-control method: 84

Percentage of non-pill users who are: 71

Percentage of Canadian women who say they would never trust a man to take a male birth control pill: 63

Breath Fresheners

One-quarter of Canadians currently smoke cigarettes, but most were planning to quit in 2004. Whether that means there will be no smokers in 2005 remains to be seen.

Rate by which 35- to 54-year-old Canadians are more likely to smoke than those 55 and older: 2 to 1

Percentage by which university grads are less likely than the national average to smoke: 9

Likelihood that a female smoker plans to quit: 7 in 10

Likelihood that a male smoker plans to quit: 5 in 10

How They Plan to Quit

Of those planning to quit, half (50%) say they will go cold turkey rather than gradually reduce the number of cigarettes they smoke. However, that does not necessarily mean that survey respondents plan on "going it alone" when it comes to quitting smoking. In a subsequent question, 45% of those planning to quit indicate that they are planning to do so with a smoking-cessation aid such as nicotine patches, a gum or a prescription drug.

If at First You Don't Succeed . . .
Of the Canadians we spoke to who smoke cigarettes, 43% indicated that they had tried to quit during the year 2003. Three-quarters (76%) were unsuccessful.

Percentage of Canadian smokers who have considered not taking a flight because they would not be able to smoke: 10
Percentage who have been tempted to smoke in the toilet of a plane: 8
Percentage who have considered joining the "mile-high club": 19

Oral Hygiene
Nearly all Canadians (95%) consider good oral health to be an important factor in maintaining good overall health. And to 98% of all Canadians, dentists are important to maintaining overall health, on par with physicians. Just 3% are unaware of any link between good oral health and good overall health.

Chances that a Canadian thinks dental hygienists are more important than chiropractors: 3 to 1
Percentage of Canadians who brush their tongues: 55
Provinces whose residents change their toothbrushes most frequently: Saskatchewan and Manitoba
Rate by which a Manitoban is more likely than a British Columbian to change his or her toothbrush every three months: 2 to 1
Percentage of Canadians who replace their toothbrush once a year or less: 8
Province whose residents visit the dentist most frequently: Ontario
Rate by which an upper-income Canadian is more likely than a lower-income Canadian to visit the dentist every six months: 2 to 1
Of those Canadians who do not visit the dentist regularly, percentage who have no teeth: 14

Why women have cleaner mouths

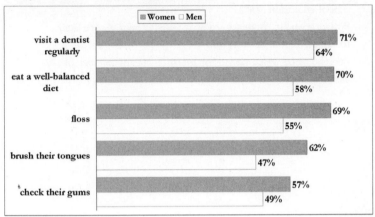

	Women	Men
visit a dentist regularly	71%	64%
eat a well-balanced diet	70%	58%
floss	69%	55%
brush their tongues	62%	47%
check their gums	57%	49%

Gender most likely to have cavities: men
Percentage of Canadians who've never had a cavity: 46
Province whose residents are least likely to have cavities:
Quebec
Percentage of Canadians who have never had a dental
procedure: 12
Percentage of Canadians 18–54 who floss: 67
Percentage of Canadians 55+ who do: 52

Giving Blood

Percentage of adult citizens Canadians believe to be blood
donors: 26
Percentage who actually donate: 3.7

This is a serious disparity. And while Canadians tend to overestimate the number who donate, they also exaggerate their own intentions to donate, with almost three in ten Canadians (28%) saying they will donate blood in the next year. More specifically, 15% say they will donate in the next six months and 13% say they will donate in six months to a year. One-third of Canadians (36%) say that they will not donate blood in the next year but might at some time in the future or that they will never donate blood (35%).

Respondents most likely to say they will donate in the next six months: Albertans (20%) and those with less than a high school education (23%)

Province whose residents are least likely to say they are likely to donate blood: Sakatchewan

Percentage by which Canadians overestimate the number of blood donors in Canada: 501.9

Food

It's good food and not fine words that keeps me alive.

—Molière

IT'S BEEN A weird few years for food.

The Atkins and South Beach diets dominated the tables of North America, as all those things we were supposed to eschew rather than chew—say, bacon and eggs—became fashionable, at least for the moment.

Dieticians (and quacks) disputed the right and the wrong way to eat, but a tragic incident at JD's Café and Night Spot left no doubt that there are *really* wrong ways to eat: a 36-year-old man died after a spicy-chicken-wing-eating contest. Not funny. *Sad.*

Also a bit sad were the results of a study by Professor John Komlos comparing the heights of Americans and Europeans. It seems that Europeans are increasing in height at quite a pace—the average Dutchman now stands 6 foot 1, three inches taller than the average American. In the 1800s, male Americans stood an average of three inches taller than the average Dutchman. It seems that poor diet in Americans—we're talking junk food, folks—has U.S. residents growing outward, not upward. And since Canadian streets are also lined with fast food outlets, it stands to reason that we're getting more squat as well.

Even average British males are now taller than Americans, although it's too early to assess the effect that food reform at hoary Oxford University might have on students' height. They were asked to consider a motion that would stop all the traditional food-throwing after final exams. It seems that the tame days of egg-pelting had evolved into tossing things like pigs' blood and long-dead fish.

But we digress.

Canadians, by and large, believe ourselves to be healthy eaters. But closer examination shows that we may be fibbing to ourselves.

When does a fib turn into a bald-faced lie? Our polls show that most Canadians don't come close to the daily diet that is recommended by the famous Canada Food Guide, the bible of responsible dieticians. This may not come as a surprise: we're a nation of snackers. And when a healthy snack does not appeal, junk food will do just fine.

Canadians *say* that nutrition is important to them, that they read food labels, that they exclude myriad products and ingredients from their plates and that, when necessary, they turn to diets. But most also admit that they really don't know very much about what's good for them. Oh, Canadians are trying to play the food game more intelligently all right. But a good number of them concede that they don't understand the rules.

Almost three in four Canadians say they eat a well-balanced and healthy diet, or some facsimile—with a few gaps here and there. Just over one in five acknowledges not doing quite that well, and 4% admit they don't eat well at all.

Twice as many young Canadians (32%) as older Canadians (17%) admit that their diet needs improvement. Similarly, Canadians in lower-income households (34%) say they don't eat healthy, compared to those in higher-income households (24%).

Detailed Confessions

The main culprits, as described by our respondents:

- **Not enough fruits and vegetables: 32%**
- **Too many sweets: 23%**
- **Too much junk food: 13%**
- **Too much oil and fat: 11%**

Now here's a bit of sorry news. Despite North Americans' fixation with what they look like and how long they're going to live, the overall importance that Canadians place on nutrition is in decline.

The Weight Watch

Again, on weight we see a pretty even split: while 43% of Canadians indicate they eat what they want and give little thought to their weight, an equal proportion (40%) claim to occasionally give up certain foods in order to maintain a healthy weight.

Who's dieting? Currently, just over two in ten Canadian adults (22%) are following a weight-loss diet. Age, gender, region, education and income do not seem to play a role in whether or not adults are currently on a diet.

Then again, nearly eight in ten (77%) say they did not start a diet or weight-loss program over the past year. One in seven (15%) started a specific diet or weight-loss program once this year, while 8% of Canadians have been on two or more diets this year (4% twice, 2% three to four times and 2% five or more times).

The most likely to say they have *not* been on a diet in the past year? Men, of course—82% of them. And people who have not finished high school—84% of these say they have not been on a diet. So educated women are more likely to diet, although many dieticians consider North America's obsession with diets to be a sad alternative to eating healthy choices and portions on a consistent basis.

Perhaps this is because other things have come to seem more important than eating nutritionally. For one thing, many of us are concerned simply with eating *less*. Fewer than half of us eat what we like, without concern for our weight, and diets are more and more common.

And more alarming than the fear that our food will make us fat is the possibility that it will make us sick—or dead. More than three-quarters of us say we are concerned about the safety of the food we eat. We're worried about mad-cow prions, *E. coli* and other bacteria—to the point that there was talk of outlawing fresh sushi in Ontario—and we're worried about genetically modified food.

That's a lot to worry about. One thing we don't worry about, though: yogourt. Ninety-one per cent of Canadians believe yogourt is healthy. That's one thing we can agree on.

What We Think about Our Diet

Generally, Canadians think they are healthy eaters. In fact, almost three in four (73%) say they eat a well-balanced and healthy diet or mainly healthy foods with some gaps. But even though Canadians think they are healthy eaters, only about half (53%) believe nutrition is extremely (17%) or very (36%) important to them in choosing the foods that they eat.

Province whose residents are most likely to claim to eat healthy: British Columbia

Rate by which a young Canadian is more likely than an older one to admit that his or her diet needs improving: 2 to 1

Percentage of Canadians who felt in 1994 that nutrition is important: 66

Percentage in 1997: 62

Percentage in 2003: 53

Percentage of British Columbians who claim that nutritional content is very important in their grocery-shopping decisions: 71

Percentage of Albertans who feel the same way: 54

Are Our Eating Habits Getting Worse or Our Consciences More Acute?

The proportion of Canadians who rate their eating habits as "fair" or "poor" has been increasing steadily over time. Checking the rear-view mirror: 1994, 15%; recently, 21%. The main factors mentioned as contributing to this group's poorer eating habits include a "busy lifestyle" (19%) and "eating takeout or fast foods" (12%).

Active control over foods consumed increases with age. While Canadians 55 years of age and older are trying to avoid cholesterol (70%, versus 53% of 18- to 34-year-olds), salt (64% versus 51%), MSG (63% versus 55%), sugar (55% versus 37%) and polyunsaturated fats (48% versus 42%), fewer young Canadians are concerned about consuming these ingredients. Canadians between the ages of 18 and 34 are most actively trying to eat more red meat (51%) and organic foods (41%).

How we try to eat better

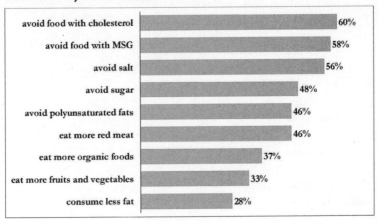

avoid food with cholesterol	60%
avoid food with MSG	58%
avoid salt	56%
avoid sugar	48%
avoid polyunsaturated fats	46%
eat more red meat	46%
eat more organic foods	37%
eat more fruits and vegetables	33%
consume less fat	28%

Chances that a British Columbian is trying to avoid
MSG: 8 in 10
Chances that a Canadian man is trying to eat more red
meat: 1 in 2

Do We Read the Labels?

Despite our desire to eat healthier, one in five Canadians admits to never reading the nutritional and calorie information (22%) or the list of ingredients on food packages (20%) when they are shopping.

• **Canadians 55 years of age and older and women are both more likely to always read the nutritional and calorie information (29% and 36%) and the list of ingredients (31% and 32%) on a package of food when they are purchasing it.**

Province with highest concentration of label-readers:
British Columbia
Lowest concentration: Alberta

What do we look for on labels?

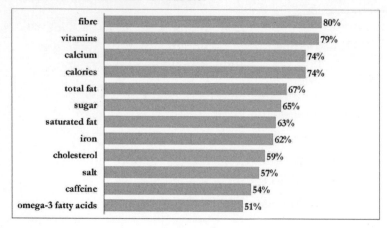

fibre	80%
vitamins	79%
calcium	74%
calories	74%
total fat	67%
sugar	65%
saturated fat	63%
iron	62%
cholesterol	59%
salt	57%
caffeine	54%
omega-3 fatty acids	51%

• **In deciding between food options, more Canadians are influenced by wanting to maintain good health (95%) and by personal weight considerations (72%) than they are by selecting prescribed food for a specific diet (52%) or by negative media coverage (46%).**

How Well Do Canadians Follow the Canada Food Guide?

According to the Canada Food Guide (produced by Health Canada), Canadian adults are advised to eat 5 to 10 servings of fruit or vegetables; 5 to 12 servings of cereals, grains and bread; 2 to 3 servings of meat, fish, poultry, eggs or beans; and 2 to 3 servings of dairy products, such as milk, cheese and yogourt, each day.

Asked about what they ate the day before they were surveyed, most Canadians reported having at least one serving of fruit or vegetables (93%); of cereals, grains and bread (93%); of meat, fish, poultry, eggs or beans (92%); and of dairy products (89%) during the previous day. Further, four in five (80%) reported consuming butter, margarine, oil or salad. Fewer, but still a majority (60%), reported having candy, chips, pop or a sweet dessert.

Percentage of Canadians who consume the minimum recommended five servings of fruit or vegetables: 17

Chances that a Canadian has not consumed the recommended serving of grains and cereals: 9.5 in 10
Ratio of upper-income Canadians who have had their daily serving of fruits or vegetables to lower-income Canadians who have: 2 to 1

What Do We Know about Nutrition?

We seem to think everyone knows more about nutrition than we do. Or maybe we all know a nutritionist. While eight in ten Canadians agree that nutrition is important to them, only three in ten consider themselves very knowledgeable about food and nutrition compared to family and friends.

- **Older Canadians (55+, 56%) are significantly more likely than younger Canadians (18–34, 32%) to strongly agree that nutrition is important to them and that they always watch what they eat.**
- **Similarly, older Canadians (91%) are more likely than younger Canadians (86%) to say that nutrition is important in choosing the foods they eat.**
- **Women are more likely than men to agree that nutrition is very important to them (83% versus 76%) and that nutrition is an important factor in choosing the food they eat (92% versus 85%).**

Canadian Weight-Watching

While 43% of Canadians indicate they eat what they want and give little thought to their weight, an equal proportion (40%) claim to occasionally give up certain foods in order to maintain a healthy weight.

Percentage of Canadians currently on a diet: 14
Percentage who have been on a diet in the past year: 28
Most weight-conscious region: Atlantic Canada
Least weight-conscious: Quebec
Odds by which a Canadian woman is more likely than a man to be on a diet: 2.5 to 1
Percentage difference between high school graduates, college graduates and university graduates in the likelihood that they have been on a diet in the past year: 0

Percentage of Canadians who intend to diet "in the new year": 16
Ratio of women who are watching their weight to men who
are: 2.4 to 1

Do We Make Our Meals from Scratch?

Most Canadians (94%) consumed at least one main meal made from "scratch" in the previous seven days. (Although "scratch" ain't what it used to be.) On average, Canadians claim that five out of their seven dinners were made from scratch during the previous week.

Percentage of men and of women who had takeout or
delivered meals during the previous seven days: 37 and 29
Chances that a Quebecker or Maritimer claims to have eaten
nothing but home-cooked meals for the past week: 1 in 3
National average: 1 in 4
Ratio of frozen-food eaters in Ontario to those in Quebec:
3 to 5
Factor by which a young Canadian is more likely than an older
Canadian to order delivery: 3

What have you eaten in the past week?

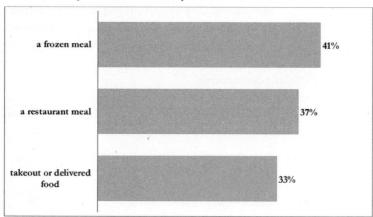

a frozen meal — 41%

a restaurant meal — 37%

takeout or delivered food — 33%

Grabbing a Quick Bite

What we think of as fast food continues to be dominated by take-out or delivered meals as opposed to frozen dinners or meals eaten in a restaurant.

Eight in ten (81%) of those who claim they had at least one takeout or ordered-in meal during the previous seven days ate at least one meal that was fast food (such as pizza, fried chicken or hamburgers). Almost one in three (30%) of these individuals had two or more fast food meals in the previous week.

Regionally, fewer Canadians living in British Columbia are eating fast food in restaurants (72%) or takeout/ordered-in (31%) than anywhere else in Canada. However, the proportion eating between three and seven fast food meals (heavy users) was the same for British Columbia as elsewhere, suggesting that other regions simply have more occasional fast food users but similar levels of heavy users.

Although half (50%) of all Canadians say they snack less often than they did three years ago, the other half snack just as much (28%) or more often (22%).

Factor by which a young Canadian is more likely than an older Canadian to have eaten takeout or delivery in the past week: 3

Factor by which a young Canadian is more likely than an older Canadian to eat snack food at least once per day: 6

Chances that a low-income Canadian has eaten fast food or frozen food in the past week: 1 in 2

Chances that an upper-income Canadian has: 1 in 3

Percentage of Canadians who never eat snack foods: 19

Factor by which a Quebecker is more likely than an Ontarian to claim not to have changed snacking habits over the past year: 2

Most Common Times to Snack

When do you snack?

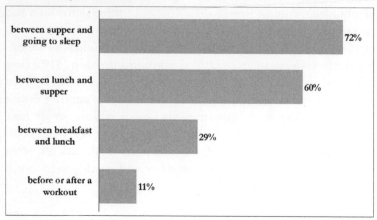

between supper and going to sleep	72%
between lunch and supper	60%
between breakfast and lunch	29%
before or after a workout	11%

Snack Time

For a strong majority (68%) of snack-eating Canadians, convenience is the determining factor behind the choice of snack food. However, a majority (59%) do not purchase their snack foods on the spur of the moment.

Those snack eaters aged 18–24 are much more likely (60%) to purchase snack foods at the spur of the moment than those aged 25–34 (47%), 35–54 (38%) or 55 and over (27%).

> Percentage of Canadian snack-eaters who prefer snack foods with some nutritional value: 78
> Factor by which fruit is more popular than fruit bars as a Canadian snack: 20
> Province that chooses the healthiest snacks: Quebec
> Province that chooses the least healthy snacks: Ontario
> Chance that a Canadian will eat snack food today: 1 in 2

Food Safety

Three-quarters (74%) of Canadians say they are concerned with the safety of the food they eat, nearly half of whom (35% of the total) are "very concerned" about the safety of their food. Just one-tenth of Canadians indicate being "not at all concerned" about the safety of the food they eat.

Concerns about food safety are highest in Atlantic Canada (83%) and lowest in Saskatchewan/Manitoba (69%), and Canadians 55 and older (77%) are more concerned than 18- to 34-year-olds (69%).

What do you worry about in your food?

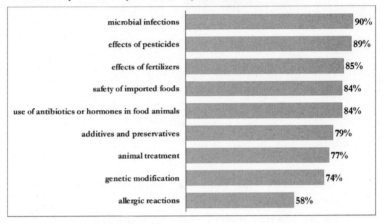

microbial infections	90%
effects of pesticides	89%
effects of fertilizers	85%
safety of imported foods	84%
use of antibiotics or hormones in food animals	84%
additives and preservatives	79%
animal treatment	77%
genetic modification	74%
allergic reactions	58%

What Are We Concerned About?

When asked to name where in the five steps of the food supply chain they feel there is the greatest chance for a food safety problem to develop, Canadians who are "very concerned" (35%) or "somewhat concerned" (39%) say it is during the "processing of foods" (41%). Fewer say it is in restaurants or other food service outlets (21%). Eighteen per cent say it is at the farm level, followed by the grocery store (12%) and the home (7%).

How worried are you about mad cow disease?

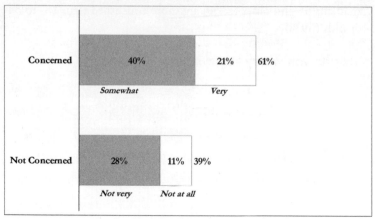

Province most concerned about mad cow disease: Ontario
Province least concerned: Quebec
Percentage difference between Atlantic Canadians and
Albertans who believe that someone in Canada will be
infected with mad cow disease: 19

Despite their concerns about mad-cow disease and the safety of the food they eat, 76% of Canadians agree with the statement "I trust Canada's food inspection agency to protect me from food-borne illnesses such as mad cow disease."

Genetically Modified Foods or Ingredients

Sixty-three per cent of Canadians indicate that if they were food shopping in a grocery store and the food they were considering purchasing was genetically modified or contained genetically modified ingredients, they would be less likely to buy the product. Respondents from B.C. (73%), Ontario (65%) and Quebec (64%) were most likely to feel strongest in their view, followed by Alberta (56%), Atlantic Canada (55%) and Saskatchewan/Manitoba (49%).

One-third (32%) of respondents indicated that it would make no difference to them in their purchase behaviour—with 47% indicating this in Saskatchewan/Manitoba followed by Alberta (41%), Atlantic Canada (38%), Quebec (32%), Ontario (28%) and B.C. (24%).

While Canadians are wary of foods that contain genetically modified ingredients, they are less certain as to whether or not we should embrace or abandon this technology given the global economy and international trade.

Forty-five per cent indicated that Canada should embrace GM technology because it is "the way of the future and it will give us a competitive advantage in the global economy." Those most likely to agree with this statement included people in Saskatchewan and Manitoba (50%), Alberta (49%), Ontario (46%) and Atlantic Canada (46%). Those aged 18 to 34 (50%) and men (48%) were most likely to agree with this statement.

Province with the highest percentage of shoppers who prefer genetically modified foods: Ontario
Rank of British Columbia among provinces opposed to genetically modified foods: 1
Percentage of Canadians who are trying to eat more organic foods: 37

Children and Obesity
Ninety-four per cent of Canadians believe that "the number of overweight and inactive children is a serious health issue in Canada today."

Percentage of Canadians who agree that "provincial governments should make it mandatory for all students from kindergarten to Grade 12 to have at least 30 minutes of physical activity each school day": 91
Percentage difference between those with children and those without among those who agree that phys. ed. should be mandatory: 0
Chances that a Canadian thinks that "the influence of television/Internet and video games on children is so powerful that it is difficult for parents to get their kids to be more physically active": 8 in 10
Percentage who say they "don't know": 1
Chances that a Canadian believes that fast food restaurants don't "offer enough low-fat nutritious choices for children": 7 in 10

Chances that a Canadian does not believe that "food companies and fast food restaurants are acting responsibly in their advertising of foods and beverages to children": 6 in 10

How Good Are Boomers at Counting Calories?

We provided baby boomers (40–59 years of age) with a list of ten food and beverage options and asked them to estimate how many calories were in each. As the results indicate, some major misunderstandings or myths clearly exist: the calorie counts of eight items were significantly overestimated, while they were significantly underestimated in two cases.

Beer and What Goes with It

Nearly nine in ten boomers (86%) think "beer will cause you to get fat or gain weight." We asked boomers to estimate the number of calories in a 12-ounce bottle of beer, and the average guess was 447.26—more than triple the actual number (140).

- **Residents of B.C. came closest (274.70), followed by Atlantic Canadians (275.06). Women guessed 396.41, while boomers 50–59 averaged 378.87.**
- **Those most likely to be furthest from the mark were Quebeckers (811.61), men (488.04) and boomers aged 40–49 (482.21).**

Average calories in a rye and cola: 171
Average estimate by baby boomers: 400.36
Average estimate by Quebeckers: 699.01
Average calories in a "a half-cup serving of dry roasted peanuts": 456
Average estimate by baby boomers: 321.36
Percentage of Canadians who think wine is "good for your heart": 79

Pop and Chips

The average guess for a 12-ounce can of cola was 340.35 calories, which is 233% of the actual number (146).

- **Those most likely to be closest are Atlantic Canadians (250.53), boomers aged 50–59 (273.58) and women (273.86).**
- **Those most likely to be furthest from the mark are residents of Quebec (442.87), men (395.18) and boomers aged 40–49 (360.83).**

There are 230 calories packed into a small (43-gram) bag of potato chips. Our boomers' average guess was 415.44, which is 181% of the actual amount.

- **Those most likely to guess accurately are Atlantic Canadians (289.82), boomers aged 50–59 (343.46) and women (410.64).**
- **Residents of British Columbia (493.71), boomers aged 40–49 (452.72) and men (419.42) are most likely to overestimate by the greatest amount.**

Tall Latte

On average, Canadian baby boomers think there are two-thirds more calories in a 12-ounce tall latte (333.43) than there actually are (200).

- **The best guessers tend to be Quebeckers (229.93), boomers aged 50–59 (273.58) and women (303.45).**
- **Those likely to wildly overjudge the caloric content are residents of British Columbia (403.68), boomers aged 40–49 (365.49) and men (360.84).**

Orange Juice

The calories in a 5-ounce glass of orange juice (118) were overestimated by a mere 32% on average (155.69).

- **Atlantic Canadians almost scored a bull's-eye at 116.81, followed by boomers aged 50–59 (129.20) and women (146.02).**
- **Residents of Saskatchewan/Manitoba were at the other end of the scale, with an average guess of**

287.86, followed by boomers aged 40–49 (169.25) and men (163.80).

Bran Muffins

The caloric content of a regular-sized 125-gram bran muffin was also underestimated, this time by almost 42% (average estimate: 210.37, compared with the actual 360).

- **Men averaged the closest estimate (237.03), followed by Quebeckers (234.19) and boomers aged 40–49 (219.59).**
- **Those most likely to be furthest from the mark are residents of Saskatchewan/Manitoba (176.51), women (179.01) and boomers aged 50–59 (192.42).**

Vitamins

Almost two-thirds of Canadians take a multivitamin at least once in a while; just over one-quarter of Canadians take one on a daily basis.

Percentage of Canadians currently on diets who take vitamin supplements: 34
Percentage of Canadians who think dieters should take vitamin supplements: 69
Percentage by which a Manitoban is more likely than an Atlantic Canadian to have taken a multivitamin: 50

Carbs

Seventy-two per cent of Canadians are aware of the terms "good carbs" and "bad carbs," used to describe the nutritional value of different carbohydrates. However, a significant proportion say they do not fully understand the difference between the types of carbohydrates—only 11% of Canadians believe they understand the distinction.

- **Albertans (83%) are the most aware of the terms "good carbs" and "bad carbs," while Quebeckers (52%) are the least aware.**
- **Women (79%) are more likely than men (64%) to be aware of the terms.**

- **While older people are more concerned with nutrition overall, it is younger Canadians who are more likely to be aware of the "good carb"/"bad carb" differentiation. Significantly more 18 to 24 year olds (72%) are aware of this than groups over 25 years old. Similarly, more of those 25 to 49 years old (61%) are aware than are those over 50 years old (53%).**

The majority of Canadians remain unaware that there may be risks associated with significant carbohydrate limiting and high protein consumption. Just over half (53%) say they are aware that this type of diet poses potential health risks; a further 32% did not know enough to answer the question.

Percentage of Canadians who think of baked potatoes as "good carbs": 51
Percentage of Canadians who think of rice as "bad carbs": 86
Percentage of Canadians aware that low-carb diets may not supply sufficient energy for brain activity: 60
Percentage of Canadian who enjoy eating carbs: 71
Percentage of Quebeckers who enjoy eating carbs: 48

Relationships

**Absence is to love what wind is to fire;
it extinguishes the small, it kindles the great.**

—Comte de Bussy-Rabutin

A WONDERFUL STORY appeared in the *Globe and Mail* on January 3, 2004. It featured several Canadian marriages that have lasted more than 60 years. Sixty! These people got hitched during the Second World War and, despite the odd bump on the road, were still enjoying life together six decades later.

Alma Harbridge, 79, married husband Doug, now 80, on April 24, 1943—so long ago that her wedding band wore off her finger. The couple held hands in their wedding picture, and they still hold hands today. "I am not the least bit bored," Alma told reporter Erin Anderssen. "When you love someone, things have a way of working out. It was a quality decision—once it's made, nothing changes it."

Claude Levasseur, 87, of Langley, B.C., had to give up the bottle to hold on to his wife Jean, 78, who was on her way out the door after the first 30 years because he was drinking too much. He quit, and she stayed. Says Claude, "I decided on my own I had better do something about this, or I'm going to lose everything here." He says he is baffled by men who leave their wives and hook up with someone new: "I don't get the drift of that. I don't see how they do it."

Beryl Cainey, 84, of Halifax, says, "Do you want to know the secret? When we have a fight, we make up and go on. You say things and you learn to stop saying things." Pam Pineo, 82, of Nanaimo, B.C., still married to Bill, 83, says, "Kids today don't give each other a chance. They don't learn to talk things through."

Well, some do and some don't. In the last Canadian census, Statistics Canada found that Canadians entered the new millennium with a marriage-to-divorce ratio of about 2 to 1—there were 153,234 marriages in Canada in 2001, and 71,783 divorces.

The Numbers Aren't All That Bad

Just under three-quarters (73%) of adult Canadians report being in some kind of non-platonic relationship—formal marriages, common-law marriages, partnerships, girlfriends and boyfriends, boyfriends and boyfriends, things like that. Nearly 94% of these relationships have at least a year's standing. So, how well are those relationships going? We focused on the marriages—contractual or common-law—and discovered that 8.5 in 10 people bonded within those marriages say they're happy.

Getting It Right

What is it about marriage that works for the vast majority of Canadians who practise this fine art?

It probably has something to do with some combination of these "sharing your soul" factors, which is, after all, what marriage is *supposed* to be all about (other than the biblical mandate to go forth and procreate, of course, which is treated as more of an option these days):

- **81% said they tell their partners about their dreams and aspirations**
- **75% say their partners know them best**
- **90% say they have never been cheated on in their marriage**
- **59% say they have never held a secret from their partner**

Before we go on, you are going to raise the issue of whether these people are telling us the truth. Hey, if the afternoon soap operas are anywhere close to reality, half the married folks in North America are fooling around—not one out of ten.

Well, we've probed the psyches of a lot of people over the years, and we try to be pretty careful about how we ask our questions. There is no doubt that the odd person fibs to us, but all our probing strongly suggests that we're getting the real goods—if the percentages are off due to untruthfulness, they're off by a couple of percentage points, no more. And that's the truth.

So you know someone who knows someone whose husband is bonking his secretary and momma doesn't know about it—it happens, but not as often as you think. We love to think we're living in a decadent world—four out of ten people we interviewed believe that even happily married people have affairs—but it's not quite as wild out there as you may think.

Flirting—Try It at Home!

Eight out of ten Canadians in married relationships (78%) say they flirt with their partners. So there is a lot of flirting going on, and not much of it is just going in only one direction, if you get our drift.

While Canadians appear to be happy about the amount of flirting done with their partner, four in ten (40%) say they'd like to see *more*. However, we discovered that six out of ten women (61%) and five out of ten men (51%) don't *want* more flirting. So you're going to have to feel your way along on this one on your own.

If you're older, maybe you don't want to get carried away. More older Canadians (64%) don't want any increase in flirting, compared to about half of their younger and middle-aged counterparts. That sounds a bit cranky, but these things happen.

How Canadians flirt with their mates

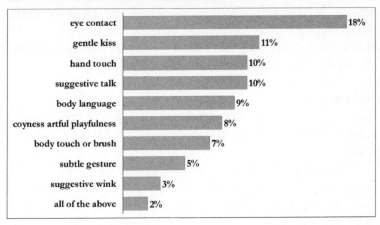

eye contact	18%
gentle kiss	11%
hand touch	10%
suggestive talk	10%
body language	9%
coyness artful playfulness	8%
body touch or brush	7%
subtle gesture	5%
suggestive wink	3%
all of the above	2%

Tidiness Is More Important Than Flirtatiousness

This could be a Canadian thing, but when we ask how partners could improve the relationship, more flirting isn't the first thing that comes to mind. It's less messiness.

Yes, it's time to talk about the main problem areas, and—not surprisingly—the priorities differ between men and women.

If I could change one thing about you, you would...

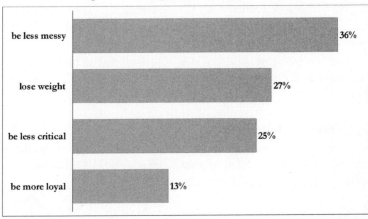

be less messy	36%
lose weight	27%
be less critical	25%
be more loyal	13%

By the way, here's a surprise: of those who responded that their main wish was that their partner be less messy, 46% were women, while only 26% were men. In Canada, as in the rest of the world, there is clearly still an argument to be made that men are pigs. Or that women are too fussy. Then again, one out of four times it looks like it's the other way around.

Behaving Badly

Even in Canada, where so many people are happy in their relationships, we do seem to find all kinds of ways of behaving . . . um . . . *badly.*

Canadians lie and cheat and seek revenge against their former lovers. But maybe not as much (or as little) as you think. You would think we'd all be vulnerable in the affairs of the heart, but there seem to be two ways to protect yourself. Canadians with university educations seem consistently more successful in romance than those without, and Quebeckers seem to fare much better than their peers around the country.

About 10% of Canadians who are currently married, divorced, separated or living common-law admit they have had or are having an extramarital affair, and 6% of Canadians who have not had an affair say that they are likely to have one in the future. Men are more than twice as likely than women to say that they are likely to have an affair in the future.

One-fifth of Canadians say that someone that they were or are married to has had an affair, and two-thirds of Canadians (66%) know a family member or friend who had an affair.

Canadians know adultery is wrong and that it is destructive. And yet they keep doing it (more and more, it seems). Read on, and find out why.

Long-Term Relationships . . . or Not

As noted above, fully three-quarters (73%) of adult Canadians report being in some form of relationship, and 94% of those relationships are more than a year old.

Average lifespan of a Canadian relationship: 17.7 years

How old you are has almost no correlation to your likelihood of being single. Those who are single and not in a relationship are more likely to be over 55 years of age (31%) or between 18 and 34 (29%).

However, where you live can make a huge difference. Quebeckers (37%) are more likely than those in other regions to say they are single and not in a relationship. The lowest proportions of completely single Canadians are found in Ontario (22%), Atlantic Canada (21%) and Saskatchewan/Manitoba (19%).

Marriage

Percentage of married Canadians between 35 and 54 years of age who wish they could go to bed married and wake up single: 19

Setting the Mood

Perhaps we're not the staid lot the world seems to think we are. Canadians have an impressive arsenal of techniques for putting their partners in the mood.

Mood-setting rituals of romantic Canadians

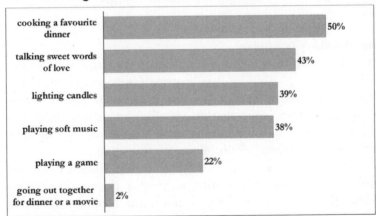

Base: Those Canadians who say they flirt.

Province in which you're most likely to be the object of a mood-setting campaign: Quebec
Odds that a Canadian will include a risqué photograph of himself or herself in a Valentine's Day card: 1 in 50

Rate by which those who say their Valentine's experiences have "left room for improvement" outnumber those who describe them as "fantastic": 3 to 1

Percentage of Canadians who feel '70s rock band KISS would get them in the mood: 5

Percentage likely to be put in the mood by Tchaikovsky: 17

Girls' Talk

When problems do arise in their marriages, women (66%) are more likely than men (26%) to try to talk it through. Interestingly, younger married men (33%) are more likely than their middle-aged (25%) or older (22%) counterparts to say they start the conversation with their spouse.

A majority (53%) of married Canadians say that when they talk with their spouse about problems, they feel they can reach a decision that both can live with, while one-quarter (27%) say they personally stay calm and reasonable in such discussions. On the opposite side, one in ten (8%) claims to get into heated arguments when discussing these problems, while one in twenty gets frustrated and shuts down (6%) or avoids discussing things that might be upsetting (4%). Fewer than 1% indicate they get into a physical fight.

But, We Don't Talk About ...

It appears that not every issue in Canadian marriages is up for discussion. One-quarter (23%) of married Canadians say that they have not discussed with their spouse an attraction to another person (surprise!). Other issues that aren't talked about include doubts about their marriage (16%), using the Internet to view pornography (9%) and extramarital affairs (4%). (Surprise again.)

Married men are more likely than married women to not tell their spouse about an attraction to another person (28% versus 18%), about using the Internet to view risqué material (16% versus 2%) or about an extramarital affair (6% versus 2%).

Dreams Canadians hide from their spouses

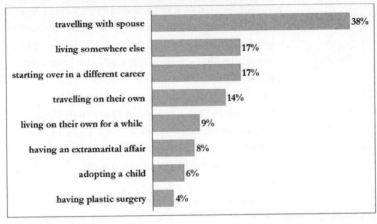

travelling with spouse	38%
living somewhere else	17%
starting over in a different career	17%
travelling on their own	14%
living on their own for a while	9%
having an extramarital affair	8%
adopting a child	6%
having plastic surgery	4%

While one fifth of married Canadians say they have dreams they have not told their spouse about, twice that number (41%) say they have kept a secret from their non-married partner.

Things Canadians hide from their spouses

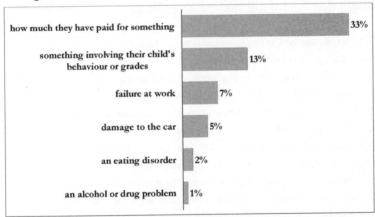

how much they have paid for something	33%
something involving their child's behaviour or grades	13%
failure at work	7%
damage to the car	5%
an eating disorder	2%
an alcohol or drug problem	1%

 • **Regionally, Quebeckers (33%) are the least likely to say they have kept a secret from their partners, compared with 47% in Saskatchewan/Manitoba, 46% in Ontario, 44% in Alberta and 44% in Atlantic Canada.**

- **Women are more likely than men to withhold how much they've paid for something (37% versus 30%), damage to the car (7% versus 3%) and, if they have children, child's behaviour or grades (16% versus 8%). Meanwhile, men (10%) are more likely than women (4%) to have kept failure at work from their spouse.**
- **Married Canadians from upper-income households (36%) are more likely than their counterparts from lower-income households (26%) to indicate they have not shared with their spouse how much they have paid for something.**

Knowledge of your past is one of the most private matters between partners. Half of married Canadians indicate that their partner knows everything about their love life before their marriage. This compares to one-quarter (26%) who say that their spouse knows some things but has not pressed for the whole story. One-tenth (13%) indicate that their spouse knows only the amount they are willing to share, while 8% say that their partner knows nothing because they haven't asked about it. One per cent say their partner knows nothing because they refuse to discuss it.

Percentage of Canadian men who have fantasized about an affair and not told their wives: 11
Ratio of secret dreams of adopting a child to dreams of an extramarital affair, among Canadian women: 2 to 1
Percentage of middle-income Canadians who have not told their spouses of their desire to get a dog: 16
Factor by which a lower-income Canadian is more likely to have disclosed his or her romantic past: 2 to 1
Percentage by which the likelihood that a married, upper-income Canadian will keep a secret from his or her spouse exceeds the likelihood that a middle-income Canadian will do the same: 50

What We *Should* Talk About

Here are the things Canadians wish their partners would talk about: Four in ten (44%) say they wish their spouse would ask them questions about themselves. Almost as many (42%) wish they could talk openly about spiritual matters with their spouse, while 40% wish they could talk with their partner about their sex lives. One-third (36%) indicate they wish they could ask their spouse to be more affectionate, and the same proportion (33%) say they wish they could talk with their partner about not having enough fun in their lives. One-fifth (21%) wish they could tell their spouse that they don't feel respected in their marriage.

My Spouse Knows Me Best ...

While it may not signal that most Canadians view their spouse as their best friend, a majority (75%) believes that their spouse is the person who knows them best. Trailing far behind are parents (8%), friends (5%), a child (5%), other relatives (2%), a former lover (1%) and colleagues at work (1%). Four per cent indicate that no one really knows them well, and 1% say they don't know.

- **Men (80%) are more likely than women (69%) to say that their spouse knows them best, while women are more likely than men to say friends (7% versus 3%), their child (6% versus 3%) or another relative (3% versus 1%) holds this distinction.**
- **Canadians who have only been married once (76%) are more likely than those who have been married more than once (63%) to say their spouse knows them best. Those who have had multiple marriages are more likely than those in their first marriage to say their child (8% versus 4%) or people at work (3% versus 0%) are the ones that know them best.**

Likelihood that a married couple will get into a heated argument while discussing problems: 1 in 2

Percentage of Quebeckers who wish that the topic of sex was open to discussion: 76

National average: 40

Men and Women Behaving Badly

Almost half (43%) of us say we've had our hearts broken.

Province where you're most likely to have your heart
broken: Saskatchewan
Least likely: Quebec
Rate by which someone with a high school education is more
likely to have his or her heart broken than someone with a
university education: 42%
Chance that a Canadian has been left standing at the altar
or personally knows someone who has: 1 in 10
Province in which you're most likely to be left standing at
the altar: British Columbia
Least likely: Manitoba
Gender most likely to be left standing at the altar: male

Being Cheated On

One-third of us have been cheated on by a partner. It seems that a lot of wild oats are sown during younger, less committed early romances. However, by the time Canadians are married, either their oats have been domisticated, or they've all been sown. Over a life-time of relationships:

- **Men (33%) and women (35%) are equally likely to have been cheated on by a partner.**
- **Young Canadians (40%) appear to be bearing the brunt of infidelity, compared to their middle-aged (34%) and older (27%) counterparts.**
- **Regionally, Quebec residents are the least likely to have been cheated on (26%), whereas British Columbia residents are the most likely (42%).**
- **Lower-income earners also experience more hardships of the heart (42%) compared to middle-income (34%) and higher-income (29%) earners.**
- **Canadians with university education are the least likely to have been cheated on (25%), while all others were equally as likely to have experienced the unfaithfulness of a partner (less than high school, 37%; high school, 38%; college, 38%).**

And Cheating

Just over one in ten Canadians would cheat on their partner if there were no chance of being caught.

- **Men (10%) are twice as likely as women (5%) to say they would cheat if there were no chance of being caught.**
- **Younger Canadians (12%) are more likely to cheat than middle-aged (6%) and older (5%) Canadians.**
- **Regionally, British Columbia (9%) and Ontario (9%) residents are more likely to cheat, whereas Atlantic Canadians (3%) are the most faithful to their partners.**
- **Middle-income (9%) to higher-income (8%) earners are the most likely to cheat if there was no chance of being caught, whereas lower-income earners (6%) are the least likely to cheat.**
- **High school graduates (11%) are the most likely to be unfaithful, while those with less than high school (5%) and university education (5%) are the least likely.**

Getting Back

One in ten Canadians has sought revenge on a partner after a breakup.

- **Men (7%) and women (8%) are equally likely to seek revenge on a partner after a breakup.**
- **Revenge-seeking appears to decline as income goes up. Lower-income earners are the most likely to have sought revenge (10%), while higher-income earners are the least likely (7%).**
- **Canadians with less than high school education are most likely to seek revenge (11%), while university graduates are the least likely (5%).**

Rate by which a Quebecker is more likely to seek revenge for a broken heart than is a Manitoban: 6 to 1

On the Side

Two-thirds (63%) of us disagree that people only have affairs if their marriage is already a failure

A strong minority (39%) of Canadians agree that "even happily married people often have affairs." (Not surprisingly, perhaps, men are roughly 50% more likely to hold this view.) But while Canadians do not necessarily think that bad marriages cause affairs, Canadians overwhelmingly think that affairs are bad for a marriage. Eighty-six per cent disagree with the statement "in the long run, an affair is often a good thing for a marriage." (Interestingly, 14% of Canadians think adultery is good for a marriage.)

Percentage of Canadians who have had an affair: 10

Percentage who say they are likely to have one: 6

Percentage of Canadians who say that someone they were married to has had an affair: 20

Rank of "loneliness" among reasons for having an affair: 1

Rank of "sex" and "love": tied for second

Percentage of men who say they would have an affair for sex: 29

Percentage of women who say they would: 8

Percentage of Canadians who have never been married who say they would have an affair for sex: 30

Percentage of married or divorced Canadians who say they would: 16

Factor by which a divorced Canadian is more likely than a married Canadian to have an affair for love: 2

To Forgive or Not to Forgive

Canadians seem unsure about what they would do if their spouse had an affair. Despite many Canadians (52%) agreeing with the statement, "if my spouse had an affair but the affair was over I would forgive them," a similar number of Canadians (55%) agree with the statement, "if my spouse had an affair, I would sever the relationship and end the marriage." However, only 15% strongly agree that they would forgive their spouse, compared with 30% who strongly agree that they would end the marriage—thereby suggesting that at the end of the day, Canadians would be more likely to sever a relationship than to forgive.

- Men (56%) are more likely than women (48%) to forgive an affair, and both sexes are equally likely to sever the relationship (54% and 55%).
- Younger Canadians are least likely to forgive (45%) and most likely to sever (71%), while older Canadians are most likely to forgive (59%) and least likely to sever (41%).
- Married people are equally likely to forgive an affair (53%) as they are to end their marriage (52%), while divorced people say they would be much more likely to end a marriage (64%) than to forgive (46%). Canadians who have never been married are slightly more likely to say they would end a marriage (64%) rather than forgive an affair (54%).
- Sixty-three per cent of divorces can be attributed to an affair.

Telling Tales

Canadians are tight-lipped about others' affairs, with most Canadians (67%) disagreeing with the statement, "if I knew someone was cheating on their spouse I would tell the spouse."

- Women (33%) are more likely than men (27%) to tell the spouse of an adulterer about an affair.
- There is a strong inverse relationship between age and likelihood to tell a spouse about an adulterer's affair. Younger Canadians (45%) are much more likely than middle-aged (28%) and older (15%) Canadians to say they would tell the spouse.
- Quebeckers (21%) are less likely than other Canadians to say they would tell the spouse.
- Canadians who have never been married (45%) are more likely than those who are married (28%) or divorced (27%) to say they would tell an adulterer's spouse about an affair.

The Other Woman

Just under half of Canadians (45%) say that women who have affairs with married men with families are home-wreckers who should get no sympathy, even if the man initiates the affair. Women (49%) are more likely than men (41%) to express agreement with this view. Canadians with high school education or less (53%) are more likely than those with a university degree (34%) to agree.

Are expectations changing? Canadians do not express surprise when a marriage breaks up due to infidelity. In fact, 79% say that when they read or hear about a women leaving her husband for another man they are not surprised in the same way they would have been years ago. Older Canadians are more likely to agree with this view than are younger Canadians (76%). Only slightly fewer (76%), express the same view regarding the situation of a man leaving his wife for another women.

Canadians also appear to hold the view that the state of politicians' marriages is a private matter. Eight in ten (81%) agree that when leading politicians leave their spouse for another person, it's nobody's business and we should respect their privacy.

Love as It Should Be

Asked to identify from a number of famous fictional couples which best typifies their current relationship, one in three Canadians who are in a relationship and who provided a response choose the battling friends turned lovers Harry and Sally, from the film *When Harry Met Sally* (34%), while almost as many opt for Homer and Marge from *The Simpsons* (30%). Just slightly fewer (27%) believe their current relationship is closer to that of Scarlett O'Hara and Rhett Butler, from the 1939 classic *Gone with the Wind*, while 8% say that Tony and Carmela from *The Sopranos* best typify their current relationship. Just under one in four of Canadians (37%) did not provide a response, including 12% who are "not currently in a relationship" and 25% who said they "don't know."

• **Middle-aged respondents are the most likely to select Harry and Sally (47%, compared to 32% of younger and 18% of older respondents). Meanwhile, younger respondents are more likely to opt for Homer and Marge (40%, compared to**

27% of older and 23% of middle-aged respondents). Older respondents are more likely to say that the couple that best typifies their current relationship is Scarlett O'Hara and Rhett Butler. (50%, compared to 21% of middle-aged and 17% of younger respondents).

Movies Canadians think best depict their relationships

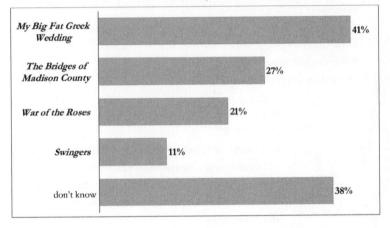

My Big Fat Greek Wedding — 41%

The Bridges of Madison County — 27%

War of the Roses — 21%

Swingers — 11%

don't know — 38%

Same-Sex Marriage

On Tuesday, June 10, 2003, Ontario's Court of Appeal ruled in favour of same-sex marriages, deeming the Canadian legal definition of traditional marriages to be unconstitutional. Asked if they "support or oppose same-sex couples being allowed to marry and register their marriage with their provincial government," a slim majority (54%) of Canadians say they support same-sex marriages.

Now, most courts in the country have also ruled the federal law that recognizes only opposite-sex unions for marriage unconstitutional, and the federal Supreme Court has weighed in, tossing the hot issue of defining "marriage" back to the federal government. Interestingly, it would appear that Canadians hold different views on how the term "marriage" should be applied, giving the federal government a number of options regarding this issue: 39% believe same-sex marriage should be "fully recognized and equal to conventional heterosexual marriages"; 32% believe it should be "allowed to existed in civil law but not have the same legal weight as a conventional marriage"; and 27% believe that it is "wrong and should never be lawful." In fact, 35% believe that the government should invoke the "notwithstanding" clause of the Canadian constitution.

Percentage of young Canadians who believe same-sex marriages "should be fully recognized and equal to conventional heterosexual marriages": 52

Percentage of Canadians over 35 who do: 33

Province the residents of which are most likely to believe same-sex marriage is "wrong and should never be lawful": Manitoba and Saskatchewan

Least likely: British Columbia

- **Support for same-sex marriage is unchanged since 1999.**
- **Residents of Quebec (65%) and British Columbia (64%) are more likely than residents of Ontario (49%), Atlantic Canada (49%), Alberta (47%) and Saskatchewan/Manitoba (43%) to support same-sex marriages.**
- **Women (60%) are more likely than men (48%) to support same-sex marriages.**
- **Canadians in a common-law relationship or living with a partner (77%) and single or never-married Canadians (64%) are more likely than widowed (37%), married (47%) or divorced or separated (48%) Canadians to support same-sex marriages.**
- **University graduates (65%) are more likely than others (50%) to support same-sex marriages.**
- **A young Canadian is twice as likely to support same-sex marriages as is an older Canadian.**

Pets

Cruel, but composed and bland,
Dumb, inscrutable and bland,
So Tiberius might have sat,
Had Tiberius been a cat.

—Matthew Arnold, dog person (1822–1888)

They say a certain amount o' fleas is good fer a dog—
keeps him from broodin' over bein' a dog.

—Edward Noyes Westcott, cat person (1846–1898)

ANYONE WITH A child, or with a clear memory of being one, knows how difficult our ambivalent relationship with animals can be to understand. They are our friends. And we eat them. We are scandalized by other cultures' habits of eating animals we like to cuddle, or play fetch with, or ride; but a trip to a petting zoo for an encounter with a lamb or cow (or chicken, goat, pig or duck) can be enough to put us off our lunch, and to scar forever the child who realizes what he or she has been eating.

We love animals. And that is probably good. It is well-known that those who are cruel to animals are likely to be cruel to humans. Who knows the exact point at which we stopped eating certain species and started feeding them instead? Sadly, the name and particulars of humanity's first pet are lost in the mists of unrecorded time.

The UNDP Human Development Report says that Americans spend more than $10 billion U.S. a year on pet food, and we Canadians spend more than $1 billion U.S.—our surveys suggest about $1.6 billion Canadian.

Since expenditures on food usually represent less than half of what it costs to keep a cat or a dog, that means that both Canadians and Americans spend more on their pets than they do on foreign aid. We also know that the UN weapons inspection team in Iraq spent more per capita on its sniffer dogs' food than the average Iraqi received as part of the "Oil for Food" program.

The American Society for the Prevention of Cruelty to Animals (ASPCA) estimates that in the first year, dog owners will spend $780 U.S. to care for a small dog, $1,115 U.S. for a medium-sized dog and $1,500 U.S. for a large dog. Cats cost in the neighbourhood of $640 U.S. in the first year. Costs go down in subsequent years (spay/neuter costs are behind you) but inevitably rise as pets get older and vet costs go up.

The ASPCA reckons that even a lowly hamster costs in the neighbourhood of $330 U.S. a year. Hamsters don't eat that much, but their pooping gets costly: two-thirds of that ASPCA estimate is gobbled up in litter costs.

The Most Important Question

Ratio of cats to dogs in Canada: 1.31 to 1

The most important question here, of course, is "Are you a dog person or a cat person." (Or both. Or neither.)

If you label yourself a dog person, you will be seen as a person who values camaraderie over independence. If you are a cat person, it's vice versa. These perceptions may be unfair, but it's just the way the world will look at you, so get used to it.

Some Canadians, of course, swoon over virtually any kind of pet. You see them gushing over almost any kind of kept creature in any location (although that approach might not work so well in Nigeria, where debt collectors walk around with leashed hyenas and baboons).

At the other end of the spectrum, everyone knows one or more people who regard all pets as messy, unnecessary nuisances. (W. C. Fields felt this way about both pets and children.)

But getting back to clear-cut dog people and their rivals, the cat people. More than half of all Canadian households are home to at least one inhabitant who is either a dog or a cat.

Yes, there are more cats in Canada (about 7.2 million) than dogs (about 5.5 million), but dogs are generally bigger. Furthermore, while cats cohabit fairly well when people are out of the house—licking each other and sleeping a lot—cohabiting dogs have been known to encourage one another to eat furniture.

So let's just say it's easier to own two cats than two dogs. The fact is, about one third of Canadian households have dogs, and about one third have cats. In short, let's call it even.

How Canadians Look at Pets and Their Owners

Canadians are generally sympathetic to animal rights: 70% in our survey agreed with the statement, "animals are defenceless and deserve our protection." Only 5% disagreed. Women were 77% in agreement. And while Alberta is beef-cattle country, its 77% positive response rating was second only to Atlantic Canada's 81%.

When asked where their pet ranks in the family hierarchy, respondents gave the following answers:

- **Member of the family: 57%**
- **Baby of the family: 26%**
- **A pet, not a family member: 15%**
- **And then, one sad little number—My pet is mainly for others in my family to enjoy, not me: 2%.**

Percentage of Canadians who agree that "Pet owners treat their pets more like people than animals": 51

Percentage of Canadians who believe pets are a good substitute for human companionship: 43

Percentage of Canadians who agree with the statement, "When I see someone's pet misbehaving, I am more annoyed with the owner than the animal": 61

Percentage of Canadian pet owners who allow animals in their beds: 69

Gender more likely to permit a pet in bed: female

Percentage of Canadians who carry a photo of a pet in their wallets: 57

Percentage who would willingly go into debt for a pet: 53

Percentage of Canadians who talk to their pets: 98

Canadiana

A Canadian is somebody who knows how to make love in a canoe.

—Pierre Berton

BAD NEWS ABOUT the Canadian identity: while 44% of Canadians point to the CN Tower in Toronto as Canada's most famous landmark, not one of our respondents could precisely locate the following powerful symbols of the country's identity:

1. The World's Largest Axe
2. The Giant Squid
3. The World's Largest Easel
4. The Giant Fiddle

Can you believe that?

Our readers, of course, will already have identified the correct locations of these national landmarks: (1) Nackawic, New Brunswick, (2) Glover's Harbour, Newfoundland, (3) Altona, Manitoba, (4) Cavendish, Prince Edward Island.

Wait, there's more. Only 1% were able to locate the World's Largest Oil Can at Rocanville, Saskatchewan. And only another 1% knew that the World's Largest Inukshuk (an Inuit stone sculpture that features balanced rocks—but you knew that) sits in Vancouver.

The good news is that 8% of respondents were aware that the

Pysanka Easter Egg is in Vegreville, Manitoba, and another 8% could place the Giant Anchor in Halifax, Nova Scotia. Almost off the map: 38% knew that the Big Nickel is in Sudbury, Ontario, and 45% knew that Bonhomme Carnaval can be found in Quebec City.

Almost everybody knew that Niagara Falls is in Niagara Falls.

Not as Smart as We Think We Are?

The deficiencies in our geographical understanding of Canada, sadly enough, coexist with some corresponding historical deficiencies. If it is held as a national truth that we Canadians are smarter than Americans—as Rick Mercer is always suggesting—you sure can't prove it by how much we know about our own history.

A recent Canada Day poll demonstrates that Americans have a better knowledge of their own history and civics than we Canadians do of ours. In total, 1,003 adult Canadians and 1,000 adult Americans were surveyed on their knowledge of their country's historical and civic facts. The Yanks creamed us: 63% of Americans scored five or more correct responses out of ten to pass the quiz, to only 39% of our Canadian respondents.

In both countries, the highest scores came when people were asked who their country's first political leader was. Fully 90% of Americans knew that their first president was George Washington, while only 54% of Canadians knew that their first prime minister was Sir John A. Macdonald. And that was our *best* mark.

"Life, liberty and the pursuit of happiness" is America's constitutional slogan, and 87% of Americans polled knew that. Unfortunately, 22% of Canadians thought it was *ours*. It is not. Ours is "Peace, order and good government." Not as sexy, but it is ours, and maybe we should know that.

While 72% of Americans correctly identified the government of the United States as a representative republic, 13% of them said that their government is a constitutional monarchy. If so, one might ask, who is the monarch?

While 56% of Canadians could correctly identify Canada's form of government as a constitutional monarchy, they enjoy only a two-to-one margin over the 26% who think that Canada is a republic. If so, where are the bananas?

How bad is this, eh? While 79% of Americans could identify the first line of their national anthem ("Oh say can you see, by the dawn's early light") only 37% of Canadians could identify the first line of their national anthem. When you take a look at the anthem, should memorizing the first line be that difficult, even if you have to start lip-synching when you get to the second line?

> O Canada!
> Our home and native land!
> True patriot love in all thy sons command
>
> With glowing hearts we see thee rise,
> The True North strong and free!
>
> From far and wide,
> O Canada, we stand on guard for thee.
>
> God keep our land glorious and free!
> O Canada, we stand on guard for thee.
>
> O Canada, we stand on guard for thee.

To answer our question correctly, you must memorize only two words, one of which has one letter in it, and the other of which is the name of the country you live in. *It can be done.*

At Which Point Darrell and John Make a Stunning Confession

Okay, we're not so smart either. We don't have to confess to this little blunder of our own, but we will. When we first released the results of this survey, we noted that only 37% of Canadians knew the first line to "Oh Canada." That's right—"*Oh* Canada"!

So . . . dunce caps all around.

That's enough about this quiz, but perhaps now is the best time to discuss something we learned in another survey that also relates to our national anthem.

Take this for what it's worth:

Some women's groups recently advocated a change in the line in the above anthem that says "in all thy sons command," on the grounds that there are also daughters in Canada, and that women are weary of having an anthem that is gender-biased.

That line doesn't exist in the French version of the anthem, so we asked only English-speaking Canadians whether they thought the line should be changed. (Remember, these people made up the majority of the respondents in the poll in which only 37% could remember *the first line* of the anthem.)

How many of them could have been expected to remember the words to the *third* line? Our bet would be not many. And yet 77% of respondents said they thought it would be a bad idea to change that third line to make it more inclusive. Among men, 79% opposed change; among women, 74%.

This raises the possibility of a new Canadian motto: Don't change what you don't know.

Royal Confusion

We Canadians are of tangled minds regarding the monarchy.

First, a brief tutorial. If you are among the 26% of Canadians who think that Canada is a republic, we will repeat: we are not. What we are is a constitutional monarchy; the Queen of England is Canada's head of state.

If that doesn't make huge sense in terms of pure logic, it doesn't necessarily have to. It's a historical thing.

So, what do Canadians think should be done about this illogical but historical situation? Essentially, the numbers tell us that they think the situation should change and stay the same. At the same time. No, *really.*

About half of Canadians (48%) think that our constitutional monarchy is outmoded and that we should have a republican form of government with an elected head of state, similar to the American system. Moreover, nearly two-thirds of us (65%) believe that the royals are simply celebrities and should not play any formal role in the government of Canada. (Remember, the Queen's representative in Canada is the governor general, who must sign all federal bills before they become law. That is a *formal* responsibility.)

However, another question in this series revealed that 79% of Canadians support our current system of government, which is . . . yes . . . a constitutional monarchy. Support is highest in Atlantic Canada, at 87%, but support runs at 73% even in Quebec.

Why do we support our constitutional monarchy when we don't think the monarchy should play a formal role in our government, which it must do if we are going to remain a constitutional monarchy?

Good question. Apparently the reason is that the majority of us feel that having a constitutional monarchy helps define Canada's identity: 62% of Canadians say that's why they support a constitutional monarchy even though 65% of them don't think we should have a constitutional monarchy. God knows what would happen if there were ever a referendum on this issue.

Maybe we just don't want to hurt the Queen's feelings. Well over eight in ten of the Queen's Canadian subjects (84%) feel that she has done a good job as monarch. And she is our favourite royal: 30% opt for her, 22% for Prince William and only 9% for Prince Charles.

So, where does that leave us?

When you get by that thing about a solid majority of us believing that our monarch should not play any formal role in our government, then move by the part where we want to keep our constitutional monarchy because it so defines us, you finally get to the question of whether Canadians want to hold on to our constitutional monarchy once Queen Elizabeth II dies and her currently far less popular son takes over.

Which is where you discover that 48% of Canadians think that her death should darned well mark the moment at which we finally break our formal ties to the British monarchy. But wait—51% think that we should *not* break them.

So it's a split. "Split" is perhaps a good description of Canada's personality on this issue.

Likelihood that a Canadian thinks Canada is a republic and not a constitutional monarchy: 1 in 4

Percentage difference between those whose favourite royal is Prince William and those who prefer his father, Prince Charles: 21

Percentage difference between the number of Quebeckers who think the monarchy should be replaced with a republic and those in Saskatchewan/ Manitoba who feel the same way: 19

Percentage difference between the number of Quebeckers who think the Queen has done a good job and the national average: –17

Ratio of the number of Quebecers who think Canada should

sever its ties to the monarchy once Queen Elizabeth's reign
ends to the national average: 1.54 to 1
Of Ontarians who think so: 0.73 to 1

Is Monarchy Outmoded?

Half of Canadians (48%) say that the constitutional monarchy is
outmoded and that they would prefer a republic system of government with an elected head of state, like in the United States.

Support for a republican system of government, by province

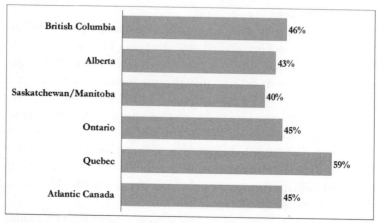

Province	Support
British Columbia	46%
Alberta	43%
Saskatchewan/Manitoba	40%
Ontario	45%
Quebec	59%
Atlantic Canada	45%

Just Celebrities?

Two-thirds (65%) of Canadians believe the royals are simply
celebrities and should not have any formal role in Canada.

Percentage of Quebeckers who think of the royals as mere
celebrities: 84
Percentage of Atlantic Canadians who do: 53

But We Support It ...

Eight in ten Canadians (79%) support the constitutional monarchy
as Canada's form of government, where we elect governments whose
leader becomes prime minister.

- Support for the constitutional monarchy is highest in Atlantic Canada (87%) and Saskatchewan/ Manitoba (84%) and Alberta (83%), followed by Ontario (80%) and British Columbia (79%).
- Quebeckers (73%) are least likely to express support for the constitutional monarchy system.
- Younger Canadians (86%) are more likely to express support for the current form of government than middle-aged Canadians (78%), while older Canadians (74%) are least likely to support the current system.

Because It Helps Define Us

Six in ten Canadians (62%) feel that the constitutional monarchy helps to define Canada's identity and should continue to be Canada's form of government.

- Regionally, this view is more likely expressed by residents of Atlantic Canada (71%) and Alberta (68%), followed by those in Saskatchewan/ Manitoba (67%), Ontario (65%) and British Columbia (63%), while only half (52%) of Quebeckers believe this to be so.
- Younger (66%) and older (64%) Canadians are more likely to feel that the constitutional monarchy helps to define Canada's identity than their middle-aged counterparts (57%).

Plus, We Think the Queen Is Good at What She Does

Eight in ten (84%) of the Queen's Canadian subjects believe that she has done a good job as monarch.

- Women (87%) are more likely than men (80%) to indicate that the Queen has done a good job as monarch.
- Canadians from middle-income households (89%) are more likely than their counterparts in either upper-income (83%) or lower-income (78%) households to agree.

> • **Quebeckers (67%) are the least likely to say that the Queen has done a good job in her role.**

And That She Should Stick with the Job

Two-thirds of Canadians (67%, 45% strongly) feel that Queen Elizabeth II should not abdicate or step down as Queen now, to allow her son Prince Charles, the Prince of Wales, to become King of England immediately. This compares to just three in ten (28%) who agree that the Queen should step down now to allow Prince Charles to become king.

> • **Once again, Quebeckers buck the national trend, with 50% disagreeing and with 42% agreeing with this proposal.**
> • **Younger Canadians (31%) are more likely than older Canadians (25%) to indicate that the Queen should step aside in order to allow Prince Charles to become king immediately.**
> • **Canadians in middle-income households (31%) are more likely than those in upper-income households (25%) to indicate that the Queen should step down now.**

She's Also the Favourite of the Family

Favourite British aristocrat

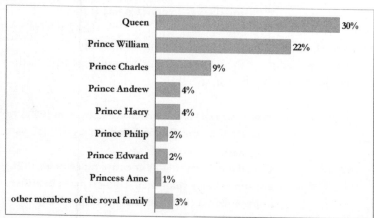

Queen	30%
Prince William	22%
Prince Charles	9%
Prince Andrew	4%
Prince Harry	4%
Prince Philip	2%
Prince Edward	2%
Princess Anne	1%
other members of the royal family	3%

The Queen is the favourite of 40% of Canadians aged 55 and older. This compares to only 30% of 35- to 54-year-olds and 20% of 18- to 34-year-olds.

Regionally, the Queen is the top choice of those in Ontario (34%) and Atlantic Canada (34%), followed by British Columbia (33%), Alberta (32%) and Saskatchewan/Manitoba (30%). Residents of Quebec (20%) are the least likely to cite the Queen as their favourite living royal. Quebeckers (23%) followed by Atlantic Canadians (19%) are the most likely to indicate that they do not have a favourite member of the royal family.

Looking to the Future

Canadians are split over the future role of the British monarchy in Canada when Queen Elizabeth's reign ends. Half (48%) say that when this event happens, Canada should end its formal ties to the British monarchy. Regionally, Quebeckers (74%) are in the highest agreement with this proposal. This is in comparison to residents of Saskatchewan/Manitoba (48%), British Columbia (43%) and Atlantic Canada (43%). Albertans (36%) and Ontarians (35%) are the least likely to agree to this idea. Men and women are split on this subject, with more men (53%, versus 42% of women) agreeing.

If ties to the monarchy were severed, four in ten Canadians (39%) indicate that they would prefer Canada's new official head of state to be a symbolic, elected governor general with limited responsibilities.

- **Albertans (54%) are by far the most likely to prefer an elected governor general, followed by those in British Columbia (40%), Saskatchewan/ Manitoba (40%) and Ontario (all at 40%), Atlantic Canada (36%) and Quebec (33%).**
- **Women (43%) are more likely than men (35%) to prefer an elected governor general.**
- **Canadians without a high school diploma (44%) are more likely than those with a university degree (34%) to indicate preference for this option.**

A similar number (37%) say they would prefer that Canada become a republic in which the prime minister becomes the official head of state in addition to the current role as head of government.

- **Regionally, support for this option is statistically consistent across all regions of the country.**
- **Men (42%, versus 31% of women) are more likely to prefer this option to replace the monarch as Canada's official head of state.**
- **Those in upper-income (42%) and middle-income (38%) households are more likely than those in the lowest-income households (30%) to choose this option.**

Fifteen per cent, on the other hand, would like the new head of state to be a symbolic governor general with limited responsibilities who is appointed by the prime minister. Regionally, residents of Quebec (23%) lead the country in selecting this option, followed by those in British Columbia (17%), Atlantic Canada (17%), Ontario (13%), Saskatchewan/Manitoba (9%) and Alberta (5%).

But Why Bother?

Half (52%) of Canadians say that the issue of the monarchy and Canada's form of government is not important to them, so why go through the fuss of changing something that seems to work okay?

And What About that Other Sovereignty—In Quebec?

It is probably not surprising that support for the queen is lowest and support for a republican government is highest in Quebec. Quebequois ambivalence to confederation is part of what makes Canada what it is. In fact, the *Oxford English Dictionary* cites a 1979 article in the Montreal *Star* as the first appearance in English of the word "sovereignist."

The question of how sovereignism is faring today is not altogether clear, as it is not at all clear what people mean by "sovereignty." If a referendum were held today on Quebec sovereignty, conditional on economic and political partnership with the rest of Canada, it would be a nail-biter. Those opting for sovereignty weigh in at 48%, while those voting against it have the support of 45%. The matter would likely be decided by the 7% of Quebeckers who don't know who they would vote for. Men, for some reason, are much more likely to vote for sovereignty, by a ratio of 55% to 42%.

However, when "sovereignty" is defined as attaining the status of a separate nation, without economic or political partnership with what remains of Canada, support drops considerably. Those opting for sovereignty would generate only 35% support, while those voting against would tip the scales at 58%. The undecided vote does not change under this definition, and the difference between men and women increases to a ratio of 43% to 28%.

If the Queen is the Favourite Royal, Who's the Best Prime Minister?

Enough of the royals. Who do Canadians think was our best prime minister during the twentieth century? The late Pierre Elliott Trudeau gets the nod, at 43%. More than four out of ten people in every province agreed, with the exception of Manitoba/Saskatchewan, at 33%—where the late Mr. Trudeau created a touch of controversy by asking "Why should I sell your wheat?"

- **More than four in ten in all of the regions of Canada named Prime Minister Trudeau as the best of the twentieth century, with the exception of Saskatchewan/Manitoba (33%).**
- **Canadians aged 35 to 54 (50%) are more likely than younger Canadians aged 18 to 34 (42%) and those over 55 years of age (34%) to name Trudeau as the best prime minister.**
- **Canadians with higher levels of education are more likely to award Trudeau with the honour of being the best Canadian prime minister (university, 48%; some post-secondary, 44%; high school or less, 37%), as are Canadians with higher household incomes (higher than $60,000, 46%; $30,000 to $59,000, 44%; less than $30,000, 39%).**

Favourite prime ministers, other than Trudeau

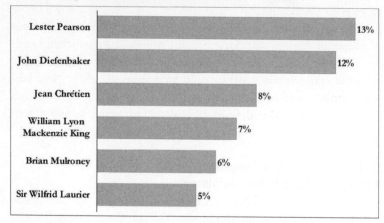

Lester Pearson	13%
John Diefenbaker	12%
Jean Chrétien	8%
William Lyon Mackenzie King	7%
Brian Mulroney	6%
Sir Wilfrid Laurier	5%

- **Lester Pearson receives his highest levels of support from British Columbians (18%), Canadians aged 55 or older (21%), the university-educated (16%), and Canadians with high household incomes (15%).**
- **Saskatchewan/Manitoba residents have not forgotten the political career of John Diefenbaker; they are more likely to name him the twentieth century's best prime minister (29%). Canadians who are 55 or older (20%) and those who have less than a high school education (20%) are also more likely than the national average (12%) to choose Diefenbaker.**
- **Jean Chrétien is more frequently chosen as the country's best prime minister by Canadians aged 18 to 34 (13%) and by Canadians who have a high school diploma (15%) or less (10%).**
- **Quebeckers (11%) are almost twice as likely as the national average (6%) to say that Brian Mulroney is the best prime minister that Canada had during the twentieth century.**

Chances that the average Canadian considers John
Diefenbaker the twentieth century's best prime minister:
1 in 8.3
Chances that a resident of Saskatchewan or Manitoba
does: 1 in 3.5
Chances that the average Canadian considers Brian Mulroney
the century's best: 1 in 16.6
That a Quebecker does: 1 in 9

As for the Canadian Anthem, It's the Best Already

As noted previously, amid attention to a petition raised by women's groups and their representatives to change a line in the lyrics of "O Canada," three-quarters (77%) of English-speaking Canadians think that changing the line in the national anthem from "in all our sons command" to wording which does not refer to only one gender is a "bad idea." Two in ten (21%) think changing the line is a "good idea."

- There is no significant difference between the opinions of men (20% say "good idea" and 79% say "bad idea") and women (22% say "good idea" and 74% say "bad idea").
- English-speakers from Alberta (87%) are most likely to say changing the lyric is a "bad idea," while those from British Columbia (74%) and Ontario (74%) are least likely.
- University graduates (32%) are more likely to say changing the lyric is a "good idea" compared to those with some post-secondary education (15%), high school graduates (16%) and those with less than a high school education (13%).

Ratio of men who think changing the lyric is a good idea
to those who think it is a bad one: 1 to 4
Ratio of women who think it is a good idea to those
who disagree: 1 to 3.4
Ratio of university graduates to those with only a high school
education who think that changing the lyric is a good idea: 2 to 1

Comparing Accomplishments: What Makes a Great Canadian?

There are many things that Canadians say make a Great Canadian. Out of a list of four items, the largest number of Canadians (82%) say that "contributing to the advancement of human knowledge" is an important factor in determining whether someone is a Great Canadian. This is followed by "making a contribution to the local community" (77%) and "strengthening our national identity" (71%). In last place is "making Canada known on the international stage" (62%).

• Quebeckers (73%) are much more likely to say that "making Canada known on the international stage" is an important consideration in determining whether someone is a Great Canadian, and much less likely (62%) than the rest of Canada to choose "strengthening our national identity."

Most worthy accomplishments, in Canadians' opinion

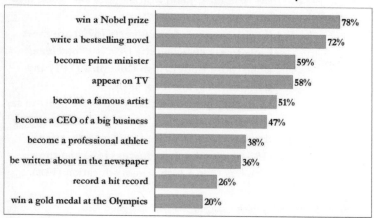

win a Nobel prize	78%
write a bestselling novel	72%
become prime minister	59%
appear on TV	58%
become a famous artist	51%
become a CEO of a big business	47%
become a professional athlete	38%
be written about in the newspaper	36%
record a hit record	26%
win a gold medal at the Olympics	20%

• Quebeckers are more likely than other Canadians to say that it is a bigger accomplishment to be on TV (65%) than in the newspaper (30%).

- **Roughly two out of three British Columbians (62%) and Atlantic Canadians (61%) say it is a bigger accomplishment to become a famous artist than to become a CEO. Quebeckers are much more likely to say it is a bigger accomplishment to become a CEO.**

But Who Knows the Basics Better?

Another Canada Day poll shows Americans know their history and civics far better than Canadians.

Six in ten (63%) Americans passed the quiz (scoring five or more correct responses out of ten), compared to 39% of Canadians.

Summary Chart			
Canadian Questions	**% Correct**	**American Questions**	**% Correct**
1. Who was the first prime minister of Canada? *Macdonald*	54%	1. Who was the first president of the United States? *Washington*	90%
2. What part of the Constitution protects Canadians' rights and freedoms? *The Charter of Rights and Freedoms*	29%	2. What part of the Constitution guarantees Americans' rights and freedoms? *The Bill of Rights*	32%
3. Which of the following slogans is associated with Canada's Constitution? *Peace, Order and Good Government* / Life, Liberty and the Pursuit of Happiness / Liberty, Equality, Fraternity	41%	3. Which of the following slogans is associated with the U.S. Constitution? Peace, Order and Good Government / *Life, Liberty and the Pursuit of Happiness* / Liberty, Equality, Fraternity	87%
4. Name one of the wars in which Canada was invaded by the United States: *War of Independence / War of 1812 / American Revolution*	38%	4. Name one of the wars in which the United States invaded Canada: *War of Independence / War of 1812 / American Revolution*	18%

Summary Chart			
Canadian Questions	**% Correct**	**American Questions**	**% Correct**
5. In 1944, Canadians joined in an event called D-Day. What happened on that day? *Invasion of Normandy / Europe / France*	47%	5. In 1944, Americans joined in an event called D-Day. What happened on that day? *Invasion of Normandy / Europe / France*	44%
6. Who was the first Canadian in space? *Marc Garneau*	33%	6. Who was the first American in space? *Alan Shepard*	14%
7. What is the first line of Canada's national anthem? *O Canada! Our home and native land*	37%	7. What is the first line of the U.S. national anthem? *Oh say can you see by the dawn's early light*	79%
8. The government of Canada is best described as: a representative republic, *a constitutional monarchy* or a cooperative association?	56%	8. The government of the United States is best described as: *a representative republic,* a constitutional monarchy or a cooperative association?	72%
9. What year did Confederation occur? *1867*	45%	9. What year was the Declaration of Independence issued? *1776*	61%
10. In what decade in the twentieth century were Canadian women first given the right to vote in elections? *1910s*	13%	10. In what decade in the twentieth century were American women given the right to vote in elections? *1920s*	36%
Canadians who passed quiz	39%	Americans who passed quiz	63%

Generally, Americans outperformed Canadians throughout the survey. However, Canadians were more than twice as likely as Americans to be able to name the first person their country sent into space (33%). Only 14% of Americans correctly identified Alan Shepard as the first American in space. Canadians (38%) were also more than twice as likely as Americans (18%) to be able to name one of the wars in which Canada was invaded by the United States.

Canadians (47%) and Americans (44%) displayed similar knowledge of the significance of D-Day and the part of their respective constitutions that protects a citizens' rights and freedoms (29% versus 32%).

The question that asked respondents to pick from three options the one that best described their country's system of government, produced interesting incorrect responses in the U.S. and Canada. As we have noted, while 72% of Americans correctly identified the government of the United States as a representative republic, more than one in ten respondents (13%) volunteered that the government of the United States is best described as a constitutional monarchy. While 56% of Canadians could correctly identify Canada's form of government as a constitutional monarchy, fully one in four (26%) believed that Canada is a representative republic.

Results by Age

In both countries, older individuals performed better than younger ones. In Canada, on average 44% of those aged 35 and older passed the quiz (scoring at least five correct responses out of ten) compared to 26% of those 18 to 34 years old. In the U.S., 46% of 18- to 34-year-olds passed the quiz compared to seven in ten of those 35 to 54 (69%) or 55 and older (73%).

The answers on which older Canadians scored better than younger Canadians include naming the invasion of Normandy/France/Europe as the event that occurred on D-Day (53% aged 35+ versus 35% aged 18 to 34), naming Marc Garneau as the first Canadian in space (41% aged 35+ versus 17% aged 18 to 34).

In the U.S., older individuals knew that the government of the United States is best described as a representative republic (75% aged 35+ versus 67% aged 18 to 34), that the Declaration of Independence was issued in 1776 (66% aged 35+ versus 48% aged 18 to 34) and that women gained the right to vote in elections in the 1920s (42% aged 35+ versus 24% aged 18 to 34) as compared with younger age groups.

Rate by which an Ontarian is more likely than a Quebecker to answer correctly: 2 to 1

Results by Gender

Men in both countries performed better than women. In Canada, 45% of men passed the quiz, while 33% of women passed. The questions on which men scored significantly higher than women included describing the events of D-Day as the invasion of Normandy/France/Europe (59% men versus 36% women), and naming the first Canadian in space as Marc Garneau (41% men versus 25% women). However, equal numbers of Canadian men (13%) and women (12%) correctly named the 1910s as the decade in which women gained the right to vote in federal elections. (Interestingly, it would not be until 1940 that Quebecoise women could vote in provincial elections, and 1951 until women in the Northwest Territories could vote in their region.) And more women (44%) than men (29%) were able to recite the first line of Canada's national anthem.

In the United States, 67% of men pass the quiz compared to 57% of women. The questions on which men scored significantly higher than women include describing D-Day as the invasion of Normandy/Europe/France (59% men versus 30% women) and naming the year the Declaration of Independence was issued (66% men and 56% women).

Tracking Our Progress

Analysis of previous Canada Day polls suggests that despite our best efforts, Canadians' knowledge of their country may still be declining. The 1998 Canada Day quiz revealed that 44% (versus 41% in 2001) could correctly identify Canada's constitutional slogan. The 1997 Citizenship Survey found that 32% of Canadians could identify the Charter as the part of the constitution that protects their rights and freedoms (versus 29% in 2001). A 1997 Canada Day poll of 18- to 24-year-olds found that 36% could name the year of Confederation (versus 27% of 18- to 34-year-olds in 2001).

Percentage of Canadians who think the slogan "Life, Liberty and the Pursuit of Happiness" applies to the Canadian Constitution: 22

Percentage of Americans who described the U.S. system of government as a constitutional monarchy rather than a representative republic: 13

Percentage of Canadians who correctly identify Sir John A. Macdonald as Canada's first prime minister: 56

Percentage of Americans who correctly identify George Washington as the first president of the United States: 90

Percentage difference between Canadians 35+ and those aged 18–34 who know Marc Garneau was the first Canadian in space: 24

Percentage decline between 1997 and 2001 in the number of 18- to 34-year-old Canadians who could name the year of Confederation: 25

Do You Remember Vimy Ridge?

On the 85th anniversary of the Battle of Vimy Ridge, a poll revealed that Canadians lack knowledge about the country's involvement in the First World War. In all, six in ten Canadians (60%) failed a three-question quiz designed to test their knowledge of Vimy Ridge and the war. Four in ten Canadians (40%) passed the quiz, and the average score was 43%. One-third (34%) failed to answer any of the questions correctly, while another quarter (26%) managed to get only one of the three questions correct. Only one in five (20%) was able to answer all three questions correctly. Despite their poor performance on the quiz, most Canadians (81%) agree that the Canadian military is "an important part of our national identity."

- British Columbians performed best, with 63% of the population passing the quiz, while Quebeckers performed the worst, with only 4% of the population passing the quiz.
- Men (46%) were more likely to pass than women (35%).
- The percentage who passed increased with age, from 31% among younger Canadians to 41% among middle-aged Canadians and 50% among older Canadians.

"In Flanders Fields"

Canadians did the best on identifying the name of the famous poem written by Captain John McCrae, who served as a medical officer in World War I. Nearly six in ten Canadians (57%) were able to name "In Flanders Fields." Looking only at Canadians outside Quebec, the percentage who correctly answered this question rises to 74%. Four in ten (38%) said they "don't know," while 6% mentioned something other than the correct answer.

Only a third (36%) of Canadians could identify Vimy Ridge as one of the battles for a key ridge on the Western Front and that is considered Canada's most famous single victory in the First World War. Instead, half of Canadians (50%) simply said they "don't know."

- **The ratio of men who answered this question correctly to women who did was 3:2.**
- **Once again, Quebeckers performed the worst, with only 6% correctly answering this question. However, even in the rest of Canada, only 46% correctly answered the question.**
- **Men (43%) were much more likely to correctly answer the question than women (29%).**

Leading the War Effort

When asked the multiple choice question "which of the following three people was the Canadian commander in the First World War whose plan led to the victory at Vimy Ridge?," one-third (34%) correctly chose Arthur Currie. In fact, Canadians were equally likely (34%) to choose American World War II general Douglas MacArthur. Meanwhile, one in ten (11%) chose nineteenth-century British naval commander Horatio Nelson, and one-fifth (21%) simply said they "don't know."

Likelihood that a Quebecker could identify the title of the famous poem written by Captain John McCrae as "In Flanders Fields": 1 in 25

Likelihood that a resident of the rest of Canada could identify it: 3 in 4

Ratio of men to women who could identify Vimy Ridge as the site of Canada's most famous single victory in the First World War: 1.48 to 1

"The Canadian Military Is an Important Part of our National Identity"

Most Canadians (81%) agree that "the Canadian military is an important part of our national identity." This includes 54% who "strongly agree" and another quarter (27%) who "somewhat agree." Only one in five (18%) disagrees (8% "strongly," 10% "somewhat").

Regionally, Quebeckers (70%) are least likely to agree, while Atlantic Canadians (93%) are most likely to agree that the Canadian military is an important part of our national identity. Canadians under 35 (76%) are less likely than those aged 35 and older (83%) to agree with the statement.

On a similar note, more than three-quarters (78%) of Canadians agree that "not enough is being done to honour Canada's war veterans." Half (50%) of Canadians "strongly agree," while another 28% "somewhat agree." In contrast, one in five (20%) disagrees (6% "strongly," 14% "somewhat") that not enough is being done to honour our war veterans.

Quebeckers (68%) and British Columbians (76%) are least likely to agree that not enough is being done, while Atlantic Canadians (86%) are most likely to agree.

Two-thirds (64%) of Canadians disagree with the statement that "commemorating military events like the Battle of Vimy Ridge glorifies war." Four in ten (40%) say they "strongly disagree," while one-quarter (24%) "somewhat disagree." One-third (33%) of Canadians agree with the statement (12% "strongly," 21% "somewhat"). Nearly one-half (46%) of Quebeckers agree. British Columbians (23%) are least likely to agree.

Remembrance

Two-thirds (65%) of Canadians say that Remembrance Day (November 11) has a greater meaning for them personally than does September 11 (33%)—the anniversary of the terrorist attacks in the United States.

- **Residents of British Columbia (81%) are the most likely to agree, while Quebeckers (45%) are the least likely.**
- **Younger (40%) and middle-aged (34%) Canadians are more likely to say that September 11 has a**

greater meaning for them personally than are older Canadians (24%).

- Canadians who have family in the Canadian Armed Forces or Reserves (7% of the population) are more likely to indicate that Remembrance Day has a greater meaning for them personally than are those without family members in the Canadian military by a ratio of four to three. Eight in ten Canadians (83%) who have family in the Canadian Armed Forces or Reserves indicate that Remembrance Day has a greater meaning for them personally, compared to 64% of those without family members in the Canadian military.

Half (52%) of Canadians said they would attend a formal Remembrance Day service in 2004. This is down slightly from the number who indicated that they would attend a formal service the year before (58%).

Percentage of lower-income Canadians who attend Remembrance Day ceremonies: 59
Percentage of upper-income Canadians who do: 47

Vimy and Dieppe

In comparison to Canadian ignorance of our troops' achievements at Vimy Ridge and in the First World War generally, only one-third (31%) of Canadians were able to name Dieppe as the French seaside town in which almost 1,000 Canadian soldiers lost their lives during a raid on August 19, 1942. One-fifth (22%) named some other location, while just under half (47%) said they "don't know."

- Men (38%) were more likely than women (24%) to correctly name Dieppe. Over half of women (55%, versus 39% of men) said they "don't know."
- A higher proportion of older (38%) and middle-aged (34%) Canadians were able to name Dieppe than of younger Canadians (18%). Six in ten (59%) of those between 18 and 34 said they "don't know."

- **Canadians with a university degree (42%) were more likely than those with some university or other post-secondary education (29%), those without a high school diploma (24%) and those with a high school diploma (22%) to correctly name Dieppe.**
- **Canadians from upper-income households (36%) were more likely than those from lower-income households (24%) to name Dieppe.**

A Bigger Military Buck
As for the future of Canada's military, three-quarters (75%) of Canadians agreed that the budget of the Canadian military needs to be increased. One-quarter (23%) disagree with this view.

Percentage of Quebeckers who think the military should receive more funding: 53
Percentage of the rest of Canada that does: 82

If you want to spend more money on the military, whose money would you like to take away?

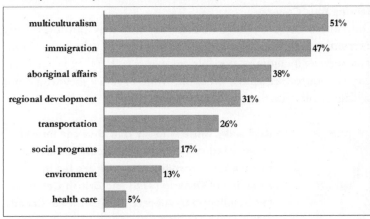

• Canadians with family in the military who agree that the military budget should be increased are more likely than their counterparts without family in the military to favour taking funds from multiculturalism (67% versus 50%), regional development (46% versus 29%) and the environment (24% versus 12%).

What Kind of Armed Forces Do We Want

As for what form of military Canada should have, a majority (53%) would opt for a better-funded and better-equipped all-purpose armed forces capable of undertaking traditional defence and combat roles at home and abroad. Of the other options tested, one-third (32%) say that the Canadian military should be downsized and reconfigured as a small but well-equipped peacekeeping and disaster-assistance force ready to be deployed anywhere in the world on short notice, while one in ten (13%) says the Canadian military should be reduced in size and refocused around specialized combat roles such as military engineering, snipers or special forces and be supplied with the best equipment available for these roles.

Serving Your Country

Only one-third (33%) of Canadians say that they can foresee any international conflict that would compel them to volunteer for military service, including a possible combat role. Fifty-six per cent say they cannot foresee such a situation, while 11% say they would not be able to serve due to age or handicap.

• Regionally, those who say that they can foresee an international conflict that would compel them to volunteer for military service are led by residents of Ontario (37%) and British Columbia (37%), followed by Alberta (32%), Atlantic Canada (31%), Quebec (28%) and Saskatchewan/ Manitoba (22%). Quebeckers (66%) are more likely than those in Ontario (52%), Alberta (50%) and British Columbia (48%) to say that they cannot foresee such an international conflict.

War on Ice: The 2002 Olympic Gold Medals

On Thursday, February 21, 2002, the Canadian Women's Olympic hockey team defeated Team U.S.A. for the gold medal. Three days later, this feat was replicated by the men's Olympic hockey team.

Six in ten Canadians (60%) indicated that they watched portions of the 2002 Salt Lake City Winter Games on television, and almost half (48%) of the adult Canadian population indicated in this survey that they had tuned in to at least one of those two games for the gold medals, with four in ten (37%) claiming to having watched both games.

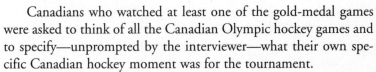

Province the residents of which were most like to watch the men's game: Manitoba and Saskatchewan
Least likely: Quebec
Province the residents of which were most likely to watch the women's game: Ontario
Least likely: Quebec

Canadians who watched at least one of the gold-medal games were asked to think of all the Canadian Olympic hockey games and to specify—unprompted by the interviewer—what their own specific Canadian hockey moment was for the tournament.

The favourite moments were the final men's hockey goal for the gold medal (16%: 21% in Ontario, and 24% among those aged 18 to 34), the final women's hockey goal for the gold medal (10%: 19% in Saskatchewan/Manitoba, and 14% among women), the victory/gold medal win (7%), seeing the teams celebrate after they won their final games (6%), the women's hockey Canadian gold victory (4%), the Canadian national anthem being played at the gold-medal ceremonies (3%), the loonie at centre ice (2%), the men's hockey Canadian gold-victory (2%) and Wayne Gretzky's press conference (2%).

Percentage of Canadians who believe our hockey golds in Salt Lake prove that Canada is the best hockey-playing country in the world: 75
Gender most likely to believe this proof: female
Percentage of Canadians who felt "a greater sense of unity with my fellow Canadians than I did before": 70

The CBC and Canadian Culture

The CBC holds a special, organic and even defining status as an icon of Canadian culture. We wanted to get a fix on where this element of our identity ranks today amid the competition of other media. Taxpayers spend a lot on the CBC, and we wanted to find out whether they're getting what they're paying for. Compared to other radio and TV services, the personal value Canadians ascribe to the CBC, though still strong, is declining. At the same time, Canadians have an enduring and growing confidence that the CBC is the best way to protect Canadian culture, and they want Ottawa to renew CBC funding and to ensure a cultural identity distinct from the United States.

Number of Canadians who believe that the CBC is important in helping to maintain and build Canadian culture and identity: 8 in 10

Number of Canadians who agree that the CBC is one of the things that helps distinguish Canada from the United States: 9 in 10

Rank of the CBC among 13 groups/organizations examined in terms of public confidence or trust to protect Canadian culture and identity on television: 1 (76%).

Number of Canadians who would recommend CBC funding cuts: 1 in 10

Number of Canadians who believe it's important for the CBC to produce programs in and about their part of the country: 8 in 10

Number of Canadians who agree that "the CBC provides value for taxpayers' money": 8 in 10

Number of Canadians who agree with the statement, "I want to see the CBC survive and prosper": 9.5 in 10

Canadian Content

The majority of Canadians (81%) believe that Canadian content and programming are important overall, in terms of their impact on helping to maintain and build Canadian culture and identity and as a symbol of culture and identity. While both CBC Radio and CBC Television are seen as contributing to Canadian identity and culture by a significant number of Canadians, CBC Television is the focus for a majority.

Six in ten (61%) Canadians believe that there should be a required minimum level of Canadian programming on Canadian television. Furthermore, almost as many believe that the current regulations requiring one hour of Canadian programming in prime time is too little (57%).

Canadian programming we think has the highest value

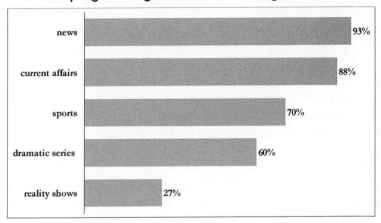

We also asked the question, "This fall there will be 5 Canadian drama series on TV, down from the 12 that were on TV three years ago. These Canadian drama series have been replaced with other types of Canadian programming, like reality shows. Do you think that this is a good thing or a bad thing in terms of the direction of Canadian programming for the future?" Almost twice as many Canadians say this is a bad thing (61%) as say it is a good thing (34%).

The CBC and the Competition

Compared to other television and radio sources that they use, Canadians ascribe a higher level of personal value (64% rate 5–7) to what they watch and listen to on the CBC—even though CTV beats CBC in most ratings, including News.

Furthermore, among English-speaking Canadians, the CBC is chosen by almost twice as many respondents (46%) as CTV (25%) or Global (20%) as having the most balanced reporting about Canada's political parties. Among French-speaking Canadians, the CBC (35%) and TVA (32%) are named by almost equal numbers.

Canadian Culture and Identity

So what does it all mean? CBC is an institution and trusted icon for Canadianism—but viewing stats, excepting "Hockey Night in Canada," say we're most likely to surf right by it when we turn on the tube. Canadians are extremely proud of their culture and identity (94% agree): an overwhelming 92% agree that it is something we should be proud of, including 70% who strongly agree. Canadians also see a role for government in doing this: fully 89% agree that it is important for the Canadian government to work to maintain and build a culture and identity distinct from the U.S.

Percentage of Canadians who think Canadian culture and identity are stronger than Americans': 43
Percentage who think they're weaker: 26
Percentage who think we'll be worse off in 5 years: 39

Media Concentration

Canadians are cautiously confident in the performance of the media in presenting news and information that is objective and balanced. While few Canadians believe that this is always the case, a very small proportion believe that the media are never objective and balanced.

	Always	Sometimes	Never	No opinion
In Canadian newspapers	15%	77%	6%	2%
On Canadian TV stations	20%	77%	3%	1%
On Canadian radio stations	19%	74%	3%	4%

Moreover, twice as many Canadians believe that the news and information presented on Canadian TV and radio stations is more objective and balanced than it was five years ago. Assessments of Canadian newspapers are more divided.

	More	Same	Less	No opinion
In Canadian newspapers	28%	44%	25%	4%
On Canadian TV stations	38%	42%	18%	2%
On Canadian radio stations	32%	47%	15%	7%

Questioning on related attitudes toward media concentration shows that over three-quarters (78%) of Canadians believe that owners of media outlets have gone too far in trying to inject their own personal politics into what their outlets report, while about two-thirds (68%) believe that media concentration undermines Canada's democracy and (62%) agree that there is too much media concentration in Canada today. However, two-thirds (64%) also believe that Canadian media need to be concentrated to some extent in order to be competitive.

Given this concern, the vast majority of Canadians believe that the federal government should do something about media concentration (only 9% say the government should do nothing). Each of the three options presented for action receive support: asking the CRTC to act (32%), holding a public inquiry (28%) and strengthening the CBC to provide a counterbalance (22%).

Percentage of Canadians who continue to see a need for the CRTC and its activities in Canada today: 83
Who believe that Canadians currently have at least a moderate sense of their culture and identity: 82
Who believe that Canadians currently have a strong or very strong sense of their culture and identity: 39

Canadians Are Funny

Comedy has been described as one of Canada's greatest exports and it appears that Canadians agree, with over eight in ten (85%) indicating that there is an identifiable Canadian sense of humour. This belief is strongest among residents of Alberta (92%) and Saskatchewan/Manitoba (92%). At the lower end, 82% of British Columbians and 83% of Ontarians agree with this view.

Canada's international reputation for comedy is believed by two-thirds (63%) of Canadians, who think that those outside of Canada perceive Canadians to be funny people. This view is strongest among residents of Atlantic Canada (72%) and Quebec (68%). In comparison, only 57% of Ontarians agree with this view. Younger (73%) and middle-aged Canadians (67%) are more likely to think that others find Canadians funny than are older Canadians (47%).

The Funniest in the World

- **Quebeckers (43%) are the most likely to cite Canada as the country with the funniest or most humorous people, whereas Ontarians (16%) are least likely to mention their own country. As well, younger (28%) and middle-aged (28%) Canadians are more likely than older (20%) Canadians to express this view.**
- **Albertans (27%) are more likely to choose Australia than those in other regions, while Quebeckers (5%) are the least likely to think that Aussies are the funniest or most humorous.**
- **The United States is more often mentioned by Quebeckers (18%) and Ontarians (17%) than by residents of Alberta (6%) or Atlantic Canada (6%). Younger Canadians (18%) are more likely to believe this to be the case than older (12%) or middle-aged (11%) Canadians.**
- **Middle-aged (14%) and older (16%) Canadians are more likely than their younger counterparts (8%) to cite England as the land of the most humorous or funniest people.**
- **And, not surprisingly, Quebeckers (15%) are more likely than those in any other region to mention France as the country with the funniest or most humorous people.**

Newfoundlanders Are Funny

When asked which province, excluding their own, has the funniest or most humorous people, one-third (33%) of all Canadians identified Newfoundland and Labrador. Quebeckers and Ontarians are viewed as the most humorous by 13% and 12%, respectively. Lower levels of support are expressed for British Columbia (7%), Nova Scotia (6%), Alberta (5%) and New Brunswick (4%). At the bottom of the list are Saskatchewan (2%), Manitoba (2%) and Prince Edward Island (1%).

- Interestingly, with few exceptions, the highest level of support for each province comes from its neighbours. For example, the biggest supporters of Quebeckers are those from Ontario (19%), while Quebeckers reciprocate, with the highest level of support for Ontario coming from that province (22%). Similarly, Alberta's highest support is from its neighbours Saskatchewan/Manitoba (19%) and British Columbia (10%).
- Canadians in the lowest-income (13%) and middle-income (16%) households are more likely to cite Ontarians as being the funniest or most humorous in the country, compared with Canadians from the highest-income households (6%).

Jim Carrey Is Canada's Favourite Home-Grown Comedian

When Canadians are asked on an open-ended basis who their favourite Canadian comedian or comedy troupe of all time is, Jim Carrey tops the list, with support from just over one in ten (12%). Wayne and Shuster (7%), John Candy (7%), the Air Farce (6%) and Yvon Deschamp (5%) round out the top five mentions.

- An interesting difference is between the choices of the age groups. Canadians between 18 and 34 (23%) are 11 times more likely than those 55 years of age or older (2%) to choose Jim Carrey as their favourite Canadian comedian, with those between 35 and 54 closer to the national average (10%).
- Older Canadians (22%) are much, much more likely to cite Wayne and Shuster as their favourite funny Canadians than are younger Canadians (0%), with the middle-aged group closer to the national average (6%).
- Quebeckers differ from those of the other regions in their choice of favourite home-grown comedians. None of the top favourites of Quebeckers was mentioned by anyone outside of that province. The top five favourites of

Quebeckers are Yvon Deschamps (19%), Rock et Belles Oreilles (5%), Jean Michel Anctil (5%), Lise Dion (5%) and Daniel Lemire (4%).

Percentage of Canadians who believe that Canadian humour is more sophisticated than American humour: 71
Ranking Canadians assign to Canada when asked to name the country with the funniest people in the world: 1
Likelihood that a Canadian would name Italy when asked to name the country with the funniest people in the world: 1 in 33
Ratio of those aged 18 to 34 who name Jim Carrey as their favourite Canadian comic to those aged 55 and up: 11.5 to 1

Canadian Landmarks

When Canadians are asked to name, on an open-ended basis, three of Canada's most monumental landmarks, it's the CN Tower (44%) that tops the list, with Niagara Falls (33%), the Canadian Rockies (32%), and the Parliament Buildings in Ottawa (26%) next in line. Others, such as Banff National Park (5%), the Great Lakes (3%) and the Montreal Olympic Stadium (3%), were also cited.

- Residents of Ontario are most apt to believe the CN Tower (58%) and Niagara Falls (44%) are Canada's most monumental landmarks.
- Residents of Saskatchewan/Manitoba (46%), British Columbia (42%) and Alberta (41%) are most likely to choose the Canadian Rockies.
- Atlantic Canadians are most likely to choose the Parliament Buildings in Ottawa (41%).
- Men (53%) are more likely than women (35%) to think the CN Tower is Canada's most monumental landmark.

When then asked to choose among a specific list of five monumental Canadian landmarks, the Canadian Rockies (32%) top the list as the monumental landmark that "most symbolizes Canada," followed by the Parliament Buildings in Ottawa (28%), Niagara Falls, the CN Tower (9%), and the Calgary Tower (1%).

Residents of Alberta (60%) and British Columbia (58%) are most likely to choose the Canadian Rockies, whereas residents of Saskatchewan/Manitoba (32%), Ontario (31%) and Quebec (30%) are most likely to choose the Parliament Buildings in Ottawa. Residents of Ontario (33%) and Quebec (31%) are most likely to choose Niagara Falls, while Atlantic Canadians are most likely to choose the CN Tower (37%).

Respondents were then provided with a list of monumental landmarks and asked where they are located in Canada. (The zeroes, of course, are not absolute zeroes—just statistical zeroes.)

The World's Largest Inukshuk: 1% specifically answered Vancouver; 2% correctly said British Columbia

The Pysanka Easter Egg: 8% specifically answered Vegreville; 6% correctly said Alberta

The World's Largest Oil Can: 1% specifically answered Rocanville; 2% correctly said Saskatchewan

The World's Largest Easel: 0% specifically answered Altona; 2% correctly said Manitoba

The Big Nickel: 38% specifically answered Sudbury; 9% correctly said Ontario

Bonhomme Carnival: 45% specifically answered Quebec City; 25% correctly said Quebec

The Giant Squid: 0% specifically answered Glover's Harbour; 16% correctly said Newfoundland

The World's Largest Axe: 0% specifically answered Nackawic; 3% correctly said New Brunswick

The Giant Fiddle: 0% specifically answered Cavendish; 4% correctly said Prince Edward Island

The Giant Anchor: 8% specifically answered Halifax; 12% correctly said Nova Scotia

The Neighbours

No chapter on Canadiana would be complete without some reference to the Americans.

Three in four Canadians (75%) agree with the statement that "Canadians are too modest about their accomplishments." Similarly, 74% of Canadians say that Americans do a better job of celebrating their accomplishments than Canadians.

Apparently this isn't because the Americans have more to celebrate. We found that 71% of respondents disagreed with the statement that "Americans have more important people and accomplishments to celebrate than Canadians."

So what is it? Why aren't we as good at celebrating our accomplishments if we have just as many as the Yanks do? Well, this is just a hunch, but think back a page or two, to the spot where the Americans trounced us in the battle of the history quizzes.

Perhaps Americans are better at celebrating their accomplishments because more of them are *familiar* with what their country has accomplished. Hmmm?

One final note here. Mavis Gallant, the famous Canadian writer who spent most of her life in France, put a question to Robertson Davies, the famous English author who spent most of his life in Canada: "I said to him once, 'Why don't Canadians love Canada the way Americans love America?' and he said: 'It's not a country you love, it's a country you worry about.'"

Oh, oh, Canada.

And speaking of Americans . . .

The Americans

Living next to you is in some ways like sleeping with an elephant. No matter how friendly and even-tempered is the beast, if I can call it that, one is affected by every twitch and grunt.

—Pierre Trudeau, describing Canada's relationship with the United States.

IT'S DIFFICULT TO imagine what it would mean to be Canadian without reference to the United States. We evaluate our policies according to how the Americans might feel about them. We congratulate ourselves on our sophistication and right-mindedness in contrast to what we see as American parochialism and backwardness. We berate ourselves for our parochialism in contrast to American sophistication. We imbibe a steady diet of American culture, and resent America for its cultural imperialism. We sneer at them for their medieval health care system, and fawn over them for their free-market swashbuckling. We celebrate America as our biggest trading partner, and complain about the influence it has on our economy.

America is something of a bugbear of the Canadian mind. That may well be what makes us Canadian: the compulsion to gaze over the border and look at the colour of the grass.

Of course, we don't always like what we see. As the booing of the American national anthem at a few hockey games last year suggests, America can be hard to like sometimes. Ask anyone in the world. But antipathy towards the U.S. is perhaps more nuanced in Canada than it is elsewhere around the globe. Only fifteen percent of Canadians would say "at the heart of it, I am actually anti-American—I don't like or respect anything that the United States and its people stand for or what it is about." Furthermore, a strong majority of Canadians (70%) agree that "I value and respect the United States and its citizens."

But they go on to say "—it's just that I disagree fundamentally with their government." That is to say, we seem to like Americans, but at this time in our history, their current president, George W. Bush, is deeply disliked—still, despite his late 2004 visit to Ottawa to munch on Alberta cattle and to Halifax to belatedly thank Maritimers for billeting stranded 9/11 airline passengers. Fairly or not, he is seen as largely ignorant of the subtleties of international relations and intemperately given to bombing as a foreign policy tool. He has alienated many former allies, so it is pretty much in keeping with his diplomatic record that Washington's reputation has suffered here in Canada.

While Bush's military adventures have, predictably, stirred up a hornet's nest of resistance and condemnation around the world, it is in no small part what Canadians see as his insensitivity to Canadians' sense of friendship with America that has so tarnished his image here. A very strong majority of Canadians (85%) agree that "Canada is a solid friend and close, dependable ally of the United States." But we feel we're not always taken seriously—and in this we're probably right. Canadians know perfectly well that we are America's biggest trading partner and their primary source of energy, but Americans seem not to be aware of these important facts. So even if Canadians sometimes boo their national anthem, and gloat over their failures, and resent their successes (particularly in hockey), we want Americans to know that this cantankerousness is nothing more than a form of friendship.

A lot of us really like the U.S. And it hardly needs to be said that there is a great deal to like. For innovation, for sheer energy, so say nothing of wealth, America has no rival. Think of its running shoes, its stealth bombers, its movie studios, its pickup trucks, its stock markets—America dominates the world by the staggering scale of its economy and its appetite for new stuff. Few Canadians are really interested in turning their backs on America.

In fact, as many as 980,000 Canadian adults say we should fully join the United States, huge numbers support closer economic and political union, and the allure of moving to the U.S. is hardly a new phenomenon. While reports of a riptide of brain drain may be an exaggeration, the fact is that 19% of employed Canadians say that "if they could, they would prefer to live and work in the United States." That's a lot of people. (Of course, that means that 81% of employed Canadians have no interest at all in moving south.) Interestingly, Quebeckers and British Columbians—those most likely to take issue with American policy—are the Canadians most likely to want to move to the U.S., at 24%.

All the same, there are many differences between us. Sputtering right-wing commentators in the U.S. are right about one thing: we *are* soft on decriminalized marijuana, gay marriage, and capital punishment. But the fact is that enormous numbers of Americans are too. When we speculate on how similar Canadians are to Americans, we have to ask: which Americans? There are all kinds of smart, cosmopolitan, articulate Americans out there, many of whom oppose the war, and many of whom voted against Bush (and as events in Ohio suggest, there may be more of these people than we thought). Not all Americans are creationists, and not all Canadians are the socialists and bleeding-heart liberals decried by the likes of Bill O'Reilly. Often, opinion will differ more between British Columbia and Alberta than it will between Canada and the U.S. So it doesn't always make sense to think of Americans as different from us; some fellow Canadians will be just as different.

The fact is that we tend to see in America what we want to see. If we're angry about the invasion of Iraq, some Canadians see the U.S. a nation of mouth-breathing hicks and glassy-eyed fascists. If we're angry with Canada, for whatever reason, we see an America defined by its commitment to freedom and prosperity.

The whole world can't be wrong—almost three-quarters of every country in the world believes that America is aggressive and dangerous and seems not to give a moment's thought to anyone else. But all those American-loving Canucks can't be all wrong either. We've all been to the U.S., and have all met friendly men and women we can get along with, even if we sometimes disagree. After all, an overwhelming majority (86%) of Canadians agree that while Canadians and Americans can be insensitive to each other, we have one of the best relationships of any two countries in the world.

Where Are the Americans Heading?
Is the U.S. heading in the "right direction" or are they "on the wrong track"? Canadians were split on this question. Just under half (45%) of Canadians believe that the United States is heading in the right direction, while an equal portion (43%) say that they are heading on the wrong track.

> Province the residents of which are most likely to believe
> that America is heading the wrong way: Quebec
> Province most likely to believe the opposite: Ontario
> Rate by which a Canadian with a university degree is more
> likely than a high school dropout to believe that the U.S. is
> heading in the wrong direction: 50%

Bush

> Chances a Canadian sees George Bush Jr.'s re-election as a
> "bad thing": 6 in 10
> Chances an American sees George Bush Jr.'s re-election as a
> "good thing": 6 in 10

George W. Bush has not earned the reputation as the most cosmopolitan or sophisticated of American presidents. But even Canadians who like him don't believe that he knows much about the country immediately to his north. Three-quarters (75%) of Canadians do not believe that American President George W. Bush has a good understanding of Canada or of the Canadian people. This belief is strongly held by 46% of Canadians.

> Rate by which a university-educated Canadian is more
> likely than a high-school dropout to believe that Bush does
> not understand Canada: 33%
> Percentage of Canadians who believe there is nothing
> Canada can do about American policies that affect us
> negatively: 50

Percentage of Canadians who believe the U.S. doesn't care
how its actions affect Canada: 70
Percentage who believe that the federal government just gives
in to whatever the U.S. government wants: 59
Percentage who believe the U.S. is not justified in withholding
reconstruction contracts from countries that did not support
the invasion of Iraq: 71

We Want Them to Like Us, Even If We Don't Care for Them

It seems we are easily wounded. President Bush's delayed apology
over the deaths of Canadian soldiers by American "friendly fire" in
Afghanistan, and his omission of Canada as one of the allies in his
War on Terrorism in his speech to Congress after 9/11 helped foster
a view that he did not value Canada's friendship and partnership.
Four in ten Canadians were "angry" about this cold shoulder (and
perhaps still are). It would appear that there are Canadians who
don't like Bush, but who want him to like us all the same.

Rate by which a resident of British Columbia is more likely
than a resident of Manitoba or Saskatchewan to feel angry
with Bush: 50%
Rate by which university-educated Canadians are more likely
than high-school dropouts to be angry with Bush: 45%

So Much for the War on Terror

To answer the perceived threat of global terrorism, the Bush administration has made some policy moves that would have been
unthinkable only a short time ago, both domestically and internationally. The cost—monetary, diplomatic, juridical, to say nothing
of the cost in lives—has been high. Do Canadians think the expense
has been worth it?

For many, the answer is an emphatic "no." More than a third
(36%) of Canadians say Bush's actions and decisions on the international stage have made the world "less safe." And four in ten
(42%) Canadians say that George W. Bush's decisions and actions
on the international stage have had "no effect" on the safety of the
world today. Meanwhile, just 9% say the president's actions and
decisions internationally have made the world "more safe."

Province the residents of which are most likely to believe
Bush has made the world less safe: Quebec.
Provinces least likely to believe so: Manitoba and
Saskatchewan
Rate by which a university graduate is more likely than a
high school dropout to believe Bush has made the world
less safe: 2 to 1

President Bush Visits Ottawa

President Bush may have made strides in rebuilding relations and good will between his administration and the Canadian government on his first official visit to Canada in November 2004, and was relieved to be greeted by Canadians using all fingers (rather than the single digit favoured by Trudeau). But his efforts don't seem to have burnished his reputation much. Only one in ten Canadians (10%) say that based on what they have seen, read, or heard about Bush's official visit to Canada, their impression of President Bush has become "better." But an almost equal proportion of Canadians (7%) say that their impression has become "worse." Meanwhile, a strong majority of Canadians (78%) say their opinion of Mr. Bush has not changed after his visit.

Province the residents of which are least likely to say their
opinion of Bush has improved: British Columbia
Most likely: the Atlantic provinces

Talking to Americans

The primary difference between Canadians and Americans seems to be over the question of whether we're different at all. Only half of Americans believe there is any difference. On the other hand, 80% of Canadians believe that we are "fundamentally different in values and outlooks." As it turns out, another difference, as we'll see below, is that on this topic at least, we are right, and they are wrong.

Province the residents of which are most likely to believe
we're different from Americans: British Columbia
Province the residents of which are least likely to think so:
Alberta
Percentage of Americans who claim that "my religious faith is
very important to me in my day to day life": 82

Percentage of Canadians who do: 64

Rate by which an American is more likely than a Canadian to "very much" agree that faith is important in day-to-day life: 100%

Percentage of Americans who believe that same-sex marriage is "wrong and it should never be lawful": 47

Percentage of Canadians who do: 27

Percentage of Americans who support the death penalty: 71

Percentage of Canadians who do: 42

(Percentage of Quebeckers who do: 29)

Percentage of Americans who believe their children are getting a good education: 59

Percentage of Canadians who do: 84

Percentage of Americans who think decriminalizing marijuana is "a sound idea": 36

Percentage of Canadians who do: 51

The Invasion of Iraq

Perhaps no gesture defines the Bush administration more vividly than the invasion and occupation of Iraq. Certainly nothing galvanized opinion around the world against the U.S. as much as this operation. To many, the Bush administration's motives were seen as impure, to say the least, and the *casus belli* as disingenuous. Bush's announcement that those who were not with him were against him made many all too willing to declare themselves against him. At any rate, Canadians certainly weren't with him.

When asked whether Prime Minister Chretien did the right thing by not supporting the United States in its war against Saddam Hussein, three-quarters of Canadians (74%) say he did. And as the U.S. seems to be increasingly ensnared in Iraqi resistance, this certainty is growing (up three points over the past year).

Rate by which a Quebecker is more likely than an Albertan to believe we did the right thing in refusing to invade Iraq: 2 to 1
Rate by which men are more likely than women to believe we did the wrong thing: 2 to 1

Of course, not all Canadians who are glad we did not end up in Iraq believe that the Americans shouldn't have gone. Keeping in mind all that has unfolded since the U.S. invaded Iraq in March 2003, two-thirds of Canadians (63% in 2004, up sharply 16 points from 47% in December 2003) believe that the United States made a mistake.

Fooling Some People Some of the Time

If Bill Clinton earned a reputation for prevarication, to most Canadians Bush was seen as a liar on his most audacious gambit. Two-thirds (67%) of Canadians agree that Bush "knowingly lied to the world in order to justify his war in Iraq." Men are significantly more likely than women to disagree with the notion that Bush lied (32% as opposed to 24%).

Percentage of Canadians who say the United States and its allies were not justified in taking military action against Iraq based on the premise that Iraq possessed weapons of mass destruction: 59

Percentage who still believe that Iraq possesses as-yet undiscovered caches of weapons of mass destruction: 35

Percentage of Albertans who believe this: 51

Percentage of Quebeckers who do: 27

It's one thing to refuse to believe Bush when he's talking about details, but even more damning when he's talking about the substance of his policies. A majority of six in ten Canadians (61%) agrees that for all the lives and money spent in Iraq, a true democracy will never come to the region.

Percentage of Albertans who believe that Bush did the right thing in invading Iraq: 54

Percentage of Albertans who believe that democracy will never come to Iraq: 65

Rank of Albertans among Canadians who support Bush: 1

Rank of Albertans among Canadians who believe democracy will never come to Iraq: 2

Percentage of Canadians who believe the world is a better place without Saddam Hussein: 87

Rate by which a Quebecker is more likely than an Ontarian to disagree with this view: 3 to 1

Doomed to Repeat It?

But as evidence that Canadians are not anti-American, there is the following very generous appraisal of their ability to learn from history: seven in ten Canadians (69%) agree that because of the quagmire of its Iraqi adventure, the United States "will learn a valuable lesson: that it is better for them to work with countries around the world rather than to act on their own in issues of world crisis."

Interestingly, it is the provinces that support the invasion the least that are most likely to believe that the U.S. has learned a lesson. Similarly, women support the American invasion much less than men do, are more relieved we did not join the U.S., and are more likely than are men to believe that America has learned from its mistakes. However, while the least educated Canadians supported the invasion the most, it is they who are most likely to believe that the U.S. has learned a valuable lesson.

Percentage of high school dropouts who believe the U.S. has learned from its mistakes in Iraq: 82
Percentage of university-educated Canadians who do: 58

How Support for the Invasion of Iraq Has Changed

Asked in 2004 which of a series of statements comes closest to their own point of view, half (48%) of Canadians say, "regardless of Saddam Hussein having been removed from power, I still oppose the war in Iraq because it was not sanctioned by the United Nations and there has not been any credible evidence to date that Iraq had weapons of mass destruction in the months leading up to the war." Three in ten (28%) Canadians say "I supported the war in Iraq and feel it was justified even if no weapons of mass destruction have been found yet because Saddam Hussein has been removed from power and reconstruction is underway," and two in ten (21%) report having changed their minds; they say, "I initially opposed the war in Iraq, but now feel it was a good thing even if no weapons of mass destruction are found because Saddam Hussein has been removed from power and reconstruction is underway." The remaining 3% "don't know."

Only province the residents of which are more likely to
have supported the war than to have opposed it: Alberta
Percentage of Canadians with university degrees who
believe that the removal of Hussein without U.N sanction
was unjustified: 58
Percentage of all other who share this belief: 44

How is Hussein to Get a Fair Trial?

Asked what forum would be the most likely to produce a fair trial
for Saddam Hussein, Canadians tilt decidedly international—a total
of 58% support some type of international forum (International
Tribunal, 30%, or International Court of Justice as in the Hague,
28%) as opposed to a more local Iraqi court (30%) or an American
military tribunal (5%).

Percentage of Canadians with university degrees who believe
that Hussein should be tried by the International Court of
Justice: 58
Percentage of all other who share this belief: 24

Where to Draw the Line

There is one thing that Canadians and Americans more or less agree
on: what Americans think of Canadian sovereignty. When asked
how they view Canada, seven in ten (69%) Americans say they
think of Canada as an entirely separate country, while three in ten
(30%) say they view Canada as just another state.

The notion that Canada is a separate country is highest among
residents of the Western states (77%), while it is lowest among those
furthest from the Canadian border—residents in the Southern
states (64%). That is to say, Southern Americans (33%) are more
likely than Western Americans (23%) to view Canada as just
another state like Michigan or Oregon.

The standard of geography taught in American schools may be
declining. While 25% of middle-aged Americans believe that
Canada is just another state, fully 35% of young Americans do.

Then again, 13% of Americans believe they have a king.

Percentage of upper-income Americans who think of
Canada as a separate nation: 76

Percentage of lower-income Americans who do: 59

Percentage of Canadians who believe that Americans think of
Canada as a separate country: 64

Percentage of Quebeckers who do: 42

Percentage of British Columbians who do: 78

Rate by which a Quebecker is more likely than a British
Columbian to believe that Americans think of Canada as just
another state in the republic: 170%

Percentage of Americans who believe Canada is a major player
in world affairs: 52

Percentage of Canadians who do: 76

Is Sovereignty Overrated?

An interesting question: how many Canadian would like to see their country become another American state? The quick answer is: not many. Seventy-two percent like things as they are.

However, this means that a quarter of us (23%) think that the U.S. and Canada should enter into a formal economic union with free trade and a common currency. A third of Quebeckers (32%) feel this way, compared to 17% of the residents of Manitoba and Saskatchewan.

And finally, 980,000 Canadian adults say we should join the United States. That's right. Four percent of Canadians feel that Canada should join the United States and become one or more states within the republic. Close to one in ten (7%) Quebeckers select this option as the best possible relationship for the two countries.

Friends and Allies

It is nice to be loved, and to know that your friendship is valued. But it can sting to discover that your warm feelings are not reciprocated. So it can be hard being friends with America. While 60% of Canadians say that the United States is Canada's closest friend and ally, only 18% of Americans name Canada in this role—a majority of Americans (56%) cite Great Britain. That is, a Canadian is more than three times as likely to name the U.S. as a closest friend and ally as an American is to name Canada.

When asked who Canada's largest trading partner is, eight in ten (82%) Canadians (correctly) indicate the United States.

When the mirror question is asked of Americans, only 14% (correctly) name Canada—one-quarter believe it to be Japan (27%) or China (25%).

Percentage of British Columbians who see the U.K. as our greatest friend and ally: 32
Percentage of Quebeckers who do: 9
Percentage of Quebeckers who see France in this role: 17
Percentage of Americans who see France as *their* greatest friend an ally: 2
Rate by which a midwestern American is more likely than a southerner to see Canada as America's greatest friend and ally: 2 to 1

Pulling our Weight

We often hear that we are expected to pull our weight in military matters. The good news is that most of us have clear consciences. Residents of both countries were asked whether they agree or disagree with the statement that "Canada is doing its share to ensure its border is secure and protected from terrorists entering the United States." In Canada, 73% agree with this statement. In the United States, 58% agree.

Percentage of Canadians who think we should *not* join Bush's "Star Wars" defence scheme: 69
Percentage of Americans who think we should: 73
Percentage of Canadians who disagree that "a terrorist attack will likely be launched from Canada in the future into the United States": 73
Percentage of Americans who do: 70
Rate by which an Albertan is more likely than a Manitoban or Saskatchewanian to believe that a terrorist attack on the U.S. is likely to be launched from Canada: 2 to 1

Doing Business

Percentage of Canadians who think the best way to improve
business relations with the U.S. is to change presidents: 27
Percentage of Americans who do: 19
Percentage of Canadians who think things would improve
with a new prime minister: 22
Percentage of Americans who do: 9

NAFTA

In 2004, seven in ten (70%) Canadians supported Canada's participation in the North American Free Trade Agreement (NAFTA)
with the United States and Mexico, up from 64% in January 2003.

Percentage of young people who support NAFTA: 78
Percentage of older people who do: 65
Rate by which an upper-income Canadian is more likely
than a lower-income compatriot to support NAFTA: 33%

The proportion of Canadians who think the free trade agreement has benefited Canada has also increased from 40% in January
2001 to 51% today. One-quarter (25%) of Canadians today think
NAFTA has hurt Canada, down from 32% in January 2001, and
one-fifth (19%) continues to think it has had no impact (22% in
January 2001).

These numbers lead to some unexpected inferences: not all of
those who support NAFTA think it is good for Canada, and not all
who oppose it think it is harmful. In fact only 66% of free-trade
supporters think the agreement has benefited Canada (compared to
15% of those who oppose it), whereas only 61% of non-supporters
think the agreement has hurt Canada. Fully 12% of supporters
think the deal has actually hurt their country. One wonders why
they support it.

Rate by which an upper-income Canadian is more likely
than a lower-income Canadian to believe the deal has
benefited Canada: 50%
Rate by which an American is more likely than a Canadian
to doubt the safety of Canadian beef: 6 to 1

Environment and Energy

Despite broad support for the NAFTA agreement, which earmarks a proportion of Canadian energy for American markets (which means that Alberta could not increase its supply to Ontario if that were to mean diminishing exports to the U.S.), 90% of Canadians believe that "Canada should establish an energy policy that provides reliable supplies of oil, gas and electricity at stable prices and on protection of the environment, even if this means placing restrictions on exports and foreign ownership of Canadian supplies."

Another 91% agree that "Canada should maintain the ability to set its own independent environmental health and safety standards and regulations, even if this might reduce cross-border trade opportunities with the United States."

Could it be that the debates of the 1988 federal election are not yet resolved?

We're All for Free Trade, But Let's Be Serious

Among the things Canadian like about free trade, foreign ownership of Canadian companies is not to be found. Seven in ten (70%) Canadians agree that the "Federal Government should have the power to stop an American company from purchasing a Canadian company." Six in ten (61%) go so far as to say that they are "angry that the Federal Government is not doing more to stop U.S. and other foreign ownership from buying Canadian-owned companies." Moreover, two-thirds (67%) of employed Canadians say "they buy Canadian-made products whenever they can, even if it means they have to pay a bit more than for the same product made in another country." It would seem that we like free trade as long as we don't have to give up our protectionism.

Greenbacks All Around: No Thanks

Most Canadians (77%) think "there will be a common North American currency within the next 20 years." However, six in ten Canadians (58%) believe such a currency would be a "bad thing for Canada." Most Canadians think it's coming, and they don't want it.

Moving Over

Another thing Canadians and Americans seem to agree on is the desireablility of living on the other side of the border. In the aftermath of Mr. Bush being elected to a second term, respondents were asked whether they had considered moving. Eight percent of Canadians agreed that "I have given very, very serious thought recently about moving to and taking up residence in the United States"—91% disagreed, and 1% said they didn't know. In the United States, 10% agreed with the view that "I have given very, very serious thought recently about moving to and taking up residence in Canada."

It Could Be Worse

Despite our differences, and a bit of mudslinging, an overwhelming majority (86%) of Canadians agree that while Canadians and Americans can be insensitive to each other, we have one of the best relationships of any two countries in the world. Just over one in ten (13%) disagree—with only four percent who strongly disagree.

It can't be *that* bad.

About the Authors

DARRELL BRICKER is President of North American Public Affairs for Ipsos-Reid. Prior to joining Ipsos-Reid Bricker was Director of Public Opinion Research in the Office of the Prime Minister. He holds a Ph.D. in political science from Carleton University. He lives with his wife and daughter in Toronto.

JOHN WRIGHT is the Senior Vice President and Managing Director of the Trends Division, Canadian Public Affairs, of Ipsos-Reid. He has been the lead media spokesperson for the company since 1990 on politics, policy, and consumer trends, and hosts a weekly radio show for Canada's largest News Talk station, Toronto's CFRB, called "Your Opinion Counts."